TOP FEDERAL TAX ISSUES FOR 2008
CPE COURSE

CCH Editorial Staff Publication

.CCH

a Wolters Kluwer business

Contributors

Editor.. George G. Jones, J.D., LL.M
Contributing Editors.. Torie D. Cole, J.D.
Hilary Goehausen, J.D.
Brant Goldwyn, J.D.
Chandra Walker, MPIA, J.D.
George L. Yaksick, Jr., J.D.
Production Coordinator .... Gabriel E. Santana
Design/Layout...Laila Gaidulis
Production ....Lynn J. Brown

ISBN 978-0-8080-1691-5

© 2007, CCH INCORPORATED
4025 W. Peterson Ave.
Chicago, IL 60646-6085
1 800 248 3248
www.CCHGroup.com

TOP FEDERAL TAX ISSUES FOR 2008 CPE COURSE

Introduction

Each year, a handful of tax issues typically requires special attention by tax practitioners. The reasons vary, from a particularly complicated new provision in the Internal Revenue Code, to a planning technique opened up by a new regulation or ruling, or the availability of a significant tax benefit with a short window of opportunity. Sometimes a developing business need creates a new set of tax problems, or pressure exerted by Congress or the Administration puts more heat on some taxpayers while giving others more slack. All these share in creating a unique mix that in turn creates special opportunities and pitfalls in the coming year. The past year has seen more than its share of these developments.

CCH's *Top Federal Tax Issues for 2008 CPE Course* identifies the events of the past year that have developed into "hot" issues. These tax issues have been selected as particularly relevant to tax practice in 2008. They have been selected not only because of their impact on return preparation during the 2007 tax season but also because of the important role they play in developing effective tax strategies for 2008. Some issues are outgrowths of several years of developments; others have burst onto the tax scene unexpectedly. Some have been emphasized in IRS publications and notices; others are too new or too controversial to be noted by the IRS either in depth or at all.

This course is designed to help reassure the tax practitioner that he or she is not missing out on advising clients about a hot, new tax opportunity or is not susceptible to being caught unawares by a brewing controversy. In short, it is designed to give the tax practitioner a closer look into the opportunities and pitfalls presented by the changes. Among the topics examined in the *Top Federal Tax Issues for 2008 CPE Course* are:

- FIN 48: Roadmap or Compas for the IRS?
- Nonqualified Deferred Compensation: New Requirements
- Intrafamily Transfers of Small Businesses
- Alternative Minimum Tax: A Growing Problem
- Family Limited Partnerships
- Passive Activity Loss Limitations
- IRS Audit Process
- Major Tax Law Developments in 2007

Throughout the Course you will find Study Questions to help you test your knowledge, and comments that are vital to understanding a particular strategy or idea. Answers to the Study Questions with feedback on both correct and incorrect responses are provided in a special section beginning on page 9.1.

To assist you in your later reference and research, a detailed topical index has been included for this Course beginning on page 10.1.

This Course is divided into three Modules. Take your time and review all Course Modules. When you feel confident that you thoroughly understand the material, turn to the CPE Quizzer. Complete one, or all, Module Quizzers for continuing professional education credit. Further information is provided in the CPE Quizzer instructions on page 11.1.

October 2007

COURSE OBJECTIVES

This course was prepared to provide the participant with an overview of specific tax issues that impact 2007 tax return preparation and tax planning in 2008. These are the issues that "everyone is talking about;" each impacts a significant number of taxpayers in significant ways.

Upon course completion, you will be able to:

- Understand the basics of FIN 48 and what it requires;
- Describe the plans that are excluded from the application of Code Sec. 409A;
- Identify a small business' responsibilities for federal employment taxes;
- Calculate AMT liability;
- Evaluate tax and nontax advantages and disadvantages of FLPs;
- Recognize sources of passive activity income;
- Explain the goals of the National Research Program; and
- Discuss the important cases decided against the IRS in 2007 and how the courts' decisions might affect the future tax planning and compliance of individuals and businesses.

CCH'S PLEDGE TO QUALITY

Thank you for choosing this CCH Continuing Education product. We will continue to produce high quality products that challenge your intellect and give you the best option for your Continuing Education requirements. Should you have a concern about this or any other CCH CPE product, please call our Customer Service Department at 1-800-248-3248.

NEW ONLINE GRADING gives you immediate 24/7 grading with instant results and no Express Grading Fee.

The **CCH Testing Center** website gives you and others in your firm easy, free access to CCH print courses and allows you to complete your CPE exams online for immediate results. Plus, the **My Courses** feature provides convenient storage for your CPE course certificates and completed exams.

Go to **www.cchtestingcenter.com** to complete your exam online.

One **complimentary copy** of this course is provided with certain CCH Federal Taxation publications. Additional copies of this course may be ordered for $29.00 each by calling 1-800-248-3248 (ask for product 0-0987-200).

TOP FEDERAL TAX ISSUES FOR 2008 CPE COURSE

Contents

MODULE 1: HOT BUSINESS TOPICS

1 FIN 48: Roadmap or Compass for the IRS?

2 Nonqualified Deferred Compensation: New Requirements

MODULE 2: WEALTH-BUILDING STRATEGIES

MODULE 1: HOT BUSINESS TOPICS — CHAPTER 1

FIN 48: Roadmap or Compass for the IRS?

This chapter explores Financial Accounting Standards Board (FASB) Interpretation No. 48 (FIN 48), Accounting for Uncertainty in Income Taxes. According to FASB, FIN 48 will help to bring about greater consistency in measurement associated in accounting for income taxes. However, its disclosure provisions have troubled many practitioners and taxpayers who fear it will be a roadmap for the IRS.

LEARNING OBJECTIVES

Upon completion of this chapter, you will be able to:

- Describe why FASB issued FIN 48;
- Understand the basics of FIN 48 and what it requires;
- Understand why practitioners are concerned that FIN 48 is a "roadmap" for the IRS;
- Identify the IRS' approach to FIN 48 disclosures; and
- Discuss FIN 48 and the convergence of U.S. and international accounting standards.

INTRODUCTION

FIN 48, which FASB issued in July 2006, is designed to clarify the accounting for uncertainty in income taxes recognized in an enterprise's financial statements in accordance with FASB Statement No. 109, Accounting for Income Taxes. FIN 48 sets forth a recognition threshold and measurement attribute for the financial statement recognition and measurement of a tax position taken or expected to be taken in a tax return. Very broadly, an expected tax benefit must be reflected in financial statements when an enterprise anticipates that the related tax position is more likely than not to be upheld. FIN 48 also provides guidance on derecognition, classification, interest and penalties, accounting in interim periods, disclosure, and transition.

FIN 48 applies to all tax positions taken on income tax returns, whether the return is filed with local, state, federal, or international taxing authorities. FIN 48 does not apply to sales, use, property, excise, gross receipts, or value-added taxes. Furthermore, if a non-U.S. based enterprise issues financial statements based on, or reconciled to, U.S. generally accepted accounting principles (GAAP), it is subject to FIN 48.

> **REMINDER**
>
> FIN 48 is effective for fiscal years beginning after December 15, 2006, is applicable to all enterprises subject to U.S. GAAP (including nonprofit enterprises), and applies to all income tax positions accounted for in accordance with FASB Statement No. 109.

TO WHOM DOES FIN 48 APPLY?

FIN 48 applies to all entities that prepare GAAP financial statements. FIN 48 uses the term *enterprise,* FASB explains, "because accounting for income taxes is primarily an issue for business enterprises." However, the requirements of FIN 48 apply to not-for-profit organizations, which must, for example, determine whether they have properly maintained their exempt status and whether income should be classified as exempt or unrelated business income.

FIN 48 also applies to passthrough entities and entities whose tax liability is subject to 100 percent credit for dividends paid (for example, real estate investment trusts and registered investment companies) that are potentially subject to income taxes. Partnerships are not subject to FIN 48 because the partners, rather than the partnership, are subject to income tax on partnership income. The same is generally true of S corporations, although some S corporations may be subject to income tax after conversion from a regular corporation. Likewise, an LLC is not subject to FIN 48 unless it may be subject to income taxes.

> **COMMENT**
>
> Several government and semiofficial bodies play different roles under the FIN 48 umbrella. FIN 48 was developed by FASB. The Securities and Exchange Commission (SEC) enforces it. The IRS is, at least at this time, more of an observer. It is aware that FIN 48 disclosures may be of significant interest to the government. However, because the disclosures are so new, the IRS is filtering exactly what information may be of value to it. "The IRS is a large consumer of information," a senior official in the IRS Large and Mid-Size Business Division (LMSB), said at a FIN 48 conference in Washington, DC, in July of 2007.

WHY FIN 48?

FASB Statement 109 contains no specific guidance on how to address uncertainty in accounting for income tax assets and liabilities. Consequently, FASB discovered that diverse accounting practices developed resulting in inconsistency in the criteria used to recognize, derecognize, and measure benefits related to income taxes. This diversity in practice resulted in non-comparability in reporting income tax assets and liabilities.

> **COMMENT**
>
> "The situation that existed prior to FIN 48 simply wasn't providing investors with the information they needed to make informed decisions," an SEC official said at a FIN 48 conference in Washington, DC, in July of 2007. "In many cases you had companies adopting drastically different accounting policies for the very same items. The objective of these rules is to provide information that investors need to make informed decisions."

FASB predicts that FIN 48 will improve financial reporting. All tax positions accounted for in accordance with FASB Statement No. 109 will be evaluated for recognition, derecognition, and measurement using the same criteria.

> **COMMENT**
>
> Before FIN 48, enterprises took different approaches. A tax position might be accounted for when it was filed in the tax return with the taxing authority. The enterprise could set up a reserve, an amount set aside by the enterprise to cover adjustments and additions to the enterprise's actual tax liability, if it was likely that the tax benefit would not be upheld.

> **COMMENT**
>
> After adopting FIN 48, 61 out of 130 large enterprises reported a negative adjustment to retained earnings, according to recent study. Forty enterprises reported a positive adjustment to retained earnings, and 12 enterprises reported no adjustment to retained earnings. Seventeen enterprises reported that the adjustment was immaterial.

> **REMINDER**
>
> FIN 48 applies only to income taxes. It does not apply to excise, estate, gift, and other taxes.

WHAT IS A TAX POSITION?

The term *tax position* as used in FIN 48 refers to a position in a previously filed tax return or a position expected to be taken in a future tax return that is reflected in measuring current or deferred income tax assets and liabilities for interim or annual periods. A tax position can result in a permanent reduction of income taxes payable, a deferral of income taxes otherwise currently payable to future years, or a change in the expected realizability of deferred tax assets. The term also encompasses, but is not limited to:

- A decision not to file a tax return;
- An allocation or a shift of income between jurisdictions, including transfer pricing;
- The characterization of income or a decision to exclude reporting taxable income in a tax return; and

A decision to classify a transaction, entity, or other position in a tax return as tax exempt.

STUDY QUESTIONS

1. FIN 48 is enforced by:
   a. IRS
   b. FASB
   c. PCAOB
   d. SEC

2. FIN 48 applies to:
   a. Income taxes only
   b. Income, estate, and gift taxes
   c. Value-added taxes
   d. All of the above

EVALUATION OF A TAX POSITION

The evaluation of a tax position under FIN 48 is a two-step process, described here.

Step 1: Recognition

The first step is recognition. The enterprise first determines whether it is "more likely than not" (more than a 50 percent chance) that a tax position will be sustained upon examination, including resolution of any related appeals or litigation processes, based on the technical merits of the position. In evaluating whether a tax position has met the more-likely-than-not recognition threshold, the enterprise should presume that the position will be examined by the appropriate taxing authority that has full knowledge of all relevant information. The enterprise can recognize the tax benefit if the more-likely-than-not threshold is satisfied. If the threshold is not satisfied, the tax benefit cannot be reported in the enterprise's financial statements.

COMMENT

Areas to review when one identifies tax positions for recognition and measurement include tax returns, Schedule M-3 workpapers, audits, notices of proposed adjustments, settlements, closing agreements, SEC filings, and minutes of audit committee meetings as well as minutes of board of director meetings.

COMMENT

FASB considered other thresholds besides more-likely-than-not when designing FIN 48. Initially, FASB selected "probable" as a recognition threshold. However, many practitioners disagreed. They expressed concern that "probable" was not consistently understood and applied. The probable threshold could also result in tax liabilities being overstated because "probable" would not reflect anticipated cash flows, some commentators cautioned. FASB ultimately decided on the more-likely-than-not threshold. This threshold, FASB indicated, was understood and would address concerns about the overstatement of income tax expenses.

Step 2: Measurement

The second step is measurement.

A tax position that meets the more-likely-than-not recognition threshold is measured to determine the amount of benefit to recognize in the financial statements. The tax position is measured at the largest amount of benefit that is greater than 50 percent likely of being realized upon ultimate settlement. That measurement is based on an analysis of the distribution of potential outcomes (that is, potential realized tax benefits) and their related probabilities. In the case of tax positions, the distribution is bounded from below by zero and from above by the amount taken in a tax return, FASB has explained.

COMMENT

Initially, FASB selected "best estimate" to measure tax benefits. *Best estimate* would represent "the single most likely amount in a range of possible estimated amounts." Some commentators expressed concern that this approach would yield counterintuitive results, especially where there would be a wide dispersion of possible estimated outcomes. FASB agreed.

COMMENT

It is not necessary that a legal tax opinion be obtained to show that the more-likely-than-not threshold is met, FASB has advised. "Management should decide whether to obtain a tax opinion after evaluating the weight of all available evidence and the uncertainties of the applicability of the relevant statutory or case law. Other evidence, in addition to or instead of a tax opinion, supporting the assertion also could be obtained." Ultimately, the level of necessary and appropriate evidence depends on all available information.

EXAMPLE

ABC Co. has taken a tax position that it believes is based on clear and unambiguous tax law for the payment of salaries and benefits to employees. The class of salaries being evaluated in this tax position is not subject to any limitations on deductibility (such as executive salaries are not included), and none of the expenditures are required to be capitalized (one such instance being expenditures that do not pertain to the production of inventories); all amounts accrued at year-end were paid within the statutorily required time frame subsequent to the reporting date. Management concludes that the salaries are fully deductible.

Because of the difficulty of defining an uncertain tax position, ABC Co.'s board decided that all tax positions are subject to FIN 48. However, because the deduction is based on clear and unambiguous tax law, management has a high confidence level in the technical merits of this position. Accordingly, the tax position meets the recognition criterion and should be evaluated for measurement. In determining the amount to measure, management is highly confident that the full amount of the deduction will be allowed and it is clear that it is greater than 50 percent likely that the tax position will be ultimately realized. Therefore, ABC Co. would recognize the full amount of the tax position in the financial statements.

COMMENT

Some practitioners are taking the position that anything less than "highly certain" falls within FIN 48.

EXAMPLE

XYZ Inc. has determined that a tax position resulting in a benefit of $100 on its tax return qualifies for recognition and should be measured. In a recent settlement with the taxing authority, the enterprise has agreed to the treatment for that position for current and future years. There are no recently issued relevant sources of tax law that would affect the enterprise's assessment. The enterprise has not changed any assumptions or computations, and the current tax position is consistent with the position that was recently settled. In this case, the enterprise would have a very high confidence level about the amount that will be ultimately realized and little information about other possible outcomes. Management will not need to evaluate other possible outcomes because it can be confident of the largest amount of benefit that is greater than 50 percent likely of being realized upon ultimate settlement without that evaluation.

EXAMPLE

MNO Inc. has determined that a tax position resulting in a benefit of $100 qualifies for recognition and should be measured. MNO Inc. has considered the amounts and probabilities of the possible estimated outcomes. The probable estimated outcome of $100 has a 5 percent individual probability of occurring and a 5 percent cumulative probability of occurring. The probable estimated outcome of $80 has a 25 percent individual probability of occurring and a 30 percent cumulative probability of occurring. The probable estimated outcome of $60 has a 25 percent individual probability of occurring and a 55 percent cumulative probability of occurring. The probable estimated outcome of $50 has a 20 percent individual probability of occurring and a 75 percent cumulative probability of occurring. Because $60 is the largest amount of benefit that is greater than 50 percent likely of being realized upon ultimate settlement, the enterprise would recognize a tax benefit of $60 in the financial statements.

EXAMPLE

QRS Inc. has determined that a tax position resulting in a benefit of $100 qualifies for recognition and should be measured. QRS Inc. has limited information about how a taxing authority will view the position. After considering all relevant information, management's confidence in the technical merits of the tax position exceeds the more-likely-than-not recognition threshold. However, management believes it is likely it would settle for less than the full amount of the entire position if examined. QRS Inc. has considered the amounts and the probabilities of the possible estimated outcomes. The possible estimated outcome of $100 has a 25 percent individual probability of occurring and a 25 percent cumulative probability of occurring.

The possible estimated outcome of $75 has a 50 percent individual probability of occurring and a 75 percent cumulative probability of occurring. The possible estimated outcome of $50 has a 25 percent individual probability of occurring and a 100 percent cumulative probability of occurring. Because $75 is the largest amount of benefit that is greater than 50 percent likely of being realized upon ultimate settlement, the enterprise would recognize a tax benefit of $75 in the financial statements.

UNIT OF ACCOUNT

The appropriate unit of account for determining what constitutes an individual tax position and whether the more-likely-than not recognition threshold is met for a tax position is a matter of judgment based on the individual facts and circumstances. The position must be evaluated in light of all available evidence.

EXAMPLE

ABC Co. anticipates claiming a $1 million research and experimentation credit on its tax return for the current fiscal year. The credit comprises equal spending on four separate projects ($250,000 of tax credit per project). The enterprise expects to have sufficient taxable income in the current year to fully use the $1 million credit. Upon review of the supporting documentation, management believes it is more likely than not that the enterprise will ultimately sustain a benefit of approximately $650,000. The anticipated benefit consists of approximately $200,000 per project for the first three projects and $50,000 for the fourth project.

In its evaluation of the appropriate amount to recognize, management first determines the appropriate unit of account for the tax position. Because of the magnitude of expenditures in each project, management concludes that the appropriate unit of account is each individual research project. In reaching this conclusion, management considers both the level at which it accumulates information to support the tax return and the level at which it anticipates addressing the issue with taxing authorities. In this example, upon review of the four projects including the magnitude of expenditures, management determines that it accumulates information at the project level. Management also anticipates the taxing authority will address the issues during an examination at the level of individual projects.

In evaluating the projects for recognition, management determines that three projects meet the more-likely-than-not recognition threshold. However, due to the nature of the activities that constitute the fourth project, it is uncertain that the tax benefit related to this project will be allowed. Because the tax benefit related to that fourth project does not meet the more-likely-than-not recognition threshold, it should not be recognized in the financial statements, even though tax positions associated with that project will be included in the tax return. The enterprise would recognize a $600,000 financial statement benefit related to the first three projects but would not recognize a financial statement benefit related to the fourth project.

STUDY QUESTIONS

3. The reason FASB offered for rejecting the "probable" threshold for recognition was:

a. The probable threshold took fewer tax information sources into consideration than did the more-likely-than-not threshold.

b. The alternative more-likely-than-not threshold was understood well and addressed overstatements of income tax expenses.

c. The probable threshold tended to overstate the income tax liabilities of certain passthrough entities.

d. The best estimate threshold was more accurate.

4. The unit of account that is appropriate for determining an organization's tax position meets the more-likely-than-not threshold is based on:

a. Prior periods' financial statements

b. Best estimates

c. Judgment stemming from the individual facts and circumstances

d. None of the above is the unit of account

SUBSEQUENT EVENTS

If the more-likely-than not recognition threshold is not met in the period for which a tax position is taken or expected to be taken, FIN 48 instructs the enterprise to recognize the benefit of the tax position in the first subsequent financial reporting period in which:

■ The threshold is met (for example, by virtue of another taxpayer's favorable court decision);

■ The position is "effectively settled" by virtue of the closing of an examination where the likelihood of the taxing authority reopening the examination of that position is remote; or

■ The relevant statute of limitations to examine and challenge the tax position expires.

COMMENT

Previously recognized tax positions that no longer meet the more-likely-than-not recognition threshold should be derecognized in the first subsequent financial reporting period in which that threshold is no longer met, according to FASB.

EXAMPLE

ABC Co. has evaluated a tax position at its most recent reporting date and has concluded that the position meets the more-likely-than-not recognition threshold. In evaluating the tax position for recognition, ABC Co. considered all relevant sources of tax law, including a court case in which the taxing authority has fully disallowed a similar tax position with an unrelated enterprise (XYZ Co.). The taxing authority and XYZ Co. are aggressively litigating the matter. Although ABC Co. was aware of that court case at the recent reporting date, management determined that the more-likely-than-not recognition threshold had been met. Subsequent to the reporting date, but prior to the issuance of the financial statements, the taxing authority prevailed in its litigation with XYZ, Co., and ABC Co. concludes that it is no longer more likely than not that it will sustain the position.

Paragraph 11 of FIN 48 notes that "an enterprise shall derecognize a previously recognized tax position in the first period in which it is no longer more likely than not that the tax position would be sustained upon examination," and paragraph 12 indicates that "subsequent recognition, de-recognition, and measurement shall be based on management's best judgment given the facts, circumstances, and information available at the reporting date." Because the resolution of XYZ Co.'s litigation with the taxing authority is the information that caused ABC Co. to change its judgment about the sustainability of the position and that information was not available at the reporting date, the change in judgment would be recognized in the first quarter of the current fiscal year.

CAUTION

An enterprise cannot presume that a taxing authority (federal, state or local) will not examine the tax position.

PENALTIES AND INTEREST

Penalties and interest also must be recognized. Penalties are assessed by the IRS, and other taxing authorities, when a specified confidence level is not met. Interest is assessed when the IRS and other taxing authorities determine that taxes have been underpaid. Financial statements, consistent with accrual accounting, should reflect interest beginning in the period that it would begin accruing according to the relevant tax law and should reflect penalties in the first period the tax position was taken in a tax return that would give rise to the penalty, based the provisions of the relevant tax law, FASB explained. The accrual of interest expense is based on the difference between the tax positions recognized in the financial statements and the amount recognized or expected to be recognized in the tax return. The penalties should be accrued if the position does not meet the minimum statutory threshold necessary to avoid payment of penalties.

EFFECTIVE SETTLEMENT

After FIN 48 was issued, FASB revisited the threshold used in evaluating if, after a settlement, the taxing authority would subsequently examine or reexamine any aspect of an enterprise's tax position. FASB ultimately decided to change the threshold from "highly unlikely" to "remote."

In February 2007, FASB issued proposed FASB Staff Position (FSP) FIN 48-a, Definition of Settlement in FIN 48. The FSP provided guidance on how an enterprise should determine whether a tax position is effectively settled for the purpose of recognizing previously unrecognized tax benefits. Under paragraph 10A(c) of the FSP, before a tax position may be considered settled, the enterprise must consider it highly unlikely that the taxing authority will subsequently examine or reexamine any aspect of the tax position included in the completed examination, presuming the taxing authority has full knowledge of all relevant information.

After the FSP was released, several commentators expressed concern at the language. They were not sure how to interpret the term *highly unlikely.* The FASB staff presented two alternatives to the Board. One option was to change the threshold used in evaluating whether the taxing authority would subsequently examine or reexamine any aspect of the tax position from highly unlikely to remote. The other option was not to make any change and leave the threshold at "highly unlikely." The Board decided to change the threshold from "highly unlikely" to "remote."

COMMENT

One FASB member noted that it is "simpler to use the same term [remote] we often use in accounting."

COMMENT

"We don't expect people to have a crystal ball," an SEC official said at a FIN 48 conference in Washington, DC, in July 2007.

STUDY QUESTIONS

5. How should a taxpayer report the change for previously recognized tax positions that no longer meet the more-likely-than-not recognition threshold?
   a. Derecognize the change in the first subsequent financial reporting period during which the threshold is no longer met
   b. Derecognize the change upon receiving IRS notice of examination pertaining to the tax position
   c. Issue a restatement of financial position for the period
   d. If a publicly traded company, provide investors of record a revised projected earnings statement during the current financial reporting period

6. The response to FSP FIN 48-a in defining whether a tax position is effectively settled was to:
   a. Leave the wording for determining the threshold as it stood for FSP FIN 48-a
   b. Issue revised guidelines for the taxing authority examiners clarifying criteria for effective settlement
   c. Change the threshold used in evaluating likelihood of subsequent examination of the tax position to remote
   d. None of the above was the response of FASB

SAMPLE INTERIM SEC FILINGS

ABC Inc. 10-Q May 2, 2007
(Quarterly Period Ended 3/31/2007)

Notes to Consolidated Financial Statements (Unaudited)

2. Recent Accounting Standards

Accounting for Uncertainty in Income Taxes

On January 1, 2007, the Company adopted the provisions of FASB Interpretation No. 48, Accounting for Uncertainty in Income Taxes—an interpretation of FASB Statement No. 109 (FIN 48), which clarifies the accounting for uncertainty in income tax positions. This interpretation requires the Company to recognize in the consolidated financial statements only those tax positions determined to be more likely than not of being sustained upon examination, based on the technical merits of the positions. Upon adoption, the Company recognized a $3 million reduction of previously recorded tax reserves, which was accounted for as an increase to the retained earnings balance as of January 1, 2007.

After considering the impact of adopting FIN 48, the Company had an $11 million reserve for uncertain income tax positions as of January 1, 2007. Movement in the reserve balance during the three months ended March 31, 2007, was not material. The Company does not currently anticipate such uncertain income tax positions will significantly increase or decrease prior to March 31, 2008; however, developments in this area could differ from those currently expected. Such unrecognized tax positions, if ever recognized in the financial statements, would be recorded in the statement of operations as part of the income tax provision.

The income tax reserve as of January 1, 2007, included an accrual for interest and penalties of approximately $1 million. The change in the accrual for interest and penalties for the three months ended March 31, 2007 was not material. The Company's policy is to recognize interest and penalties accrued on uncertain tax positions as part of income tax expense.

With few exceptions, periods ending after March 31, 2003, are subject to U.S., state, and local income tax examinations by tax authorities.

XYZ Inc. 10-Q May 2, 2007
(Quarterly Period Ended 3/31/2007)

Notes to Consolidated Financial Statements (Unaudited)

1. Basis of Presentation and Accounting Policies

Adoption of New Accounting Standards

The adoption of FIN 48 at January 1, 2007, did not have a material effect on the Company's financial position.

The total amount of unrecognized tax benefits as of January 1, 2007, was $339 million. Included in that balance were $101 million of unrecognized tax benefits that, if recognized, would affect the annual effective tax rate and $175 million of tax positions for which the ultimate deductibility is certain, but for which there is uncertainty about the timing of deductibility. The timing of such deductibility would not affect the annual effective tax rate. The balance of unrecognized tax benefits at January 1, 2007, comprises $63 million of unrecognized tax benefits that, if recognized, would reduce goodwill.

The Company recognizes interest and penalties accrued related to unrecognized tax benefits in income taxes. The Company had approximately $35 million for the payment of interest and penalties accrued at January 1, 2007.

As of January 1, 2007, the Internal Revenue Service (IRS) is conducting an examination of the Company's U.S. income tax returns for the years 2002 through 2004. During the first quarter 2007, the Company effectively settled the premerger XYZ Corp. IRS examinations for the 2002 and 2003 years, resulting in an after-tax benefit of $28 million.

The Company anticipates that the current IRS examination will be effectively settled within the next 12 months. An estimate of the range of the reasonably possible change to the unrecognized tax benefits that may occur as a result of the anticipated settlement cannot be made.

MNO Inc. 10-Q May 2, 2007
(Quarterly Period Ended 3/31/2007)

Notes to Consolidated Financial Statements

Note 2. Effect of Adoption of FASB Interpretation No. 48 (FIN 48), Accounting for Uncertainty in Income Taxes

Each year the company files hundreds of income tax returns in the various national, state, and local income taxing jurisdictions in which it operates.

These tax returns are subject to examination and possible challenge by the taxing authorities. Positions challenged by the taxing authorities may be settled or appealed by the company. As a result, there is an uncertainty in income taxes recognized in the company's financial statements in accordance with FASB Statement No. 109, Accounting for Income Taxes.

In 2006, the FASB issued FIN 48, which clarifies the application of FASB Statement No. 109 by defining a criterion that an individual income tax position must meet for any part of the benefit of that position to be recognized in an enterprise's financial statements and provides guidance on measurement, derecognition, classification, accounting for interest and penalties, accounting in interim periods, disclosure, and transition.

In accordance with the transition provisions, the company adopted FIN 48 effective January 1, 2007. This resulted in a $116 reduction in the previously accrued liabilities and a corresponding $116 increase in reinvested earnings at January 1, 2007. In accordance with FIN 48, the total amount of global unrecognized tax benefits at January 1, 2007, was $1,070. Of the $1,070 of unrecognized tax benefits, $714 relates to tax positions, which if recognized would reduce tax expense. The total gross accrued interest and penalties at January 1, 2007, was $134. Interest accrued related to unrecognized tax benefits is included in interest income, net of miscellaneous interest expense, under other income, net. Income tax related penalties are included in the provision for income taxes.

The company and/or its subsidiaries files income tax returns in the U.S. federal jurisdiction, and various states and non-U.S. jurisdictions. With few exceptions, the company is no longer subject to U.S. federal, state and local, or non-U.S. income tax examinations by tax authorities for years before 1999. Given the uncertainty regarding when tax authorities will complete their examinations and the possible outcomes of their examinations, a current estimate of the range of reasonably possible significant increases or decreases that may occur within the next 12 months cannot be made.

> **COMMENT**
>
> Many more individuals may be involved in an enterprise's FIN 48 analysis than in the past. In addition to accounting staff and the CFO, the enterprise's tax manager and tax staff likely will have more involvement.

SIMILAR LANGUAGE IN IRS STANDARDS

If the language in FIN 48 sounds familiar, it is. The rules for *covered opinions* under Circular 230, Rules of Practice before the IRS are similar. Circular 230 requires practitioners to:

- Identify and consider all relevant facts;
- Avoid basing the opinion on unreasonable factual assumptions;
- Consider all significant federal tax issues;
- Relate the law and judicial doctrines to the facts, come to a conclusion regarding the likelihood of the taxpayer prevailing or to explain why no conclusion has been reached, and set forth the reasons for the conclusion.

The more likely than not language also appears in the Tax Code. In Notice 2005-12, the IRS explained that the accuracy-related penalty under Code Sec. 6662A does not apply with respect to any portion of a reportable transaction understatement if, under Code Sec. 6664(d), it is shown that there was reasonable cause and the taxpayer acted in good faith with respect to that portion of the understatement.

Under Code Sec. 6664(d), a taxpayer does not have reasonable cause and did not act in good faith unless:

- The relevant facts affecting the tax treatment of the item are adequately disclosed in accordance with regulations prescribed under Code Sec. 6011;
- There is or was substantial authority; and
- The taxpayer reasonably believed that its treatment of the item was more likely than not the proper tax treatment.

A taxpayer is treated as having a reasonable belief only if the belief is based on the facts and the law that exist at the time the return is filed and the belief relates solely to the taxpayer's chances of success on the merits of the tax treatment of the issue.

DISCLOSURE PROVISIONS

The disclosure provisions of FIN 48 have generated a lot of controversy and alarm among practitioners. Some practitioners worry that FIN 48 disclosures will serve as a roadmap for the IRS to launch examinations and investigations.

COMMENT

The disclosure concerns have been challenged by some lawmakers who ask what are enterprises "trying to hide."

COMMENT

An SEC official tried to calm practitioners concerns at the July 2007 FIN 48 conference in Washington, DC, by saying, "These rules were written from the perspective of providing additional information to investors. I certainly don't contemplate a large level of interaction between the staffs of the SEC and the IRS."

The disclosures may reveal tax positions that enterprises expect will change. For example, unrecognized tax benefits could decrease because of audit settlements or the closing of the statute of limitations on certain tax years.

EXAMPLE

ABC Co. or one of its subsidiaries files income tax returns in the U.S. federal jurisdiction, and various states and foreign jurisdictions. With few exceptions, ABC Co. is no longer subject to U.S. federal, state and local, or non-U.S. income tax examinations by tax authorities for years before 2001. The IRS began an examination of ABC Co.'s U.S. income tax returns for 2002 through 2004 in the first quarter of 2007 that is anticipated to be completed by the end of 2008. As of December 31, 2007, the IRS has proposed certain significant adjustments to the ABC Co.'s transfer pricing and research credits tax positions. Management is currently evaluating those proposed adjustments to determine if it agrees, but if accepted, ABC Co. does not anticipate the adjustments would result in a material change to its financial position. However, ABC Co. anticipates that it is reasonably possible that an additional payment in the range of $80 to $100 million will be made by the end of 2008.

ABC Co. adopted the provisions of FIN 48 on January 1, 2007. As a result, ABC Co. recognized approximately a $200 million increase in the liability for unrecognized tax benefits, which was accounted for as a reduction to the January 1, 2007, balance of retained earnings. A reconciliation of the beginning and ending amount of unrecognized tax benefits is as follows:

	(in millions)
Balance at January 1, 2007	$370,000
Additions based on tax positions related to the current year	10,000
Additions for tax positions of prior years	30,000
Reductions for tax positions of prior years	(60,000)
Settlements	(40,000)
Balance at December 31, 2007	$310,000

Included in the balance at December 31, 2007, are $60 million of tax positions for which the ultimate deductibility is highly certain but for which there is uncertainty about the timing of such deductibility. Because of the impact of deferred tax accounting, other than interest and penalties, the disallowance of the shorter deductibility period would not affect the annual effective tax rate but would accelerate the payment of cash to the taxing authority to an earlier period.

ABC Co. recognizes interest accrued related to unrecognized tax benefits in interest expense and penalties in operating expenses. During the years ended December 31, 2007, 2006, and 2005, ABC Co. recognized approximately $10, $11, and $12 million in interest and penalties, respectively. ABC Co. had approximately $60 and $50 million for the payment of interest and penalties accrued at December 31, 2007, and 2006, respectively.

STUDY QUESTIONS

7. Which of the following is *not* similar in language to FIN 48's more-likely-than-not standard for taxpayers to prevail in their tax positions?

a. FASB Statement 109
b. Circular 230's covered opinion rules
c. Code Sec. 6664(d)'s reasonable cause rules
d. All of the above reflect similar language to that for tax positions in FIN 48

8. FIN 48 disclosures may reveal tax positions that enterprises expect will change. *True or False?*

EFFECTIVE DATE

FIN 48 is effective for fiscal years beginning after December 15, 2006. In the months leading up to December 15, 2006, many practitioners expected FASB to delay the effective date of FIN 48 because of the controversy surrounding it. FASB reported that it received more than 400 letters about FIN 48. Most requested a one-year delay in its effective date. However,

FASB chose not to delay the effective date after determining that taxpayers had had enough time to plan for the new standard.

> **COMMENT**
>
> The SEC was also asked to delay implementation of FIN 48 and declined to do so. The Investment Company Institute (ICI) had recommended a delay for mutual funds. "FIN 48 uniquely affects the mutual fund industry because the price at which fund shares are purchased and sold (the net asset value or NAV) is calculated each business day," the ICI told the SEC. "Unlike other corporate registrants that are required to apply FIN 48 only to their periodic financial statements, mutual funds must apply the interpretation on a daily basis. Mutual funds must begin recognizing tax liabilities in their NAVs as early as January 2, 2007. Other corporate registrants will not be required to recognize tax liabilities under FIN 48 until, at the earliest, March 31, 2007." Although the SEC declined to delay implementation of FIN 48, it told the ICI that "in light of the unique issues and challenges that the application of FIN 48 present for funds (particularly with respect to the calculation of NAV), we would not object if a fund implements FIN 48 in the first required financial statement reporting period for its fiscal year beginning after December 15, 2006." The first funds to have a fiscal year that begins after December 15, 2006, are calendar-year funds. "A calendar-year open-ended or close-ended fund would implement FIN 48 no later than its June 29, 2007 (the last business day of the semiannual reporting period) NAV," according to the SEC.

IRS RESPONSE TO DISCLOSURE CONCERNS

The IRS described the disclosure provisions in its "FIN 48 Field Examiners Guide" released in May 2007. FIN 48 requires the following disclosures that the IRS may find relevant in a tax audit situation:

(a) A tabular reconciliation of the total amounts of unrecognized tax benefits at the beginning and end of the period, which shall include at a minimum:

1. The gross amounts of the increases and decreases in unrecognized tax benefits as a result of tax positions taken during a prior period.
2. The gross amounts of increases and decreases in unrecognized tax benefits as a result of tax positions taken during the current period
3. The amounts of decreases in the unrecognized tax benefits relating to settlements with taxing authorities
4. Reductions to unrecognized tax benefits as a result of a lapse of the applicable statute of limitations

(b) The total amount of unrecognized tax benefits that, if recognized, would affect the effective tax rate;

(c) The total amounts of interest and penalties recognized in the statement of operations and the total amounts of interest and penalties recognized in the statement of financial position;

(d) For positions for which it is reasonably possible that the total amounts of unrecognized tax benefits will significantly increase or decrease within 12 months of the reporting date:

    1. The nature of the uncertainty;

    2. The nature of the event that could occur in the next 12 months that would cause the change;

    3. An estimate of the range of the reasonably possible change or a statement that an estimate of the range cannot be made; and

(e) A description of tax years that remain subject to examination by major tax jurisdictions.

In its "FIN 48 Field Examiners Guide," the IRS predicts that FIN 48 disclosures should give the IRS a somewhat better view of a taxpayer's uncertain tax positions; however, the disclosures still do not have the specificity that would allow a perfect view of the issues and amounts at risk.

EXAMPLE

There may be a contingent tax liability listed in the tax footnotes of a large multinational taxpayer with a description called "tax credits"; however, tax credits could be U.S., foreign, or state tax credits. So the "tax credits" in this example may or may not in this case have a U.S. tax impact.

COMMENT

FASB Board Member Edward Trott told corporate tax professionals in Washington, DC, in February of 2007 at the 8th Annual Tax Policy and Practice Symposium, Understanding the Global Tax Arena, sponsored by the Tax Council Policy Institute that FASB did not invent tax uncertainties. "These issues have always been there." The FASB did not craft FIN 48 to provide information to the IRS, Trott stressed. "Our focus was on the capital markets," he said. Trott explained that it is important for companies to communicate tax uncertainties to the capital markets. He predicted that FIN 48 will improve that communication.

STUDY QUESTIONS

9. FIN 48 is effective for fiscal years beginning:
   a. After December 15, 2006
   b. After December 31, 2006
   c. After January 1, 2007
   d. After December 15, 2007

10. All of the following are discussed in the IRS "FIN 48 Field Examiners Guide" as FIN 48-required disclosures *except:*
   a. The tax position as measured under international accounting standards
   b. A description of tax years that remain subject to examination by major tax jurisdictions
   c. Penalties and interest
   d. All of the above are required disclosures

IRS VIEW OF EFFECTIVE SETTLEMENT

In the tax years under examination, a tax position does not need to be specifically reviewed or examined by the taxing authority to be considered effectively settled through examination, according to the IRS in its "FIN 48 Field Examiners Guide." Effective settlement of a position subject to an examination does not result in effective settlement of similar or identical tax positions in periods that have not been examined. In general terms, this means that when an IRS examination is closed there has been effective settlement of all uncertain tax positions for the examined year, whether such uncertainties are known to the IRS and examined or not, as long as the conditions in the immediately preceding are present, the IRS stated in its "FIN 48 Field Examiners Guide."

EXAMPLE

A taxpayer did not report dividend income on its tax return based on an ambiguous tax law. Furthermore, assume the position meets the require-ments of FIN 48 and accordingly, the taxpayer creates a reserve for un-certain tax positions related to this item. The tax year is audited by the IRS but the IRS does not propose an audit adjustment and closes the case.

Assume also that the issue is not likely to meet any of the exceptions to the Service's policy against reopening examinations. Because the examination is closed and it is remote that the Service would reopen an examination of the issue, the taxpayer can reverse that contingent tax liability and record the tax benefit at this point on the U.S. GAAP financial statements because the uncertainty is now effectively removed.

TAX ACCRUAL WORKPAPERS

As of press time, FIN 48 workpapers are treated by the IRS as tax accrual workpapers. Consequently, they are subject to the IRS's policy of restraint in asking for tax accrual workpapers.

The Internal Revenue Manual defines *tax accrual workpapers* to include those audit workpapers, whether prepared by the taxpayer, the taxpayer's accountant, or the independent auditor, that relate to the tax reserve for current, deferred, and potential or contingent tax liabilities.

The agency's policy regarding requests for tax accrual workpapers is one of self-restraint: Routine audits do not include a request for tax accrual workpapers. Only transactions that involve a listed tax-shelter transaction or that are under a strict *unusual circumstances standard* will trigger a request. In requesting tax accrual workpapers under the unusual circumstances standard, the IRS reminds agents that the workpapers "should normally be sought only when such factual data cannot be obtained from the taxpayer's records or from available third parties, and then only as a collateral source for factual data." The IRS will not issue a summons for tax accrual workpapers without National Office review and approval; it cannot be done strictly on the field office level.

CAUTION

FIN 48 disclosures reported in quarterly and/or annual financial statements, and any other public documents, are not subject to the policy of restraint, and may be considered by examiners and others when conducting risk assessments, the IRS has cautioned.

In a March 2007 memorandum, IRS Chief Counsel Donald Korb presented Large and Mid-Size Business Division Commissioner Deborah Nolan some "good news/bad news" for taxpayers on FIN 48:

- FIN 48 workpapers are tax accrual workpapers and therefore may be subject to IRS summons; but
- As tax accrual workpapers, FIN 48 documentation falls under the IRS' policy of restraint.

Korb noted that FIN 48 describes financial accounting and reporting requirements. FIN 48 does not set forth documentation requirements. Rather, the documentation requirements that taxpayers and their auditors must follow are established by the Securities and Exchange Commission (SEC), the Public Company Accounting Oversight Board (PCAOB), and the American Institute of Certified Public Accountants (AICPA), and these documentation requirements remain unchanged by the issuance of FIN 48, Korb told Nolan. Korb concluded that documentation resulting from the issuance of FIN 48 is considered tax accrual workpapers.

Typical Workpaper Content

Tax accrual workpapers typically include determinations and related documentation of estimates of potential or contingent tax liabilities related to tax positions taken by the taxpayer on certain transactions. In addition, there may be an audit trail and/or complete explanation of the transactions. There may also be information on whether there was reliance on outside legal advice; an assessment of the taxpayer's position; references to promotional materials; and comments on unwritten agreements, confidentiality agreements, restitution agreements, contingency fees, expectations, and other material facts surrounding the transactions. The workpapers may include documents written by the taxpayer's employees and officers describing or evaluating the tax strategies. The scope and quality of the workpapers will vary.

> **COMMENT**
>
> IRM Section 4.10.20.2(2) defines tax accrual workpapers as "those audit workpapers, whether prepared by the taxpayer, the taxpayer's accountant, or the independent auditor, that relate to the tax reserve for current, deferred, and potential or contingent tax liabilities, however classified or reported on audited financial statements, and to footnotes disclosing those tax reserves on audited financial statements." These workpapers reflect an estimate of a company's tax liabilities and may also be referred to as the tax pool analysis, tax liability contingency analysis, tax cushion analysis, or tax contingency reserve analysis.

> **CAUTION**
>
> IRS Chief Counsel Donald Korb warned that the name given the workpapers by the taxpayer, the taxpayer's accountant, or the independent auditor is not determinative.

IRS Court Loss

In late August, a federal district court handed the IRS a defeat in a closely watched tax accrual workpapers case (*Textron v. U.S.,* DC R.I., August 29, 2007). In this case, the IRS learned that a taxpayer's subsidiary had engaged in nine listed transactions. The taxpayer complied with all IRS information document requests, except for requests seeking its tax accrual workpapers.

COMMENT

The IRS defined *workpapers* to include all accrual and other financial workpapers or documents created or assembled by the taxpayer, an accountant for the taxpayer, or the taxpayer's independent auditor relating to any tax reserve for current, deferred, and potential or contingent tax liabilities, however classified or reported on audited financial statements. The workpapers include, but are not limited to, any and all analyses, computations, opinions, notes, summaries, discussions, and other documents relating to such reserves.

The court observed that the IRS had a legitimate, good-faith purpose for requesting the workpapers, to determine the taxpayer's tax liability. However, the court agreed with the taxpayer that the attorney-client privilege and the tax practitioner-client privilege in Code Sec. 7525 protected the workpapers, which protect confidential communications relating to legal advice sought from the attorney, or legal-type advice sought from the accountant. The workpapers were not prepared for litigation but in the ordinary course of business and to satisfy requirements for financial statements filed with the SEC, the court found.

COMMENT

The work product privilege applies to materials prepared by an attorney in anticipation of litigation. It allows a lawyer to develop legal theories and strategy free from unnecessary intrusion by his or her adversaries, including the IRS.

COMMENT

"We strongly believe that the documents disclosed [to the SEC] are not work product," IRS Chief Counsel Donald Korb said after the decision. "The documents had to be prepared for regulatory purposes. This requirement removes them from work product protection," he noted. Korb indicated that the IRS is likely to appeal the district court's decision.

STUDY QUESTIONS

11. When a position subject to an IRS examination is effectively settled, similar tax positions in the taxpayer's unexamined periods are considered settled as well. *True or False?*

12. FIN 48 workpapers are subject to the IRS' policy of restraint for tax accrual workpapers. *True or False?*

EFFECTIVE TAX RECONCILIATION WORKPAPERS

Effective tax rate reconciliation workpapers are not accrual workpapers. Consequently, they are not covered by the IRS' policy of restraint. IRS Chief Counsel reiterated this view in a Chief Counsel Advice (CC-2007-15) issued in June of 2007.

The Chief Counsel noted that FASB Statement 109 (Accounting for Income Taxes, effective 1992) established financial accounting and reporting standards for the effects of income taxes that result from an enterprise's activities during the current and preceding years. FASB Statement 109 requires several types of financial statement disclosures, one of which requires the disclosure of a reconciliation of "(a) the reported amount of income tax expense attributable to continuing operations for the year to (b) the amount of income tax expense that would result from applying domestic federal statutory tax rates to pretax income from continuing operations." The specific details that make up the numbers reported in the broad categories are contained in the underlying workpapers maintained by companies.

According to the Chief Counsel, the IRS did not intend for effective tax rate reconciliation workpapers to be treated as tax accrual workpapers or audit workpapers. They are not prepared for the purpose of determining the proper amount of the reserve for contingent tax liabilities. They are not audit workpapers in the sense of workpapers retained by the auditor to document the performance of the audit. They are prepared by the taxpayer, not the auditor. They do not reflect procedures followed or tests performed by the auditor in reviewing the taxpayer's financial statements.

COMMENT

Chief Counsel's determination is not a "back-door approach" to securing tax accrual workpapers, Robert Adams, a senior official in the IRS LMSB Division, told the July 2007 FIN 48 conference in Washington, DC.

CERTAINTY

Since the release of FIN 48, the IRS has been telling taxpayers that they can gain more certainty in regard to their FIN 48 disclosures. The IRS launched a special FIN 48 initiative in the autumn of 2006 and continues to remind taxpayers that "candor, transparency, and the right motivations" generate certainty on tax issues.

Special IRS Initiative

The special IRS initiative, which was administered by the LMSB Division, aimed to expedite the examination and resolution of uncertain tax positions taken in filed returns and/or expected to be taken in tax returns yet to be filed. The IRS cautioned that the initiative was not intended to produce a different result from what would obtain under the normal pace of examination and resolution but was simply designed to speed up the process by which such examination and resolution would otherwise result.

Eligibility. Taxpayers that issue certified financial statements in accord with U.S. GAAP could raise an issue—or multiple issues—under the initiative. Promoters of listed transactions were not eligible under the initiative.

The IRS indicated that the initiative was intended to assist taxpayers that will issue certified financial statements for their current financial accounting years ending on or before March 31, 2007. Other taxpayers would have had sufficient time to address similar concerns under ordinary practices.

Some issues were expressly outside the scope of the initiative. The IRS declined to resolve:

- Any issue or transaction that was designated for litigation or for which the taxpayer had been notified that the IRS is considering designating the issue or transaction for litigation;
- Any issue or transaction for which the taxpayer was a party in a court proceeding to determine the tax treatment of any aspect of the issue or transaction;
- Any issue or transaction for which the IRS had imposed a fraud penalty or for which the IRS has notified the taxpayer that the IRS was considering imposing a fraud penalty;
- Any issue or transaction for which the taxpayer was under a tax-related criminal investigation or for which the taxpayers had been notified that the government intends to launch a criminal investigation.

Ongoing Initiatives

Besides its one-time initiative, the IRS is also encouraging taxpayers to take advantage of various agreements and initiatives to resolve "uncertain tax positions," including:

(a) Prefiling:

  1. Industry issue resolution
  2. Prefiling agreements
  3. Advance pricing agreements
  4. Compliance Assurance Program

(b) Post-filing:

  1. Joint audit planning
  2. LIFE
  3. Advanced Issue Resolution
  4. Appeals Fast Track Program
  5. Accelerated Issue Resolution
  6. Early Referral to Appeals

STUDY QUESTIONS

13. All of the following are reasons that the IRS does not consider effective tax rate reconciliation workpapers to be treated as accrual or audit workpapers *except:*

  a. The reconciliation workpapers are prepared by the taxpayer, not the auditor.
  b. The reconciliation workpapers do not reflect procedures followed or tests performed by the auditor in reviewing the taxpayer's financial statements.
  c. The reconciliation workpapers are not prepared for the purpose of determining the proper amount of the reserve for contingent tax liabilities.
  d. All of the above are reasons effective tax rate reconciliation workpapers differ from accrual or audit workpapers.

14. Which of the following was addressed in the IRS special FIN 48 initiative in 2006?

  a. An issue designated for litigation
  b. A transaction for which the IRS issued a fraud penalty
  c. The expedition of uncertain tax positions taken in filed and as yet unfiled returns
  d. An issue under tax-related criminal investigation

CLOSED TAX YEARS

Many practitioners are concerned that the IRS will reopen an exam cycle that had been closed because of FIN 48 disclosures. In its "FIN 48 Field Examiners Guide," the IRS recognized its longstanding policy not to reopen tax years that have been examined and closed. However, that policy is not absolute. A tax year that has been examined and closed may be reopened if exceptional circumstances are present.

Exceptional circumstances include fraud or misrepresentation of material facts, a substantial error based on an established IRS position existing at the time of the examination or if the failure to reopen the case would be a serious administrative omission. The IRS also has reserved discretion to reopen cases involving abusive transactions.

> **CAUTION**
>
> Because FIN 48 requires more information to be disclosed about uncertain tax positions than was the case before FIN 48 was issued, it is possible that reopenings will occur more frequently because of the potentially increased availability of information warranting reopening, the IRS observed.

A FIN 48 analysis is a multistep process. The following provides a brief overview of that process.

Brief Workflow Plan for Complying with FIN 48

1. Identify uncertain tax positions
2. Determine the unit of account
3. Determine whether the recognition threshold is met
4. Measure the tax benefit
5. Evaluate tax-planning strategies
6. Monitor changes in subsequent periods
7. Determine interest and penalties
8. Classify tax liabilities
9. Prepare required disclosures

CONVERGENCE

FIN 48 has highlighted the differences between U.S. accounting standards and international accounting standards. Although the FASB sets U.S. accounting standards, many other nations follow standards set by the International Accounting Standards Board (IASB). The IASB does not have a similar FIN 48 standard. IASB is contemplating a standard and one may be issued in the future.

In 2002, FASB and IASB signed a memorandum of understanding to develop compatible accounting standards that could be used for both domestic and cross-border financial reporting. In 2006, the two organizations released a roadmap for convergence. FASB and IASB have seven projects on their active agenda for convergence. They are:

- Business combinations;
- Consolidations;
- Fair value measurement guidance;
- Liability and equity distinctions;
- Performance reporting;
- Post-retirement benefits including pensions; and
- Revenue recognition.

By 2008, FASB and IASB also agreed to look at major differences in a few focused areas. They are:

- Borrowing costs;
- Fair value option;
- Government grants;
- Impairment;
- Income tax;
- Joint ventures;
- Research and development;
- Segment reporting; and
- Subsequent events.

SEC Action

In June of 2007, the SEC proposed a major change. The SEC proposed allowing non-U.S. companies to file financial results according to International Financial Reporting Standards (IFRS) as approved by the IASB. U.S. issuers are required to prepare financial statements in accordance with U.S. GAAP. Under the proposal, non-U.S. companies would be able to access U.S. capital markets without reconciliation with U.S. GAAP by 2009.

> **COMMENT**
>
> According to the SEC, nearly 100 countries require or allow the use of IFRS.
>
> The IASB predicted that the proposal showed the importance and relevance of the continuing IASB-FASB convergence process and would reduce significantly the barriers to capital flows between countries using IFRSs and the U.S. GAAP.
>
> "Our ultimate aim at the IASB is to have a single set of accounting standards used worldwide," Sir David Tweedie, IASB chair, said after the SEC's announcement.

STUDY QUESTION

15. An important change that would be brought about by adopting the SEC proposal regarding the IFRS is:

  a. To allow non-U.S. companies to participate in U.S. capital markets without reconciling their statements with GAAP

  b. Unification of standards between the SEC and IFRS regarding financial statement disclosures

  c. Standardization of multinational disclosures of uncertain tax positions

  d. None of the above is the proposed change

CONCLUSION

Because FIN 48 may increase the likelihood that tax benefits from transactions will not be recognized for financial reporting purposes, tax departments generally need to take the initiative and screen contemplated transactions with significant tax uncertainties using FIN 48 procedures from the get go. Doing that homework upfront will help prevent later decisions by the financial accountants not to recognize tax benefits from coming as a surprise to management.

FIN 48 requirements also have encouraged a heightened assessment and documentation environment. Companies embarking on aggressive tax planning strategies should take care to make assessment and documentation efforts begin upon initiating the position. Assessment and documentation should not become an afterthought in processing the transaction for financial-reporting purposes.

For many practitioners, FIN 48 is something to be feared. The IRS has reassured tax professionals that it is not. Indeed, the IRS appears to be learning what FIN 48 is all about just as many tax professionals are. What approach the IRS will ultimately take is yet to be decided. In the meantime, practitioners should remember that the IRS is aware of FIN 48 disclosures and is taking an increasing interest in them.

MODULE 1 — CHAPTER 2

Nonqualified Deferred Compensation: New Requirements

This chapter discusses requirements for nonqualified deferred compensation that were enacted in the American Jobs Creation Act of 2004 and subsequently interpreted in IRS and Treasury Department regulations and other guidance. These new rules and regulations come under the general umbrella of newly created Code Sec. 409A, enacted to curb abuses. The discussion of Code Section 409A in this chapter includes insights into the broad reach of the term *nonqualified deferred compensation* for purposes of these new rules, as well as the variety of resulting compliance deadlines that now loom for most businesses.

LEARNING OBJECTIVES

Upon completion of this chapter, you will be able to:

- Identify the plans, formal or informal, covered by the deferred compensation regulations;
- Describe the plans that are excluded from the application of Code Sec. 409A;
- Discuss the requirements for elections to defer compensation;
- Determine the events that can trigger a taxable "distribution";
- Explain the requirements for changing a distribution;
- Identify the effective date, transition rules, and accompanying deadlines; and
- Understand the reporting requirements for nonqualified plans.

INTRODUCTION

Enacted in the American Jobs Creation Act of 2004 (P.L. 108-357) (AJCA '04), Code Sec. 409A provides strict, detailed rules for the taxation of nonqualified deferred compensation arrangements. The term *deferred compensation* is broad in its coverage. A plan or arrangement provides for deferred compensation if the service provider has a legally binding right to compensation that, under the plan, is or may be paid in a later year. The "nonqualified" part of the term *nonqualified deferred compensation* distinguishes it from *qualified deferred compensation*. Qualified deferred compensation plans (such as 401(k) plans) allow employees to defer compensation until their retirement, with the employer in the advantageous position of getting a current deduction in the tax year it makes the contribution even though the employees will not recognize this amount as income for some years to come. With a nonqualified plan, the employer cannot take its deduction until the employee recognizes the income. Like qualified deferred compensation, nonqualified deferred compensation offers the employee the advantage of deferring recognition of income, albeit for a shorter period of time.

In 2007, the IRS and Treasury issued long-awaited final regulations (T.D. 9321) for the deferred compensation rules under Code Sec. 409A. The regulations are comprehensive. They address the definition of deferred compensation and a deferred compensation plan, exclusions from deferred compensation, and the treatment of stock rights such as options. The regulations also discuss the requirements for deferral elections, events that can trigger payment, time and form of payment, changes in payment schedules, effective dates, and transition rules.

Code Sec. 409A was enacted after Congress became concerned that employers were providing nontaxable deferred compensation for top employees with protected assets, such as funds in an offshore trust or in an account that was not available to the employer's creditors. Executives were avoiding payment of millions of dollars in income taxes through nonqualified deferred compensation arrangements. In the past, the IRS had little success at regulating these arrangements, losing cases in court or writing regulations that never saw the light of day.

Congress itself, in the House Committee Report to the AJCA '04, summarized the reasons behind new Code Section 409A succinctly:

> While the general tax principles governing deferred compensation are well established, the determination whether a particular arrangement effectively allows deferral of income is generally made on a facts and circumstances basis. There is limited specific guidance with respect to common deferral arrangements. The Committee believes that it is appropriate to provide specific rules regarding whether deferral of income inclusion should be permitted.

> The Committee believes that certain arrangements that allow participants inappropriate levels of control or access to amounts deferred should not result in deferral of income inclusion. The Committee also believes that certain arrangements, such as offshore trusts, which effectively protect assets from creditors, should be treated as funded and not result in deferral of income inclusion.

The penalties for violating new Code Sec. 409A are harsh, regardless of whether the misstep is done intentionally or out of ignorance; the deferred amount must be included in income, plus interest, plus a 20 percent penalty.

The 20 percent penalty provides a strong incentive for compliance with the statute and the regulations.

EFFECTIVE DATES AND TRANSITION RULES

Code Sec. 409A generally applies to deferrals made after December 31, 2004. It also applies to deferrals under plans prior to that date *if* the plan was materially modified after October 3, 2004.

Although Code Sec. 409A has been officially on the books and effective since January 1, 2005, the main compliance problem faced by taxpayers and their tax advisors has been that the language of the Code Sec. 409A itself is not sufficiently clear or inclusive to cover all situations. To fill in the gaps, IRS regulations and other directive guidance have been necessary. Promulgating these rules and regulations has been an arduous process for the IRS, which is required to issue proposals for public comment before binding rules could be set. And although some of these proposed and then final rules and regulations restate the obvious, others set binding requirements that are not at all intuitive or not the only logical alternative from which the IRS could chose. In recognition of this problem, the IRS has delayed the effective date of many of its otherwise-binding rules and regs.

The implementation of the IRS's rules and regulations on Code Section 409A is still a work in progress, with additional clarifications expected to be needed and issued in the future. The main body of rules and regulations, however, has now been set:

- Notice 2005-1 (December 2004)—Basic guidance with "good faith compliance" during 2005 if a pre-2005 plan is amended by December 31, 2005;
- NPRM REG-158080-04 (October 2005)—Proposed regulations that could be relied on immediately but that, with "good faith compliance," were generally not effective until January 1, 2007; rules on deferral elections, however, applied to amounts earned starting in 2006;
- TD 9321 (April 2007)—Final regulations are effective January 1, 2008, when all plans must be operationally compliant with all aspects of these regulations (except for written plan compliance, which has been delayed one year pursuant to Notice 2007-78, below); and
- Notice 2007-78 (September 2007)—Written plan documents do not have to comply until after December 31, 2008. Otherwise, however, the plan must be operated in accordance with the final regulations beginning January 1, 2008.

For periods starting January 1, 2005, and ending before January 1, 2008, a deferred compensation plan must operate in good faith compliance with Code Sec. 409A. Compliance with Notice 2005-1, the proposed regulations, or the final regulations is considered good faith compliance. A plan does not have to be amended to reflect good faith compliance for events that do not affect compliance after December 31, 2007; for example, a deferred amount that was paid out by December 31, 2007.

> **CAUTION**
>
> Several statutory provisions under Code Sec. 409A have separate effective dates. Special dates and rules apply to stock option or stock appreciation rights; offshore trust accounts; payment elections; collective bargaining agreements; plan amendments permitting certain changes in elections; initial deferral elections relating to services performed in 2005; materially modified plans; changes consistent with established practices; suspension or termination of a plan; and equity-based compensation. More details about these deadlines appear later in the chapter.

Other Guidance

In addition to the final regulations, the IRS chose to address certain subsidiary issues separately and more specifically by issuing several other pieces of guidance under Code Sec 409A. This effort included:

- Notice 2006-33—Discussion of offshore trusts and restricted assets (which expires at the end of 2007);
- Notice 2006-100—Description of reporting and withholding (which the IRS more recently announced may be extended through 2007);
- Announcement 2007-18—Provision employer measures to pay penalties owed on backdated stock options;
- Notice 2007-34—Description of the application of Code Sec. 409A to split-dollar life insurance;
- Rev. Rul. 2007-48—Coverage of Code Sec. 402(b) trusts, which are exempt from Code Sec. 409A; and
- Notice 2007-62—Discussion of the interaction of Code Sections 409A and 457 (government and exempt organization plans).

More Guidance to Come

The IRS also has already acknowledged the need to issue additional guidance on:

- Calculating income and interest inclusion from taxable deferrals;
- The treatment of losses that follow inclusion;
- Reporting of income and deferrals;
- Funding issues;
- Financial health triggers and offshore trusts;
- The consequences of plan failures; and
- A voluntary correction program.

Room for Error?

The American Bar Association Section of Taxation and other practitioners have asked the IRS to institute a voluntary compliance program (VCP) to address inadvertent noncompliance with Code Sec. 409A. The ABA Section indicated that the small business community may remain largely unaware of the new provision. The ABA Section suggested a short-term program to cover the transition period between January 1, 2005, and December 31, 2007, and another for the compliance period between January 1, 2008, and December 31, 2010. In the past, the IRS has questioned whether it has the authority to operate a VCP and the resources for a VCP, noting that it only has eight attorneys in the branch that deals with executive compensation. The Section urged the IRS to allocate the needed resources to the program.

In response, the IRS announced in Notice 2007-78 that it will establish a limited voluntary compliance program for certain unintentional operational failures. The program will allow correction of these failures in the same taxable year in which they occurred, to avoid the application of Code Sec. 409A, and will only impose tax on limited amounts where such failures occur.

Practitioners have also asked the IRS to institute a private rulings program for Code Sec. 409A, which is a no-rulings area. Again, the IRS anticipated being swamped with inquiries by practitioners who wanted the IRS to bless their plan "just in case," and questioned whether it would have the resources to administer such a program.

STUDY QUESTIONS

---

1. When is the effective date on which all written plan documents must fully comply with the final regulations of Code Sec. 409A?

   a. December 31, 2005

   b. January 1, 2008

   c. January 1, 2009

   d. None of the above is the full compliance date

2. Which of the following is **not** a compliance transition or compliance period for which the Section of Taxation of the American Bar Association requested a voluntary corrections program to help practitioners and taxpayers comply with Code Sec. 409A?

   a. January 1, 2005 through December 31, 2007

   b. January 1, 2008 through December 31, 2010

   c. January 1, 2011 through December 31, 2012

   d. All of the above were separate requests for VCPs

KEY DEFINITIONS

Service Recipient and Service Provider

The guidance uses the term *service recipient* to refer to the employer and the term *service provider* to refer to the employee or independent contractor. A service recipient is any person for whom services are performed and with respect to whom the legally binding right to provide compensation arises. Any person (including corporations, partnerships, etc.) under common control or in a controlled group with the service recipient would also be considered a service recipient. The nonqualified deferred compensation rules apply to a plan that provides for the deferral of compensation, even if the payment of the compensation is not made by the person for whom services are performed.

A *service provider* may be:
- An individual;
- A corporation;
- An S corporation;
- A partnership; or
- A personal service corporation.

Compensation

Compensation is generally an employee's compensation from the employer for the year. Compensation from the employer includes, but is not limited to, the following items if they are actually paid or made available to the employee during the year:
- Wages;
- Salaries;
- Fees for professional services; and
- Other amounts received in cash or otherwise for personal services actually rendered in the course of employment with the employer maintaining the deferred compensation plan, to the extent the amounts are includible in gross income or excludable as foreign earned income.

Compensation includes commissions paid to salespeople, profit-percentage based compensation, commissions on insurance premiums, tips, bonuses, fringe benefits, and reimbursements and expense allowances under a nonaccountable plan.

Nonaccountable plan. An *accountable plan* requires an employee to account to the employer for deductible business expenses incurred by the employee and reimbursed by the employer. Allowances and reimbursements under an accountable plan are nontaxable. If the plan does not require a proper accounting, or makes payments for nondeductible expenses, the plan is described as a *nonaccountable plan,* and the employer's payments are included in the employee's income.

An employer may elect not to include as compensation any amount contributed by the employer under a salary reduction agreement that is not includible in the gross income of an employee. This would apply to a contribution under a cafeteria plan, a qualified transportation fringe benefit plan, a 401(k) plan, or a 403(b) annuity.

Legally binding right. Compensation is subject to the deferred compensation rules if it is a legally binding right during a tax year to compensation that under the terms of a plan will be (or might be) payable to the service provider in a later tax year. A legally binding right to an amount that will be excluded from income when and if received is not a deferral of compensation, unless the service provider has received the right in exchange for an amount that will be includible in income (assuming the right is not part of a cafeteria plan).

Service recipient's right to reduce or eliminate right to compensation. A service provider does not have a legally binding right to compensation *to the extent that* compensation may be reduced unilaterally or eliminated by the service recipient or other person after the services creating the right to the compensation have been performed.

Written Plan

Under final regulations, a Code Sec. 409A nonqualified deferred compensation plan is not in compliance unless the material terms of the plan are put in writing. To be considered a *written plan,* the document or documents constituting the plan must specify, at the time an amount is deferred:

- The amount to which the service provider has a right to be paid (or, in the case of an amount determinable under an objective, nondiscretionary formula, the terms of such formula); and
- The payment schedule or payment-triggering events that will result in a payment of the amount.

The requirements for the written plan were relaxed in part for 2008 by Notice 2007-78. A written plan that fails to comply with the final regulations will not violate Code Sec. 409A before January 1, 2009, provided the plan is operated in compliance with the final regulations and the written plan is amended by December 31, 2008, to comply with the final regulations retroactively to January 1, 2008. However, elections about the time and form of payments must still be made in writing before January 1, 2008.

> **COMMENT**
>
> The government has requested comments on the provision of a model plan but has expressed skepticism about such a plan's usefulness. It indicates that any plan would have to be simple and might not be able to address possible plan variations.

A plan will be deemed to be established if the written plan is in place by the end of the service provider's tax year in which the legally binding right to compensation arose. If the deferred compensation is not payable in the subsequent year after the compensation was earned, the plan may be established by the 15th day of the third month of the subsequent year. Plan amendments that increase deferral amounts are not considered established until the amendment is included in the plan documents.

STUDY QUESTIONS

3. Which of the following is a type of payment to employees that an employer or employee may elect not to include as compensation?
   a. Contributions under a cafeteria plan
   b. Fees for professional services
   c. Amounts received for personal services during course of employment
   d. All of the above are available for the employer election

4. All of the following are required for deferred compensation arrangements to be considered written plans under Code Sec. 409A *except:*
   a. The amount to which the service provider has a right to be paid
   b. The payment schedule or payment-triggering events for payment of the deferred amount
   c. In case of amounts determinable under an objective formula, the terms of such formula
   d. All of the above are required for written plans

SPECIFIC ARRANGEMENTS COVERED BY CODE SEC. 409A

The final regulations under Code Sec. 409A generally provide that unless certain requirements are met, amounts deferred under a nonqualified deferred compensation plan are currently includible in gross income to the extent not subject to a substantial risk of forfeiture and not previously included in gross income. As discussed later in this chapter, certain significant exceptions have been carved out from this general rule and those compensation payments are not considered governed by Code Section 409A.

Other parts of the regulations or other separate guidance, however, address specific types of compensation that the IRS wants to make clear are subject to Section 409A. To prevent any ambiguity over its decision to include these types of compensation, the IRS has singled them out either in separate guidance or as separate sections within the final regulations.

Split-dollar Life Insurance

Split-dollar life insurance arrangements often combine insurance with other economic benefits. The arrangements are taxed either under an economic benefits regime (if the employer owns the policy) or as a loan (if the employee owns the policy). The rules for taxing these arrangements apply to split-dollar life insurance arrangements entered into on or after September 17, 2003, as well as to split-dollar life insurance arrangements entered into before that date if material modifications to the policy are made after that date.

Notice 2007-34 discusses the application of Code Sec. 409A to split-dollar life insurance. For split-dollar life insurance arrangements taxed under the economic benefit regime, the cost of current life insurance protection is treated as provided under a death benefit plan and thus excluded from the nonqualified deferred compensation requirements. However, the service provider must agree to report the cost of the death benefit protection as a current taxable benefit. This exclusion applies even if other economic benefits are available.

A split-dollar life insurance arrangement provides for deferred compensation if the service provider has a legally binding right during the tax year to economic benefits, such as the policy cash value, that are payable in a later tax year, and the legally binding right does not qualify as a short-term deferral. The excess of the policy cash value over the premiums is treated as earnings under Code Sec. 409A.

Split-dollar arrangements under the loan regime are not treated as deferred compensation unless loan payments are waived, cancelled, or forgiven.

Offshore Trusts and Restricted Assets

Under the economic benefit doctrine, an amount set aside from an employer's creditors to fund a deferred payment obligation is taxable to the employee at the time of funding. Putting assets in a trust is a typical example. *Rabbi trusts* have provided a device to get around the economic benefit doctrine. A transfer of assets to a trust for a key employee's benefit would not be taxable as long as the assets were subject to the employer's general creditors, even if the assets did not become available until the company developed financial problems. Some arrangements provided that the rabbi trust became a "secular" trust (fully set aside from creditors) if the company went bankrupt or became insolvent, thus protecting the employee's benefits.

Code Sec 409A(b) attacks these schemes. Setting aside assets in a trust or other arrangement that is outside the United States is a taxable transfer of property under Code Sec. 83, even if the assets are available to satisfy the claims of general creditors. The assets are taxable at the time they are transferred out of the United States. This rule does not apply if all the services were performed in the foreign jurisdiction.

Assets are also deemed transferred to the employee as of the earlier of:

- The date the plan first provides that assets will become restricted to provision of benefits in connection with changes in the employer's financial health; or
- The date assets are so restricted. Again, this rule applies even if the assets are initially available to general creditors.

Ordinarily, amounts deferred before January 1, 2005, are not subject to Code Sec. 409A. However, in Notice 2006-33, the IRS clarified that amounts set aside in offshore trusts or under a financial health trigger were governed by Code Sec. 409A(b), even if set aside before January 1, 2005. For assets set aside before March 22, 2006, the IRS provided a grace period of December 31, 2007, for employers to cure the provisions that would trigger taxation. Assets set aside on or after that date are subject to the funding provisions. Employers with assets subject to the grace period could pay out those assets by December 31, 2007, and be in compliance with Code Sec. 409A.

Any subsequent increase in value or earnings is taxable as an additional transfer at the time of the increase or when earned.

Ineligible 457 Plans

Code Sec. 409A does not apply to an eligible Code Sec. 457(b) deferred compensation plan established for government employees by a state or local government or tax-exempt entity. But in Notice 2007-62, the IRS explained that Code Sec. 409A does apply to an ineligible deferred compensation plan subject to Code Sec. 457(f), separately and in addition to the requirements under Code Sec. 457(f). Deferred amounts will be taxable under Code Sec. 457(f) at the time a substantial risk of forfeiture lapses. The same amounts may be taxable under Code Sec. 409A, which carries interest and an additional 20 percent penalty.

STUDY QUESTIONS

> **5.** Split-dollar arrangements under the loan regime are not treated as deferred compensation unless loan payments are waived, cancelled, or forgiven. ***True or False?***
>
> **6.** Under Code Sec. 409A(b), rabbi trust assets deemed transferred to the employee are taxable:
>
>   **a.** When they are written into an employee's employment contract
>   **b.** At the time they are transferred outside the United States
>   **c.** When the trust is terminated
>   **d.** Rabbi trust assets are never taxable

EXCLUSIONS FROM CODE SEC. 409A

The hallmark of deferred compensation is a legally binding right to provide compensation in a future tax year. Because of, or perhaps in spite of, this inclusive definition, there are a number of exceptions from the deferred compensation rules of Section 409A, principally for those payments already covered by other Internal Revenue Code provisions. In addition, however, other exceptions have been carved out, most notably for short-term deferrals.

Short-Term Deferrals

Amounts paid within 2½ months after the end of the year in which an amount was earned are not treated as deferred compensation but are considered short-term deferrals. This treatment also applies to payments made after an amount ceases to be subject to a substantial risk of forfeiture that becomes vested in one year and is paid within 2½ months of the following year. This result is based on the deduction rule in Code Sec. 404 that excludes these amounts from deferred compensation. Thus, a bonus would not be considered deferred compensation if the company paid a discretionary bonus within the short-term deferral period following a one-year bonus period, for example.

A payment that otherwise qualifies as a short-term deferral but is made after 2½ months may continue to qualify as a short-term deferral if the taxpayer establishes that:

- It was administratively impracticable to make the payment within the period;
- Making the payment by the end of the period would have jeopardized the solvency of the service recipient; and
- As of the date upon which the legally binding right to the compensation arose, such impracticability or insolvency was unforeseeable.

Also, the payment must be made as soon as reasonably practicable.

Because each payment is analyzed separately for purposes of the short-term deferral exception, the initial payment in a series can qualify for the short-term deferral exception even if the rest of the payments do not. This rule does not apply to annuity payments, which are treated as a single payment.

Normal Pay-Period Overlap

A deferral of compensation does not occur solely because compensation is paid after the last day of the employer's tax year under the normal schedule for compensating employees (or nonemployees) for an ordinary payroll period. For a nonemployee, the compensation could be paid by the earlier of the normal timing arrangement or 30 days after the end of the service provider's tax year.

Separation Pay

The final regulations refer to severance pay or separation pay as compensation (including separation from death or disability) for which the right to payment is conditioned upon separation from service. It is not compensation that could be received without separating from service, even if in fact it is paid upon separation from service. Separation agreements can be deferred compensation because they provide a legally binding right to compensation in a subsequent year.

However, some separation pay agreements are not treated as deferred compensation.

One example of such an agreement is a collectively bargained agreement that provides for separation pay either upon an involuntary separation or under a window program. The agreement must cover services performed for one or more employers and the employee must terminate employment with all employers. The definition of involuntary separation must have been the subject of arm's-length, good faith negotiations.

Another exclusion applies to an amount paid only upon an involuntary separation from service or under a window program. For this exclusion, the separation pay cannot exceed twice the sum of the service provider's annualized compensation, or, if less, twice the maximum taken into account under Code Sec. 401(a)(17). The amount must be paid within two years of the year of the separation from service.

An *involuntary separation from service* arises from a unilateral decision by the employer to terminate the employee's services when the employee was willing and able to continue working. The parties may identify the separation as voluntary, but this treatment may be rebutted based on the facts and circumstances. An employee's decision to separate from service for a good reason may be treated as an involuntary termination.

A good reason includes a reduction in duties or compensation, a change of duties or job conditions, a change of location, or other material negative changes.

A *window program* is a program established by the service recipient (employer) for a limited period of time (no more than 12 months) to provide separation pay to service providers who separate from service during that period under specified circumstances. A pattern of repeated periods will not be treated as a window period.

A foreign separation pay agreement is not deferred compensation, even if it provides payments upon a voluntary separation. The separation pay must be required under foreign law; the income does not have to be attributable to services performed within the foreign country.

Independent Contractors

Code Sec. 409A does not apply to an amount deferred by an independent contractor working for an unrelated service recipient if the independent contractor provides significant services to two or more unrelated service recipients. Generally, the services provided to any one recipient cannot generate more than 70 percent of the total compensation received by the independent contractor. An *independent contractor* for these purposes is someone who is actively engaged in the trade or business of providing services, other than as an employee or as a member of the board of directors of a corporation (or similar position with respect to an entity that is not a corporation).

These independent contractor rules do not apply to a service provider that provides management services to a service recipient. *Management services* encompass services that involve the direction or control of the financial or operational aspects of a trade or business of the service recipient, or investment management or advisory services provided to a service recipient whose primary trade or business includes the investment of financial assets.

Foreign Arrangements

In general, Code Sec. 409A does not apply to a foreign arrangement if the compensation would not have been subject to U.S. taxes at the time the right to compensation arose (or the right was no longer subject to a substantial risk of forfeiture) and the service provider was:

- A nonresident alien;
- One of certain types of resident alien; or
- A resident of a U.S. possession.

Compensation that would have been excluded from U.S. income taxes at the time earned by the terms of any tax treaty with the United States is not deferred compensation. The exclusion under the treaty will override other Tax Code provisions that could have applied. For a U.S. citizen or resident alien, Code Sec. 409A does not apply to amounts deferred under a broad-based foreign retirement plan. This exclusion applies only to nonelective deferrals and will apply even if the same plan permits elective deferrals.

Nonqualified deferred compensation plans do not include an arrangement under which contributions made by or on behalf of such individual are excludable for federal income tax purposes pursuant to any bilateral income tax convention or other bilateral or multilateral agreement to which the United States is a party.

Code Sec. 409A does not apply to an arrangement if all of the taxpayers involved use the accrual method of accounting.

STUDY QUESTIONS

7. Which of the following enables pay from an involuntary separation from service to be excluded from consideration as deferred compensation?

   a. The employee must be terminated because of meeting the organization's criteria for disability or official retirement age.

   b. A collective bargaining agreement provides for the separation pay upon an involuntary separation or under a window program.

   c. The separation pay is at least three times the service provider's annualized compensation.

   d. The employee is terminated from one employer but obtains employment during the same tax year with another organization.

8. Code Sec. 409A does **not** apply to amounts deferred by an independent contractor working for an unrelated service recipient if:

   a. The contractor provides services to two or more unrelated service recipients for equal compensation

   b. The contractor claims statutory employee status on his or her tax return

   c. The contractor provides significant services at the same hourly compensation rate to two recipients, with three-quarters of compensation paid by one recipient

   d. The Code Sec. 409A independent contractor exclusion applies to all of the above

Coverage by Other Code Provisions

Qualified plans. The final regulations exclude qualified plans from Code Sec. 409A because they have their own set of inclusive, well-developed rules. This exclusion applies to pension plans described in Code Sec. 401(a), annuity plans described in Code Sec. 403(a) and (b), a simplified employee pension, and a simple retirement account. The regulations also exclude welfare benefit plans such as a bona fide sick leave or vacation plan, compensatory leave, or a disability or death benefit plan. The final regulations do not clarify the definition of a bona fide sick or vacation plan or a compensatory time plan. Taxpayers may rely on the definitions in Code Sec. 457(f) until there is further guidance.

Nontaxable, excludable benefits. The provisions do not apply to medical expense reimbursement arrangements that are not taxable to the service provider under Code Sec. 105 or 106 and to other expense reimbursement arrangements that would be excludable as employee business expenses. Code Sec. 409A does apply to reimbursement arrangements that are taxable to the service provider. Deferred compensation does not include an Archer medical savings account (MSA), any health savings account (HSAs), or any other medical reimbursement arrangement that is not includible in income.

Section 457 plans. Code Sec. 409A does not apply to an eligible deferred compensation plan that complies with Code Sec. 457(b). However, a plan that that violates Code Sec. 457(b) and is described in Code Sec. 457(f) is subject to Code Sec. 409A. Because the rules under Code Sections 409A and 457(f) apply separately and are not coordinated, it is necessary to overlay the Code Sec. 409A rules to the Code Sec 457(f) rules.

Restricted property and Section 402(b) trusts. The receipt of property that is subject to a substantial risk of forfeiture under Code Sec. 83 is not deferred compensation. If a service provider receives restricted property from a plan, there is no deferral of compensation merely because the value of the property is not includible in income when the property is received. This rule also applies to an amount included in income because of a Section 83(b) election. A transfer of property includes the transfer of a beneficial interest in a trust or annuity plan governed by Code Sections 83, 402(b), or 403(c). However, the right to receive vested property in the future may be considered deferred compensation. The right to receive nonvested property in the future would not be deferred compensation.

Stock rights. Stock of the employer is identified as service recipient stock. Service recipient stock is a class of stock that, as of the date of grant, is common stock of a corporation that is an eligible issuer of service recipient stock. Service recipient stock generally cannot include preferences, though liquidation preferences are permissible. An eligible issuer of service recipient stock can only be the corporation for which the service provider provides direct services on the date of grant of the stock right, and any corporation in a chain of organizations all of which have a controlling interest in another organization, beginning with the parent organization and ending with the organization for which the service provider was providing services at the date of grant of the stock right.

> **COMMENT**
>
> The final regulations are significantly more flexible than earlier guidance in regard to stock rights and service recipient stock.

Stock options. The grant of an incentive stock option or the grant of an option under an employee stock purchase plan does not constitute a deferral of compensation. However, this exclusion does not apply to a modification, extension, or renewal of a statutory option that is treated as the grant of a new option that is not a statutory option. In such an event, the option is treated as if it had been a nonstatutory stock option from the date of the original grant. Whether the nonstatutory option has a deferral feature is determined as of the date of grant.

Backdated options. Code Sec. 409A applies to the grant of a nonstatutory stock option for service recipient stock, if the option price is or could become less than the stock's fair market value at the time the option was granted. Thus, options issued at a discount price are covered by Code Sec. 409A. If the value of the stock is rising, a discounted option could be hidden by backdating the grant of the option to an earlier date when the value of the stock was lower. Therefore, Code Sec. 409A will generally apply to a backdated option The IRS has identified backdated options as an issue of special audit interest.

STUDY QUESTIONS

9. Code Sec. 409A provisions apply to which of the following types of medical expense reimbursement arrangements?

   a. Arrangements taxable to the service provider under Code Secs. 105 and 106
   b. Expense reimbursement arrangements excludable as employee business expenses
   c. Health savings accounts
   d. Archer medical savings accounts

10. An incentive stock option or option under an employee stock purchase plan is excluded from Code Sec. 409A regulations:

   a. At all times
   b. Only as long as the employee remains employed at the organization granting the option
   c. Unless the statutory option is modified, extended, or renewed
   d. Stock options and employee stock purchase plan options are always subject to Code Sec. 409A regulations

INITIAL DEFERRAL ELECTIONS

Code Sec. 409A strictly controls the timing of compensation deferral elections. Violations trigger acceleration of income inclusion and additional tax and interest implications. An *election to defer* compensation includes:

- An election regarding the time of the payment;
- An election as to the form of the payment; or
- An election as to both the time and the form of the payment.

An election to defer does not include an election as to the medium of payment (e.g., an election to take cash or another form of property).

Salary

An employee's initial election to defer compensation must be irrevocable and generally must be made before the close of the taxable year preceding the taxable year the services are actually rendered. An election is not deemed to occur until it becomes irrevocable. Accordingly, a plan may provide that the initial election may be changed at any time prior to the last date established for making the election. An election is not revocable merely because the service provider or service recipient may make an election to change the time and form of payment under the subsequent deferral rules, or because the service recipient may accelerate the time of payment pursuant to exceptions to the prohibition on accelerated payments.

When the employee first becomes eligible to participate in an existing or new plan, the election may be made within 30 days of eligibility, for amounts earned after the election is made. For a nonelective excess benefit plan, an employee may become a participant without realizing it. The regulations allow the employee to make a one-time retroactive election in the first year after the employee accrues a benefit under a nonelective excess benefit plan.

Bonuses

One form of bonus is a discretionary bonus awarded in a year subsequent to the year services are performed. If the employer announces in 2008 that it will award bonuses in 2010 for services performed in 2009, the employee must make a deferral election before the beginning of 2009.

Performance-based Compensation

The election rules are different for performance-based compensation. *Performance-based compensation* means employee compensation contingent on satisfying preestablished performance criteria relating to a performance period of at least 12 consecutive months. Organizational or individual performance criteria are considered "preestablished" if:

- They are established in writing not later than 90 days after the commencement of the period of service to which the criteria relate; and
- The outcome is substantially uncertain at the time the criteria are established.

In no event will criteria satisfy the test if the amount will be paid regardless of performance. Nor are criteria satisfied if based on a level of performance that is substantially certain to be met at the time the criteria are established.

It is more difficult for the employer and employee to quantify the amount of total compensation and potential deferral amounts prior to actual service. Accordingly, the regulations made timing of the election more flexible for these situations.

Generally, an initial election to defer performance-based compensation must be made no later than six months before the end of the performance period. For this liberal election period to apply, the employee must perform services through the date of the election. Services must be performed continuously from the later of the beginning of the performance period or the date the performance criteria are established.

In no event may an election to defer performance-based compensation be made after the compensation has become readily ascertainable. If the performance-based compensation is a specified or calculable amount, the compensation is *readily ascertainable* when the amount first becomes substantially certain to be paid. If it is uncertain because it is based on a performance level or a vesting requirement, the amount is readily ascertainable when the amount is both calculable and substantially certain to be paid.

For making an election, performance-based compensation is split between the portions that are readily ascertainable and not readily ascertainable. The minimum amount that is both calculable and substantially certain to be paid will be deemed readily ascertainable.

Compensation based on the performance of employer stock is not performance-based compensation unless there is a performance-based vesting requirement.

Fiscal Year Compensation

In the case of an employer on a fiscal year that is not the calendar year, the employee must make the election before the beginning of the employer's fiscal year. This rule applies whether the employee is on a calendar year or some other fiscal year.

> **EXAMPLE**
>
> The employer has a tax year ending September 30. Employee Dan participates in a bonus plan under which he is entitled to a bonus for services performed during the employer's *fiscal* year that will be paid on December 15 of the calendar year in which the fiscal year ends. The amount qualifies as fiscal year compensation. If Dan elects to defer the payment of the amount related to the fiscal year ending September 30, 2009, Dan must elect the time and form of payment not later than September 30, 2008.

Commissions

A service provider earning sales commissions is treated as providing the services related to the commission in the year in which the customer remits payment to the service recipient. Alternatively, because the commission may be paid in the year of the sale, and the customer's payment may be made in a later year, the services will be those provided in the year of the sale, provided this method is applied consistently to all similarly situated service providers.

These rules apply to commissions involving a related customer, provided that substantial sales or substantial services from which commissions are earned are also provided to unrelated customers by the service recipient, and the arrangements with the related customer are bona fide, arise from the service recipient's ordinary course of business, and are substantially the same as the terms and practices that apply to unrelated customers.

Separation from Service

An employee may make an initial election to defer separation pay at any time before the employee obtains a legally binding right to the payment. This rule applies to separation pay from a voluntary or involuntary termination where the employee had no prior right to separation pay and the pay is the result of bona fide, arm's length negotiations. The separation pay can take into account previous compensation or services but cannot be based upon previously existing legally binding rights.

Teacher's Compensation

The regulations provide a special rule for teachers who want to annualize their pay and be paid over 12 months instead of the 9-month school year. A teacher may elect before the beginning of the period of service, i.e., the beginning of the school year, to defer recurring part-year compensation earned over a period of less than 12 months. No amount may be deferred more than 13 months after the beginning of the performance period.

STUDY QUESTIONS

11. Generally, an employee's initial election to defer compensation must be made:

   a. Irrevocably in a one-time retroactive election during the employee's term of employment

   b. Irrevocably prior to the last date before the deferral commences

   c. At the beginning of the taxable year in which the employees wishes to have compensation deferred

   d. By the close of the taxable year preceding the taxable year in which the services are rendered

12. Compensation based on the performance of employer stock:

   a. Is never considered performance-based compensation of the employee

   b. Is not considered performance-based compensation unless the arrangement has a performance-based vesting requirement

   c. Is performance-based compensation for corporate officers and other highly compensated employees

   d. Must be elected for deferral using the same timing restrictions as for other deferred compensation

TIME AND FORM OF PAYMENT

A nonqualified deferred compensation plan must provide that compensation deferred under the plan can be distributed only after one or more of the following events:

- The participant's separation from service (or six months after separation from service for specified employees), death, or disability;
- A time specified under the plan at the time of the deferral election;
- A change in the ownership or effective control of the employer or in the ownership of a substantial portion of the assets of the employer; or
- The occurrence of an unforeseeable emergency.

Conditioning payment on any other event will cause the plan to fail, resulting in immediate taxation and penalties to the employee unless the payment is subject to a substantial risk of forfeiture.

A fixed date and a fixed schedule of payments must be designated for each category of event. A plan may provide that the date of the event is the payment date. A plan may also provide that a payment upon one of these events is to be made in accordance with a schedule that is objectively determinable and nondiscretionary. A payment is made on a fixed date or schedule if made by the end of the calendar year in which the date occurs, or, if later, by the 15th day of the third month following the fixed date.

The plan can allow a payment to be made as soon as administratively feasible, but the payment must be restricted to a specific taxable year of the employee, or the designated period must not be more than 90 days and the service provider must not have a right to designate the tax year of the payment. A payment is treated as made upon the date specified under the plan (including a date specified in a fixed schedule) and is not treated as an accelerated payment if the payment is made no earlier than 30 days before the designated payment date. If a payment is scheduled to be paid "any time" before a particular date, it does not have a fixed date because it could be paid in a prior year. A payment within 180 days of a triggering event violates the 90-day rule. A schedule based upon the timing of payments is not a fixed schedule of payments.

Payment schedules with a fixed or formula limitation on the amount that may be paid in any particular period would meet the requirement of a fixed schedule or time and form of payment. However, a change in the formula may be a subsequent election.

Forfeiture or Voluntary Relinquishment

The payment of an amount as a substitute for a payment of deferred compensation will be treated as a payment of the deferred compensation. A forfeiture or voluntary relinquishment of an amount of deferred compensation will not be treated as a payment of the compensation, but there is no forfeiture or voluntary relinquishment if an amount is paid, or a legally binding right to a payment is created, that acts as a substitute for the forfeited or voluntarily relinquished amount.

Separation from Service

Whether an employee has separated from service depends on whether the facts and circumstances indicate that the employer and employee reasonably anticipated that the employee would not perform any more services after a certain date, or that the level of services would permanently decrease to 20 percent or less of the average level of services over the preceding three years. An employee who performs 50 percent or more of the average level of services will be presumed not to have separated from service. No presumption applies to a change to between 20 and 50 percent of services.

In lieu of payments for a phase retirement, a plan may define a separation from service as including a reduced level of services between 20 and 50 percent of prior average services, provided the definition is specified no later than the time and form of payment are specified. Notice 2007-78 allows a plan to adopt in 2008 an alternative definition of separation from service, provided the payment event does not occur in 2008.

An employee on a bona fide leave of absence or sick leave has not separated from service as long as the employee has a right to reemployment. Employees on a salary continuation or terminal leave program cannot delay their separation from service. An employee who is rehired cannot suspend the payment of deferred compensation.

In the case of a merger or acquisition, the buyer and seller can specify whether employees will be treated as having separated from service. A spin-off does not result in a separation from service, because there is no termination of employment with the same employer.

An independent contractor has separated from service upon the expiration of the contract (or all contracts) with the service recipient, if the expiration is a good-faith and complete termination of the relationship. If a renewal of the contract is anticipated, there is no good-faith termination. An individual who is both an employee and an independent contractor must separate from service in both capacities to have separated from service.

Specified employees. A specified employee cannot receive a payment on account of separation from service until six months after the date of separation (or the date of death, if earlier). A *specified employee* is a key employee of a publicly traded corporation: an officer with annual compensation exceeding $130,000; a 5 percent owner of the corporation; or a 1 percent owner of the corporation with annual compensation exceeding $150,000. Up to 50 service providers may be identified as specified employees. This delay requirement must be in the written plan, but Notice 2007-78 allows plans to be amended by December 31, 2008, to include this provision, provided the plans' operation meets this requirement.

Other Payment Events

Disability. A service provider is disabled if the service provider is unable to engage in any substantial gainful activity by reason of any medically determinable physical or mental impairment that can reasonably be expected to result in death or can be expected to last for a continuous period of at least 12 months. A service provider is also considered disabled if the service provider is, by reason of any medically determinable physical or mental impairment that can be expected to result in death or can be expected to last for at least 12 months, receiving income replacement benefits for a period of at least three months from an accident or health plan covering employees of the employer. Any person may determine whether the service provider is disabled, as long as the determination complies with the regulations. Social Security disability will be treated as disability under the regulations.

Death. A beneficiary of a deceased service provider cannot elect a different time or form of payment without complying with the rules for subsequent elections and accelerated payments, except for a domestic relations order. The rules permit a change in payments based on the different life expectancy of the new beneficiary, as for a joint and survivor annuity. Otherwise, the government refused to provide a limited window for changing the payout.

Change in control of a corporation. A change in the effective control of a corporation occurs when another party acquires 30 percent of the stock. For a nonstock, nonprofit corporation, the rules look at changes in the composition of the organization's board of directors, trustees, or other governing body.

Unforeseeable emergency. Distributions upon the occurrence of an unforeseeable emergency are allowed. An *unforeseeable emergency* is a severe financial hardship to the service provider resulting from:
- An illness or accident of the service provider, the service provider's spouse, beneficiary, or dependent; or
- A loss of the service provider's property due to casualty or other, similar extraordinary and unforeseeable circumstances beyond the control of the service provider such as imminent foreclosure or eviction, medical expenses, or funeral expenses.

The amount of a distribution made because of an unforeseeable emergency cannot exceed the amount necessary to satisfy the emergency plus the amount necessary to pay taxes reasonably anticipated as a result of the distribution.

Transition relief. Notice 2007-78 allows a plan to adopt an alternative definition of disability, change in control, or unforeseeable emergency by December 31, 2008, provided the event does not occur in 2008.

Delayed and disputed payments. The employer or service recipient may delay a payment based on an objective formula related to business performance (e.g., payments limited to percentage of cash flow). Payments may also be delayed if they would jeopardize the ability of the service recipient to continue as a going concern. Payments can be delayed if necessary to avoid the deduction limitation under Code Sec. 162(m) [excessive employee pay]. The six-month delay rule for specified employees continues to apply in this case.

If the service recipient refuses to pay an amount, whether intentional or inadvertent, the payment will be considered timely if the employee makes reasonable efforts to collect the payments, including notice to the employer within 90 days of the deadline for making the payment and further measures within 180 days to enforce the payment.

Specified time or fixed schedule. Amounts may be paid at a specified time or pursuant to a fixed schedule if the amounts are objectively determinable and the dates are nondiscretionary and objectively determinable. The amount may be identified by a formula at the time deferred. A specified time includes a designation of a defined period or periods that are objectively determinable, as long as the period does not include two taxable years. A fixed schedule may be based on the date that a substantial risk of forfeiture lapses. For example, a plan may provide that a service provider is entitled to substantially equal payments on each of the first three anniversaries of the date that a substantial risk of forfeiture lapses.

Changes in Payments

A plan may provide that a deferral election may be changed at any time before the last permissible date for making such a subsequent deferral election. When a plan permits a subsequent deferral election, the plan must require that:

- Such election not take effect until at least 12 months after the date on which the election is made, or 12 months before a payment commences at a fixed date or pursuant to a fixed schedule; and

■ The payment about which such election is made be deferred for a period of not less than five years from the date such payment would otherwise have been paid (or in the case of a life annuity or installment payments treated as a single payment, five years from the date the first amount was scheduled to be paid).

This requirement does not apply to payments on account of death, disability, or unforeseeable emergency.

Life Annuity Under Subsequent Deferral Rules

Entitlement to a life annuity is treated as an entitlement to a single payment. Accordingly, an election to delay payment of a life annuity or to change the form of payment of a life annuity must be made at least 12 months before the scheduled commencement of the life annuity, and must defer the payment for a period of no fewer than five years from the originally scheduled commencement of the life annuity.

A change in designated beneficiary before any annuity payment has been made is not a change in the time or form of payment. A change in the form of a payment before any annuity payment has been made from one type of life annuity to another with the same scheduled date for the first annuity payment, is not a change in the time and form of a payment, provided that the annuities are actuarially equivalent applying reasonable actuarial methods and assumptions. The entitlement to a series of installment payments that is not a life annuity is treated as the entitlement to a single payment, unless the plan provides at all times with respect to the amount deferred that the right to the series of installment payments is to be treated as a right to a series of separate payments.

Antiacceleration

Acceleration rules apply to elections by beneficiaries with respect to the time and form of payment, as well as elections by service providers or service recipients with respect to the time and form of payment to beneficiaries. An election to change the identity of a beneficiary does not constitute an acceleration of a payment. A change of beneficiary is not an acceleration of a payment if the change in the time of payments stems solely from the different life expectancy of the new beneficiary and does not change the commencement date of the life annuity.

However, accelerated payments are permissible in certain situations. A plan can allow the acceleration of scheduled payments under the following circumstances:

■ Domestic relations orders;
■ Conflicts of interest or ethics laws requirements;

- Limited cashouts that do not exceed a specified amount;
- Payment of employment taxes on compensation deferred under the plan (the FICA amount), or to pay the income tax withholding imposed on the FICA amount;
- Payments upon income inclusion under Code Sec. 409A for compliance failures;
- Cancellation of deferrals following an unforeseeable emergency or hardship distribution;
- Arrangement terminations in accordance with certain conditions;
- Payment of state, local, or foreign taxes arising from participation in the plan that apply to deferred amounts before being paid or made available;
- Cancellation of deferral elections due to disability, by the later of the end of the tax year of the service provider or the 15th day of the third month following the date the service provider incurs a disability;
- Offset of debt of the service provider to the service recipient, where such debt is incurred in the ordinary course of the service relationship, and does not exceed $5,000; and
- Bona fide disputes as to a right to a payment occurring as part of a settlement between the service provider and the service recipient of an arm's length, bona fide dispute.

STUDY QUESTIONS

---

13. Accelerated payments of deferred compensation are permitted in all of the following cases *except:*

    a. Payments to creditors of a service provider who is in a bankruptcy proceeding

    b. Payments of employment taxes on deferred compensation

    c. Cancellation of deferral elections due to disability of the service provider

    d. Payments upon income inclusion under Code Sec. 409A for compliance failure

---

PARTNERS AND PARTNERSHIPS

Neither the proposed nor the final regulations address the application of Code Sec. 409A to arrangements between partners and partnerships. Notice 2005-1 and the preambles to the proposed and final regulations provide interim guidance. The IRS and Treasury continue to study the issues in this area. The government has said that the treatment of passthrough entities must wait for a project under Code Sec. 83 on the treatment of a transfer of a partnership interest for services.

Notice 2005-1 indicates that the nonqualified deferred compensation rules "may apply" to arrangements between partners and partnerships. However, taxpayers may generally treat a partnership interest or an option to acquire a partnership interest, issued in connection with the performance of services, as though it were an issuance of stock. Accordingly, IRS guidance provides that:

- An issuance of a profits interest to a service provider for services performed that does not result in an inclusion of income (because the interest's liquidation value is zero) is treated as not resulting in a deferral of compensation;
- An issuance of a capital interest for services performed is treated in the same manner as an issuance of stock and generally will not result in a deferral of compensation. For example, an interest subject to a substantial risk of forfeiture does not defer compensation;
- Rules governing other stock-based deferred compensation may be applied by analogy to grants of partnership equity-based deferred compensation, such as the treatment of an option to acquire a partnership interest at the interest's fair market value;
- Arrangements providing for payments in liquidation of the partnership interest of a retiring or a deceased partner's successor may be treated as not subject to the nonqualified deferred compensation rules. For a retired partner, the exclusion applies only if the amounts are paid pursuant to a written plan of the partnership, are paid on account of the partner's retirement, and the partner did not provide any services in the year of payment; and
- Guaranteed payments made to a partner not acting in his or her capacity as a partner are subject to the nonqualified deferred compensation requirements if the payments are for services and would otherwise constitute a deferral of compensation under a nonqualified deferred compensation plan.

REPORTING DEFERRED COMPENSATION

The total amount of deferrals by an employee under a nonqualified deferred compensation plan for the year must be shown on the Form W-2 provided to the employee and the IRS. Employers need not report deferrals for an employee if the total deferrals for the year with respect to the employee under all nonqualified deferred compensation plans do not exceed $600. For withholding purposes, any amount includible in the gross income of an employee under these rules is included in the employee's wages for the year of inclusion.

Income recognized due to participation in a nonqualified deferred compensation plan that fails to meet the requirements of Code Sec. 409A is reported in box 12 on Form W-2 using Code Z - Income under Code Sec. 409A. Once the

IRS sees a Code Z amount, it will look for payment of the 20 percent penalty and interest factor. Code Z should not be used to report a distribution from a Code Sec. 409A plan.

Amounts deferred by nonemployees are reported on a Form 1099, rather than Form W-2. A payor should report amounts includible in gross income under Code Sec. 409A and not treated as wages in box 7 (nonemployee compensation) of Form 1099-MISC. In addition, a payor should report these amounts in box 15b of Form 1099-MISC. The amount reported in box 15b should include only the amounts includible in gross income under Code Sec. 409A and not included in wages under Code Sec. 3401(a).

Transitional Reporting Rules for 2005 and 2006

For calendar years 2005 and 2006, an employer was not required to report amounts deferred during the year under a nonqualified deferred compensation plan in box 12 of Form W-2 using Code Y. Likewise, a payor was not required to include such amounts in box 15a of Form 1099-MISC.

Employers and payors, including those who relied on earlier guidance for calendar year 2005, were required to file an original or corrected information return and furnish an original or corrected payee statement for 2005, reporting any previously unreported amounts includible in gross income for calendar year 2005, as determined under the new guidance for calendar year 2006. Failure to comply may result in penalties. Generally, the original or corrected returns must have been filed by February 28, 2007, and the original or corrected payee statement must have been filed by January 31, 2007.

Code Z was used in box 12 on 2005 Form W-2 to identify income recognized from a plan that violated Code Sec. 409A. For nonemployees, the income should have been reported in box 7 and box 15b on Form 1099-MISC. Code Y in box 12 on Form W-2 identified annual deferrals under a plan that satisfies Code Sec. 409A.

Reporting Rules for 2006

For 2006, an employer also had to report amounts includible in gross income as wages on line 2 of Form 941 and box 1 of Form W-2. For non-employees, a payor should have reported taxable amounts as nonemployee compensation in box 7 of Form 1099-MISC and such amounts in box 15b of Form 1099-MISC. The includible and reportable amounts equaled the portion of the total amount deferred under the plan that, as of December 31, 2006, was not subject to forfeiture and had not been included in income in a previous year, plus any amounts of deferred compensation paid or made available to the service provider during 2006.

COMMENT

Because of the need to change payroll systems and information collection systems, the IRS may postpone some of the reporting requirements on a case-by-case basis. So far, however, no general postponement has been announced.

STUDY QUESTIONS

14. Amounts deferred by employers for nonemployees are reported on:

   a. Form W-3

   b. Form 1099

   c. Form W-2

   d. None of the above is the form used

15. Employers and payors that filed information returns for 2005 reporting income includible as determined under new guidance must:

   a. File a corrected information return and payee statement for 2005 that includes previously unreported amounts of gross income

   b. Attach a statement to their 2006 returns to make retroactive corrections to the 2005 returns

   c. Report the amounts deferred under a nonqualified deferred compensation plan in box 12 of Form W-2 and in box 15a of Form 1099.

   d. None of the above is the means of correcting the information for 2005

CONCLUSION

This chapter focused on the requirements for nonqualified deferred compensation as interpreted in final regulations issued in 2007. Although more issues must be addressed, the IRS has issued guidance on all the basics that employers need to design a plan that complies with Code Sec. 409A. As the new regulations take effect in 2008, the tax community will be challenged to comply with this complex area of tax law. The IRS will also be challenged to assist taxpayer efforts to comply with the new rules while it considers when to begin an audit program in this area.

Employers, too, will be challenged. The array of compensation packages subject to the new Section 409A rules is broad and requires employers and their advisors to take a comprehensive look at how their compensation interfaces with them. Employers will not only be challenged by the complexity of the new rules, but also by the time pressures that they impose. In addition to scrambling to meet the various new compliance deadlines under the Code Sec. 409A, however, many employers also will be taking a fresh look at compensation alternatives that may help them avoid some or all of the deferred compensation requirements altogether.

MODULE 1 — CHAPTER 3

Intrafamily Transfers of Small Businesses

Millions of small business owners are approaching retirement age as the first members of the baby boomer generation reach age 60. Many small business owners want their children to take over the business after they retire. This chapter explores some of questions that practitioners can expect when a small business client announces that he or she is planning to transfer the business, most often to an adult child. Although federal tax considerations may not be at the top of clients' list of concerns, they are very important. If the transfer of a small business from one generation to the next is not structured correctly, the IRS may end up taking a much larger share of hard-earned profits than anticipated. The IRS is especially watching for abusive private annuities and family limited partnerships. Ultimately, the best approach is developed in careful consultation with the small business owner.

LEARNING OBJECTIVES

Upon completion of this chapter, you will be able to:

- Help clients develop a succession plan;
- Understand the traditional role that private annuities play in transferring a small business from one generation to the next and the IRS' crackdown on abuses;
- Describe buy-sell agreements, grantor retained annuity trusts, and family limited partnerships;
- Review some of the common methods for valuing a small business;
- Describe the allocation of purchase price; and
- Identify a small business' responsibilities for federal employment taxes.

DECIDING TO MOVE ON

At some point in the life of every small business owner there comes a time when he or she must decide whether to continue in business. The small business owner may decide to close the business completely, transfer it to a child, sell it to a third party, or start a new business. One of the most attractive options to many small business owners is to turn the business over to their adult child. However, the process is not as simple as saying "next week my daughter will take over the business." Not only does the owner have to remove him- or herself from the business managerially, he or she also has to disengage from the business emotionally—a task that may be very difficult for some small business owners who have grown their businesses into successful ventures.

> **COMMENT**
>
> This chapter uses the term *small business* to mean businesses with between 11 and 200 employees. A *micro-business* is a business with fewer than 10 employees.

> **CAUTION**
>
> According to a study by Kent State University in Ohio, 70 percent of family-owned businesses do not survive beyond the second generation, and only 13 percent continue to the third generation.

MAKING A SUCCESSION PLAN

One way to help clients to start thinking about the future of their business is to develop a succession plan. A *succession plan* sets forth the future of the business after the owner has left the daily operation. A typical succession plan includes provisions for three elements:

- The transfer of ownership;
- The transfer of assets; and
- The transfer of knowledge and skills.

> **CAUTION**
>
> Typically, in most small businesses, ownership, assets, knowledge, and skills will be transferred to the same individual(s). Nevertheless, goals are as varied as there are family situations. The current older-generation owner may need a continuing cash flow from the business on which to retire; or he or she wants all children to share in the future financial success of the business but also recognizes that only one child is suited to running the business day to day.

A succession plan also spells out:

- A successor(s) to the current business owner; and
- The timing of transfer of power and assets.

Selecting a Successor

In many cases, the small business owner may be grooming a successor. The intended successor may be a child, another family member, or key employee. Other times, children, other family members, or key employees may not have an interest in continuing the business or the ability to do so.

> **CAUTION**
>
> Many small business owners try to please everyone and give all of their children a hand in running the business. Divided management often is troubled management, especially for a business that previously had one leader.

Timing

Another important consideration is timing of transferred control. A transition in control of a small business can take place over a period of months or even years, depending on the needs and wishes of the family members and the business itself. Transitions are stressful times for everyone in the business. One of the hardest tasks for a former owner may be to gradually let go of controlling the daily business operations.

> **COMMENT**
>
> Sometimes, a business may terminate because of events completely outside of the owner's control. Hurricane Katrina taught many businesses a valuable lesson: disaster can strike at any time and without much warning. In addition to personal losses, the small business owner often loses the business itself. At the same time, employees are experiencing significant trauma in their lives after the disaster. The IRS and other federal agencies play major roles in helping small businesses recover. One of the most important tax breaks is the election that allows a taxpayer in a presidentially declared disaster area to claim disaster losses in the tax year *before* the year of loss. This provides quick relief by recognizing the losses earlier rather than later. The IRS often gives taxpayers extra time to file returns and submit payments after a disaster. Additionally, it will often abate penalties for late filing and late payment not only for income taxes but also for federal employment tax deposits.

STUDY QUESTIONS

1. Which of the following is **not** a typical element of a small business succession plan?

   a. The transfer of knowledge and skills to the next generation

   b. The transfer of ownership to the next generation

   c. The transfer of assets of the business to the next generation

   d. All of the above are typical elements of a succession plan

2. All of the following are timing issues discussed for transferring a small business **except:**

   a. How the former owner will gradually let go of controlling daily business operations

   b. How to mitigate the stress created by the transition of control

   c. How to recover business resources for a business located in a presidentially declared disaster area

   d. All of the above are timing issues for transferring control of a small business

TOOLS TO TRANSFER A SMALL BUSINESS

More likely than not, the child(ren) of a small business owner will not have the cash to buy the parent's business outright. Intrafamily transfers of small businesses are often financed by:

- Private annuities;
- Self-canceling installment notes;
- Buy-sell agreements;
- Grantor retained annuity trusts (GRATs); and
- Family limited partnerships.

All of these mechanisms create federal tax consequences, which are discussed in this section.

Private Annuities

Traditionally, a private annuity arrangement was one of the most popular ways to transfer a small business from one generation to the next. Many small business owners have most of their wealth tied up in their business. Although they want to pass the business on to family, they have the real problem of needing money on which to retire or start a second career. Private annuity arrangements often provide an ideal solution.

Private annuity arrangements have been used to transfer countless small businesses. However, as they have grown in popularity, so too have the number of arrangements that "push the envelope" on maximizing tax benefits. Pushing back, the IRS has announced that it has discovered "abuses" and, in response, recently proposed new rules to crackdown on tax evasion.

> **CAUTION**
>
> Although private annuities have been popular mechanisms to transfer a business between family members, they are far from perfect. Essentially, all the business owner has is the promise of his or her child to pay. Inflation also is a factor to consider because it will erode the value of the payments over time.

Traditional approach. The traditionally taxpayer-friendly treatment of private annuities began more than 60 years ago.

In *D. Lloyd v. Comm'r* (33 BTA 903, Dec. 9201), the Board of Tax Appeals (the predecessor of today's Tax Court) considered the taxation of gain from a father's sale of property to his son using an annuity contract. The Board found that the annuity contract had no fair market value within the meaning of the predecessor of Code Sec. 1001(b) because of the uncertainty of payment from the son. Because the annuity contract had no fair market value under that provision, the Board held that the gain from the sale of the property was not required to be recognized immediately but rather would be included in income only when the annuity payments exceeded the property's basis. In reaching its holding, the Board applied the open transaction doctrine articulated by the Supreme Court in *D. Burnet v. E.A. Logan* (SCt, 2 USTC ¶736, 283 US 404, 51 SCt 550). Under this doctrine, if an amount realized from a sale cannot be determined with certainty, the seller recovers the basis of the property sold before any income is realized on the sale.

In 1969, the IRS issued Rev. Rul. 69-74. In that ruling, a father transferred a capital asset having an adjusted basis of $20,000 and a fair market value of $60,000 to his son in exchange for the son's legally enforceable promise to pay him a life annuity of $7,200 per year—a large sum 40 years ago—in equal monthly installments of $600. The present value of the life annuity was $47,713.08. The IRS determined that:

- The father realized capital gain based on the difference between the father's basis in the property and the present value of the annuity;
- The gain was reported ratably over the father's life expectancy;
- The investment in the contract for purposes of computing the exclusion ratio was the father's basis in the property transferred;
- The excess of the fair market value of the property transferred over the present value of the annuity was a gift from the father to the son; and
- The prorated capital gain reported annually was derived from the portion of each annuity payment that was not excludible.

A few years later, the Tax Court decided the case of *Est. of L.G. Bell v. Comm'r* (60 TC 469, Dec. 32,025 (1973)). In that case, a husband and wife transferred stock in two closely held corporations to their son and daughter and their spouses in exchange for an annuity contract. The fair market value of the stock substantially exceeded the value of the annuity contract. The stock transferred was placed in escrow to secure the promise of the transferees. As further security, the annuity agreement provided for a *cognovit judgment* (an act of a debtor in permitting judgment to be entered against him or her by a creditor) against the transferees in the event of default. Because of the secured nature of the annuity, the tax court held that:

- The difference between the value of the stock and the value of the annuity contract constituted a gift;
- The difference between the adjusted basis of the stock and the value of the annuity contract constituted gain that was taxable in the year of the transfer (which was not before the court); and
- The investment in the annuity contract equaled the present value of the annuity.

IRS makes important changes. In 2006, the IRS backed away from the open transaction approach of *Lloyd* and the ratable recognition approach in Rev. Rul. 69-74. The IRS determined that neither approach "clearly reflects the income of the transferor of property in exchange for an annuity contract." The IRS discovered that taxpayers were avoiding or deferring gain on the exchange of property for an annuity contract under a ratable recognition approach or an open transaction approach. In response, the IRS issued proposed regulations (NPRM REG-141901-05) that would leave the transferor of the property and the transferee in the same before-tax position as if the transferor had sold the property for cash and then used the proceeds to purchase an annuity contract. According to the IRS, an annuity contract, whether secured or unsecured, can be valued at the time it is received in exchange for property using actuarial tables (more about these later).

Specifically, under the proposed regulations, if an annuity contract is received in exchange for property other than money:

- The amount realized attributable to the annuity contract is the fair market value, as determined under Code Sec. 7520, of the annuity contract at the time of the exchange;
- The entire amount of the gain or loss, if any, is recognized at the time of the exchange, regardless of the taxpayer's method of accounting; and
- For purposes of determining the initial investment in the annuity contract under Code Sec. 72(c)(1), the aggregate amount of premiums or other consideration paid for the annuity contract equals the amount realized attributable to the annuity contract (the fair market value of the annuity contract).

The proposed regulations would apply to exchanges of property for an annuity contract, regardless of whether the property is exchanged for a newly issued annuity contract or the property is exchanged for an already existing annuity contract. Moreover, the proposed regulations would not distinguish between secured and unsecured annuity contracts.

The proposed regulations are a significant departure from the old rules. Many tax practitioners have predicted that families will no longer use private annuities to transfer small businesses. However, because the rules are so new, it is too early to predict.

COMMENT

Generally, the proposed regulations became effective for exchanges of property for an annuity contract after October 18, 2006, and for annuity contracts received in such exchanges after October 18, 2006. However, the effective date was delayed for six months for certain transactions that pose the least likelihood of abuse. The effective date was delayed until April 18, 2007, for transactions in which:

- The issuer of the annuity contract is an individual;
- The obligations under the annuity contract are not secured, either directly or indirectly; and
- The property transferred in the exchange is not subsequently sold or otherwise disposed of by the transferee during the two-year period beginning on the date of the exchange.

Mechanics. In a traditional private annuity arrangement, the owner transfers his or her business to an individual in exchange for the purchaser's promise to make annual payments to the seller for life. The transfer of assets in exchange for the annuity must be treated as a bona fide, arm's-length transaction. Under the traditional approach, a private annuity arrangement can yield significant gift, income, and estate tax benefits:

- No gift tax is due on the transfer as long as the value of the property does not exceed the present value of the payments;
- Income tax on the appreciation attributed to the property generally is allowed to be deferred by the seller-family member under a private annuity arrangement; and
- No estate tax is due on the senior family member's death because the value of the business is not included in his or her gross estate for tax purposes, if the value of the annuity equals the value of the exchanged business interest.

Besides being an arm's-length transaction, courts have developed various factors they consider in evaluating whether a private annuity arrangement is a bona fide transfer. Some of the factors are:

■ The degree of the annuitant's control over the transferred assets;

■ The source of the annuity payment; and

■ The extent of the annuitant's continuing interest in the transferred business.

EXAMPLE

Arthur transfers ownership of his small business to his daughter in exchange for an annuity. The business is valued at $1 million. The interest rate is 5.2 percent. The annuity factor is 7.3193. To calculate the total amount of the annuity, the value of the asset is divided by the annuity factor. In this case, $1 million divided by 7.3193 is $136,625. The total amount of the annuity payment over Arthur's life is $136,625.

Secured annuity. When an annuity is secured, there is no deferral of taxation of gain. An annuity generally will be treated as secured if:

■ The stock transferred was placed in escrow; and

■ The annuity agreement provided for a cognovit judgment.

Tables. Valuations of noncommercial annuities that are based upon one life or less are valued for estate, gift, and income tax purposes using actuarial tables issued by the IRS based on an interest rate assumption equal to 120 percent of the federal midterm rate for the month in which the interest is valued, rounded to the nearest 0.2 percent. The tables are gender-neutral.

Table S, Single Life Remainder Factors, contains factors to determine the present value of the following property interests:

■ A noncommercial annuity payable over the life of one individual;

■ A life estate or the right to receive the income from property or to use nonincome-producing property for the life of one individual; and

■ A remainder or reversion taking effect after the life of one individual, including a remainder interest in property transferred to a pooled income fund.

The current version of Table S, which is effective for transactions occurring after April 30, 1999, is in Reg. § 20.2031-7(d)(7). For transfers occurring after April 30, 1989, and before May 1, 1999, the applicable Table S is in Reg. § 20.2031-7A(e). The appropriate factors for transfers occurring before May 1, 1989, and after November 30, 1983, are contained in Table A at Reg. § 20.2031-7A(d). However, remainder interests in property transferred to a pooled income fund prior to May 1, 1989, but after November 30, 1983, are obtained from Table G in Reg. § 1.642(c)-6A(d).

Table B, Term Certain Remainder Factors, is used to determine the present value of:

- A noncommercial annuity payable for a definite number of years;
- A term of years or the right to receive income from property or to use nonincome-producing property for a term of years; and
- A remainder or reversion taking effect at the end of a term of years.

The current version of Table B, which is effective for transaction dates after April 30, 1989, is in Reg. § 20.2031-7(d)(6). For transactions after November 30, 1983, and before May 1, 1989, Table B is in Reg. § 20.2031-7A(d).

Table J, Adjustment Factors for Term Certain Annuities, and Table K, Adjustment Factors for Annuities, are used to adjust the value of noncommercial annuities to account for the time value of money. Table J is used for annuities when the payments are due at the beginning of each interval whereas Table K is used for annuities when the payments are due at the end of each interval. The current versions of Tables J and K, which are effective after April 30, 1989, are in Reg. § 20.2031-7(d)(6).

COMMENT

Tables for transfers before December 1, 1983, were based on gender.

STUDY QUESTIONS

3. According to the IRS, an unsecured or secured annuity contract can be valued:
   a. At the time when payments commence
   b. At the time it is received in exchange for property
   c. At the death of the transferor as part of his or her estate
   d. None of the above

4. In a traditional private annuity arrangement, which of the following describes the tax treatment of the transfer?
   a. No gift tax is due at the time of transfer but estate tax is due upon the death of the senior family member
   b. Estate tax is not payable upon the transferor's death but income tax on the appreciation of transferred property is payable at the time of transfer
   c. No gift tax is due for transferred property worth less than the present value of the payments and no estate tax is due upon the death of the transferor
   d. None of the above is the correct tax consequence of the traditional private annuity arrangement

Self-Canceling Installment Notes

A variation of a private annuity is known as a *self-canceling installment note (SCIN)*, a vehicle in which the seller retains a secured interest by way of a note from a family member. The child's obligation to repay the note ends when the parent dies, even if amounts are still due. No estate tax is due at the death of the seller because the SCIN has no value due to its self-canceling feature. However, amounts already repaid to the seller are considered part of the seller's estate.

Installment Sales

The installment accounting method permits the reporting of gain from qualified installment sales as payments are received rather than in the year of sale. Under the installment method, sale proceeds guaranteed today, although not paid today, do not become taxable until they are actually obtained. This treatment changed in the Tax Relief Extension Act of 1999. The 1999 Tax Relief Act repealed use of the installment accounting method for accrual method taxpayers. However, one-year later, Congress reversed its decision in the Installment Tax Correction Act of 2000. Once again, accrual method taxpayers who are selling a business can use the installment method of accounting to defer the recognition of income until payments are received from a business buyer.

In an installment sale, property (such as a small business) is transferred and at least one payment is received by the seller after the close of the tax year in which the disposition occurs. An installment sale includes dispositions from which payment is to be received in a lump sum in a taxable year subsequent to the year of sale.

To use the installment method, the seller must allocate the total purchase price he or she received among all the assets sold in the transaction. Then, for each asset to which the installment method applies, the seller must compute the *gross profit percentage*—basically, the seller's gross profit (the selling price minus the tax basis of the property, selling expenses, and any depreciation recapture) divided by the selling price of the asset. Then, when the seller receives a payment from the purchaser, the principal portion of the payment is multiplied by the gross profit percentage to determine the amount that must be reported as taxable gain for the year.

EXAMPLE

Alberto sold commercial real estate to his daughter Marisa on January 1, 2006. The total price was $600,000, of which $500,000 was allocated to the building and $100,000 was for the land underneath. Selling expenses were $37,500. Alberto originally purchased the property 10 years ago for $300,000 ($250,000 for the building and $50,000 for the land). Over the years, Alberto claimed $61,168 in depreciation using the straight-line method. Alberto made no capital improvements to the building during the time he owned it.

Marisa made a $200,000 down payment and will pay the balance at 10 percent interest on a 20-year amortization schedule, except that at 5 years the unpaid principal will be due in a balloon payment.

First, separate the transaction into two portions: the building and the land.

	Building	Land
Cost basis:	$250,000	$ 50,000
Less: depreciation	− 61,168	− 0
	188,832	50,000
Plus: expenses of sale	+ 31,250	+ 6,250
Adjusted basis:	$ 220,082	$56,250

Alberto's net gains on the sale of the building alone will be the sales price minus the adjusted basis computed above, or $500,000 − $220,082 = $279,918. Because this amount is greater than the $61,168 in depreciation, all of the depreciation he claimed over the years will be recaptured and taxed in the year of the sale. The remainder of Alberto's profit on the building, or $218,750 ($279,918 − $61,168) will be divided by the selling price of $500,000 to arrive at his gross profit percentage for the building: $218,750 ÷ $500,000 = .4375, or 43.75 percent.

For the land, no depreciation was deductible, so there is no recapture. Alberto's profit on the land is the price less the adjusted basis, or $100,000 − $56,250 = $43,750. His gross profit percentage of the land would be $43,750 ÷ 100,000 = .4375, or 43.75 percent.

For every payment Alberto receives, including the down payment and the balloon, he must separate the principal from any interest. Interest is taxed as ordinary income. Of the principal, 1/6 will represent a payment for the land, and 5/6 will represent a payment for the building. Of the payment for the land, 43.75 percent will be taxed as capital gains, and the remainder is a return of Alberto's capital, which is not taxed. Of the payment for the land, 43.75 percent of each payment will be taxed as capital gains, and the rest represents either the recaptured depreciation, which was taxed in the year of the sale, or the return of Alberto's capital, which is not taxed.

CAUTION

Installment reporting is not available when a related purchaser disposes of the purchased property within two years or before the original seller receives all payments, whichever is earlier, and one of the principal purposes of the disposition is the avoidance of federal income tax. Related purchasers include spouses, brothers and sisters, ancestors, and lineal descendants; a partnership and its partners; an estate and its beneficiaries; a trust and its grantor or beneficiaries; a corporation and any shareholder owning 50 percent or more of its stock; controlled entities owned by the same parties; and parties involved in the same entity.

COMMENT

Installment sales are reported on Form 6252, Installment Sale Income.

Buy-Sell Agreements

Another common financing device for the transfers of small businesses is a *buy-sell agreement,* or a contract among owners of a business or between the business and its owners for the purchase of a departing owner's share of the business. Businesses commonly use buy-sell agreements to safeguard against the death or disability of the owners. However, a buy-sell agreement can include terms to handle the departure of an owner for any reason.

Buy-sell agreements among owners generally require the owners to purchase the interest of a departing owner at a defined price. Such contracts are referred to as *cross-purchase agreements.* In contrast, buy-sell agreements between businesses and owners may be referred to as *ownership redemption agreements* or *stock redemption/repurchase agreements.* Such agreements generally require the business to purchase a departing owner's interest at a defined price. Both types of agreements are commonly referred to as *buyout agreements.*

Insurance. The most common means of funding a buy-sell agreement is through life insurance. This assumes that the triggering event is an insurable risk. Death and disability are always insurable. The purchaser of life insurance must have an insurable interest in the life of the owner of the company at the time the life insurance is purchased. The owner of the insurance will continue to maintain an insurable interest in the insured as long as the company continues in existence.

When life insurance is used to fund the purchase of a departing owner's share of the business, the premiums are not deductible by the business or the other owners personally because whoever pays the premiums is a direct or indirect beneficiary of the policy. The proceeds from life insurance are usually not subject to income tax regardless of who owns the policy.

Tax treatment. Generally, an owner receives capital gain treatment on taxes for the proceeds of the disposition of a business interest. If the company is a corporation and the corporation owns the life insurance policies, the stock purchase will be a redemption with the stock redemption rules of Code Sec. 302 applying to the transaction.

The deceased or disabled owner will recognize capital gain treatment on a sale or exchange of a capital asset if the other shareholders own the life insurance or if it is a full redemption by the corporation. However, family attribution rules and their appropriate waivers will apply to the redemption and a practitioner should take those into account when determining the structure of the agreement. If the company is a partnership and the partnership owns the life insurance, a departing partner's income tax consequences hinge on the language in the agreement.

On the sale of a business, the IRS is especially vigilant to prevent a working owner's compensation during the year or two leading up to the sale or transfer from being turned into capital gain by keeping salary low and channeling the difference back into the business as capital. Keeping careful records of the owner's participation in the business is essential to substantiate "reasonable compensation" in the face of an overall IRS audit over the transfer of the business.

Grantor Retained Annuity Trusts

Grantor retained annuity trusts (GRATs) are a complex way of transferring assets to the next generation with minimal gift or estate taxation. Despite the administrative costs to set up and run a GRAT, however, a properly constructed GRAT can provide the most secure and effective structure to transfer a business with minimal opposition from the IRS about its gift and estate tax consequences.

Very simply, a GRAT is an irrevocable trust that pays the grantor an annuity for a term of years. The value of the annuity payments is determined by reference to actuarial tables published by the IRS using the Code Sec. 7520 rate. The remainder goes to the grantor's beneficiaries. The arrangement may be set up so the business owner receives payments in a predetermined fixed amount or as a percentage of the value of the assets in the GRAT. A GRAT is often used to transfer family businesses that operate as closely held corporations.

> **CAUTION**
>
> The transfer of assets to the trust does not qualify for the annual gift tax exclusion because the transfer is not a gift of a present interest.

The grantor is treated as the owner of the trust, for tax purposes, if he or she retains specific rights or powers over the trust. The grantor is taxed on trust income and may claim any charitable deductions or credits. The remainder—

the amount that will eventually pass to the beneficiaries—is considered a gift at the time the GRAT is created.

> **COMMENT**
>
> A GRAT may be attractive when interest rates are low. The interest rate applied to a GRAT is fixed when the GRAT is created. A lower interest rate generally translates into a lower gift tax.

The IRS imposes a gift tax on the remainder at the time the trust is created, rather than when the beneficiaries actually receive the remainder. At the end of the GRAT's term, the remainder passes to the beneficiaries free of transfer tax.

> **CAUTION**
>
> If the grantor dies before the GRAT ends, the assets revert to the grantor's estate and may be subject to federal estate tax.

> **COMMENT**
>
> An alternative planning technique involves an installment sale to an *intentionally defective* grantor trust. Most attractively, if the grantor dies before the end of the installment period, only the value of the unpaid note will be included in the grantor's gross estate. With a GRAT, the entire value of the trust assets must be included in the grantor's gross estate.

Family Limited Partnerships

Family limited partnerships (FLPs) are another mechanism to effect intra-family transfers. However, in this arrangement, the parent (donor) takes a general partnership interest and retains control over the business. FLPs are created by moving assets to a partnership, according to applicable state law. Generally, appreciated assets can be transferred without triggering a tax consequence. Although they are popular, FLPs are viewed with great skepticism by the IRS.

> **COMMENT**
>
> The general rule that assets can be transferred to an FLP does not apply if the FLP is an *investment partnership* comprising more than 80 percent of the assets as securities and cash. If an investment partnership, the FLP contributions could trigger gain recognition under Code Sec. 721(b).

In exchange for transferring assets to the FLP, the parent receives a general partner interest (a 1 or 2 percent interest) and a much larger limited partnership interest (the remaining 98 or 99 percent). The parent keeps the general partnership interest and transfers portions of the limited partnership interest to the children or to trusts for their benefit. The limited partnership interests transferred are worth less, for transfer tax purposes, than the fair market value of underlying assets. Generally, taxpayers may discount the value of gifts of FLP interests by 20 to 40 percent.

EXAMPLE

Marcus transfers his small business, valued at $1 million, to an FLP. Marcus retains a 1 percent general interest and distributes 10 percent in limited partnership interests to each of his four children. Buy using an FLP, Marcus may transfer $400,000 in assets at a discounted value for gift tax purposes between $240,000 and $320,000.

Gift tax. Although the transfer of an interest in an FLP is a taxable gift, the taxable value of the gift is a fraction of the full value of the assets. Additionally, FLP interests are considered to be completed gifts if there is an immediate economic benefit and the assets transferred to the FLP are removed from the parent's estate.

IRS view. When the IRS attacks an FLP, it usually bases its attack on the valuation of the partnership interests. Unless it can be proven that the children have a legitimate capital interest in the partnership, the IRS can disregard their partnership interests for income tax purposes. The IRS also questions the legitimacy of *deathbed FLPs* in which the FLP structure is created literally a few days or weeks before the business owner dies for the purpose of lower estate tax value. However, set up while the owner is still active and using realistic gift tax valuation discounts for transfers to limited partnership interest, an FLP can provide a legitimate way for a small business to avoid significant estate taxes.

STUDY QUESTIONS

---

5. The transfer of assets to a GRAT does **not** qualify for the annual gift tax exclusion because:

    a. The assets are not accessible by the recipient.

    b. The grantor is able to claim other benefits for the gift, such as charitable deductions or credits.

    c. The transfer is not considered to be a gift of a present interest.

    d. Asset transfers do qualify for the annual gift tax exclusion.

---

6. Transfers of interests to an FLP are **not** considered completed gifts if:

   a. Assets transferred to the partnership are removed from the parent's estate.
   b. There is an immediate economic benefit.
   c. The taxable value of the gift is a fraction of the full value of the assets.
   d. All of the above are reasons that the transfers are considered completed gifts.

VALUING A SMALL BUSINESS

Whatever financing method may be used, the small business must be valued. Any of numerous methods can be used to value a business and an owner's interest in that business. It is important to remember that in determining the value of a business and its components the transferor and transferee, as buyer and seller, are not the only parties to the transaction; the IRS is very much a party that wants its share...in tax dollars. Usually, the competing interests of a buyer and seller assure the IRS that it will collect its fair share when both buyer and seller's tax positions are added up. In an intrafamily transfer, however, there is more of a possibility that "friendly parties" will cut the IRS out of its full share, if not in resulting income tax, then in circumvented gift or estate tax. Especially in intrafamily transfers of a business, therefore, the IRS looks closely at valuation.

PLANNING POINTER

Prospective buyers will perform their own valuation of the business. Small business owners should be prepared to be peppered with many questions about finances, products and services, staff, customers, vendors, and facilities, among other aspects of the business. Typically, sellers make five years of recent financial statements available for inspection but potential buyers may ask for a more expansive review.

CAUTION

A professional valuation can tell the price that an average buyer might pay; however, it is just a starting point in real world negotiations.

Some Valuation Methods

Appraisers use a number of different valuation methods. Some of the more common are explained here.

Net book value. Net book value is an asset-based valuation method. Net book value has the advantage of ease. A value obtained under this method may accurately reflect market value if the business trades in a commodity (for example, manufactured chains, computer chips, or electronic fasteners) and does not have large investments in equipment or facilities. In contrast, net book value may undervalue a business possessing substantial intangible assets such as a customer base, a highly trained workforce, or copyrights.

Capitalized earnings. The capitalized earnings method is a historical earnings valuation method. The capitalized earnings method has the advantage of ease in computing and including the value of intangible assets. However, this method is more applicable to business purchases because it requires using a required rate of return on the business for the future. The question will always arise, whether historic information accurately reflects the current value of a high growth company or whether historical performance will accurately reflect future performance.

Appraisal. Professional appraisers may use traditional market-based valuation methods such as the comparable sales method and industry averages or they may use any of the other methods available. The key is to know what method the appraiser is using and ensure that it is an appropriate fit with the business and owners. Appraisals have the advantage of being valuations by an objective third party.

Discounted cash flow. The discounted cash flow method has the advantage of capturing expected growth and intangible asset values. However, the projections are subjective and the assumptions used to project future cash flow are not always accurate. The advantage of this method is that it attempts to look forward to the possible business potential. The disadvantages are that an appropriate discount rate must be used, the calculations are somewhat complex, and the method requires the appraiser or practitioner to have extensive knowledge of the business and industry to accurately predict the future.

Hybrid methods. The hybrid methods of business valuation combine aspects of the various other methods to determine a final valuation. The most common method used is the excess earnings method, which combines asset and historical earning value. Another method is to combine the discounted cash flow and asset values. These methods have the advantage of being the most comprehensive valuation methods. The disadvantages of these methods are their complexity and questionable accuracy of relying on projections of future events.

Goodwill. Goodwill is an important but difficult to define concept. Generally, *goodwill* is the value of a business based on expected continued customer patronage due to the organization's name, reputation, or any other factor. Goodwill is the total of many qualities that bring patronage to a business.

The IRS has provided a formula for valuing goodwill. Under the formula, the net tangible assets are valued and then goodwill is valued by capitalizing earnings in excess of a reasonable return on the net tangible assets. The procedure in applying the formula is as follows:

1. Determine the average earnings of the business for a representative period;
2. Determine the average annual value of the tangible assets used in the business for the same period;
3. Determine a fair percentage return on the tangible assets;
4. Deduct the percentage return on tangible assets from the average earnings to determine average earnings attributable to goodwill; and
5. Capitalize the average earnings attributable to goodwill at an appropriate rate. This is the fair market value of goodwill.

COMMENT

Continuous operation for a long time in the same community under the same or similar name is one of the chief factors in developing goodwill.

CAUTION

Friendship between the seller of a business and his or her customers is *not* goodwill. Goodwill also does *not* include identifiable intangible assets such as patents, leases, and franchises, and if the value of goodwill cannot be separated from the value of these assets, it is generally ignored for tax purposes.

Special Situations

Sometimes, the business entity may call for a special valuation method. This is generally true for closely held corporations. The stock of a closely held corporation is often held by a single family. Consequently, there is often very little, if any, trading of the stock. Valuing a closely held corporation is much more complex than valuing a publicly traded corporation.

Over the years, the IRS and the courts have identified various factors relevant to the valuation of closely held stock:

- The nature of the business and its history from inception;
- The general economic outlook and the condition of the particular industry involved;

- The book value of the stock and the financial condition of the business;
- The company's earning capacity;
- The company's capacity to pay dividends;
- Goodwill or other intangible value;
- Any sales of the stock and the size of the block being valued;
- The market prices of stocks of corporations in the same line of business; and
- Life insurance proceeds receivable by the company upon the death of the controlling shareholder.

ALLOCATION OF PURCHASE PRICE

When the assets of a going concern are sold to a single buyer, the buyer and seller generally must allocate the purchase price among the tangible and intangible assets for sale. The seller in that case usually wants to allocate as much of the purchase price as possible to assets that yield capital gains rather than ordinary income. The buyer's interest, on the other hand, will be to allocate as much of the purchase price as possible to assets that do not have to be fully capitalized and can be written off quickly. When the "purchase" is to a family member, however, the natural self-interests of buyer and seller can become tainted to the extent that allocations become suspect by the IRS.

These tensions are at play in all business asset sales, but they vary with changes in the parties' circumstances and in the tax laws. The Tax Code mandates that allocation on the sales of the assets of a business follow a particular method: the *residual allocation method*. This allocation method in Reg. §§ 1.1060-1(x) and 1.338-6(b) has a hierarchy of seven categories.

If a group of assets constituting a going concern is acquired in a single transaction, allocation of basis is required to determine the basis for depreciable assets and assets such as inventory that may be sold in the near future. Under the residual method of allocation, the purchase price for a group of assets constituting a going concern is allocated among the following asset classes:

- Cash and general deposit accounts;
- Actively traded personal property, certificates of deposit, and foreign currency;
- Assets that are marked to market, and certain debt instruments;
- Stock in trade, inventory, and property held for sale to customers in the ordinary course of business;
- Class V assets, which are all assets not included in any other class;
- Class VI assets, which are Code Sec. 197 intangibles except goodwill and going concern value; and
- Class VII assets, which are goodwill and going concern value.

Allocations are made first to the top category of assets, then to the second, and third. Whatever is left unallocated automatically is allocated to intangible assets in the nature of goodwill and going concern value. Consideration is allocated among different assets in each of these categories according to their fair market values.

Buyers and sellers will try to the extent possible to make allocations that serve their own tax interests. Although no asset can receive an allocation greater than its fair market value, that value cannot always be determined with mathematical precision, so there often is some room to maneuver. The buyer and seller, however, both must use whatever allocation they finally agree to.

Until a couple of years ago, sellers wanted to allocate as much as possible to goodwill and going concern value, because doing so enabled them to recognize proceeds as capital gain, not ordinary income. Buyers hated allocations to these assets, because they could not be written off. Now, however, they can be written off over 15 years.

Many other purchased intangible assets, such as covenants not to compete, that buyers used to write off over their terms, now cannot be written off over fewer than 15 years. So buyers may want to enter into consulting agreements to shift some allocation away from the covenant not to compete and to get more immediate tax benefit from their expenditures. Although covenants not to compete and consulting fees both are taxable as ordinary income, sellers have to remember that consulting agreements generally will require them to perform services, whereas covenants not to compete do not. Again, these agreements are particularly suspect in a family setting in which enforcement of the agreement is generally not as rigorous.

STUDY QUESTIONS

7. The valuation method that uses a traditional market-based valuation method such as comparable sales is the:

a. Appraisal
b. Capitalized earnings method
c. Net book value
d. Discounted cash flow method

8. The formula that the IRS recommends for valuing goodwill uses:

a. Net tangible assets
b. Discounted cash flow
c. Capitalized earnings
d. Net book value

FINAL FEDERAL PAYROLL TAX RESPONSIBILITIES

While a business is in operation, the owner is responsible for collecting and paying federal employment taxes for his or her employees. Federal employment taxes include:

- Federal income tax withholding;
- The Federal Insurance Contributions Act (Social Security and Medicare) tax, known as FICA; and
- The Federal Unemployment Tax Act (FUTA) taxes.

FICA imposes two taxes on employers and two taxes on employees:

- To finance federal old age, survivors, and disability insurance (Social Security); and
- To finance hospital and hospital service insurance for those 65 years of age or older (Medicare).

The taxes are withheld on the employee's wages at one fixed rate for Social Security and at another fixed rate for Medicare. Identical amounts are required from the employer. There is an annual limit called a *taxable wage base* for Social Security tax purposes beyond which no tax can be imposed. There is no taxable wage base for Medicare tax purposes.

COMMENT

For 2007, employers do not withhold Social Security tax after an employee reaches the taxable wage base of $97,500 in Social Security wages.

FICA and FUTA Responsibilities
While the Employer Is in Business

Employers must withhold the employee portion of those taxes from each payment of wages. The amount to withhold is based on a flat, ungraduated percentage of the employee's gross taxable wages. Neither the size nor the frequency of wage payments affects this withholding duty. Additionally, employers are responsible for the employer portion of the tax, which will be the same amount as that withheld from the employee's wages. This process continues for Social Security tax purposes until the employee's wages reach the specified taxable wage base.

Unlike FICA taxes, no employee contributions are required for FUTA taxes. Only the employer pays FUTA taxes. FUTA tax must be paid until an employee's wages reach the FUTA taxable wage base of $7,000. The base is established by law and is the same for all employees. Once an employee earns that amount, the employer no longer has further FUTA liability for that employee for the year.

Forms 941 and 944. Nonagricultural employers file Form 941, *Employer's Quarterly Federal Tax Return*, or Form 944, *Employer's Annual Federal Tax Return*, to report wages paid, tips reported to the employer, federal income tax withheld, Social Security and Medicare taxes withheld, the employer's share of Social Security and Medicare taxes, and advance earned income credit payments. A separate Form 941 is filed for each quarter, as this table shows.

Quarter	Range of Months
1	January–March
2	April–June
3	July–September
4	October–December

Form 941 is due by the last day of the month following the end of the quarter.

Some small employers may be eligible to file Form 944 instead of filing Form 941 each quarter. Form 944 generally is due on January 31 of the following year. This form is designed for employers having an annual liability of $1,000 or less for Social Security, Medicare, and withheld federal income taxes. The IRS notifies employers if they are eligible to file Form 944.

Tax deposits. The IRS takes federal employment tax deposits seriously. Deposits must be timely or the business risks incurring penalties. Employers deposit employment taxes either monthly or semiweekly. The schedule an employer uses is based on the amount of taxes reported during the four quarters in a so-called lookback period.

Monthly depositors. If a business reported taxes of $50,000 or less during the lookback period, it is a monthly schedule depositor and generally must deposit each month's accumulated employment taxes on or before the 15th day of the following month. For example, taxes for January must be deposited by February 15.

Semiweekly depositors. If a business reported taxes greater than $50,000 for the lookback period, it is a semiweekly schedule depositor and generally must deposit employment taxes on Wednesday or Friday, based on the following schedule:

- The employment taxes on payments made to employees on Wednesday, Thursday, and/or Friday, must be deposited by the following Wednesday; and
- The taxes on payments made to employees on Saturday, Sunday, Monday, and/or Tuesday, must be deposited by the following Friday.

> **COMMENT**
>
> Semiweekly depositors always have at least three banking days to make a deposit. If any of the three weekdays after the end of the semiweekly period is a holiday on which banks are closed, the taxpayer is allowed one additional day to deposit.

Whether a business is a monthly depositor or a semiweekly depositor, if it accumulates taxes of $100,000 or more on any day during a deposit period, it must deposit them on the next banking day. If this happens, the business becomes a semiweekly depositor for the remainder of the calendar year and for the following calendar year.

> **CAUTION**
>
> An employer is subject to various penalties for late payment of withholding taxes. The maximum penalty is 15 percent of the underpayment. A *responsible person* is also subject to a penalty for failure to collect withholding tax or failure to pay withholding tax once it is collected. For example, in a sole proprietorship, the responsible person is the sole proprietor. The penalty is 100 percent of the withholding amounts that should have been retained and paid to the government. The penalty is known as the *trust fund recovery penalty.* This is because employers are required to withhold employees' taxes and hold them in trust until the funds are deposited with the government. The 100 percent penalty only applies to the employee's withholding. It does not apply to the employer's share of Social Security tax payments or other taxes.

Final Returns

When a small business ceases paying wages to its employees, the first step is to file a quarterly return. On that return, the employer reports wage payments and tax withheld to date. Employers also must provide an annual reconciliation return reconciling amounts shown as having been paid on the quarterly returns for the quarterly returns for the year with amounts shown as having been withheld on the employees' wage and tax statements. Additionally, employers must provide the IRS, in a separate statement, with the address at which the employer's past tax records are located, the name of the person keeping the records, and, if the business has been sold or transferred, the name of the new owner and the date when the sale or transfer took place.

The quarterly return should be labeled "final return." The IRS will treat this quarterly return the same as the quarterly return for the fourth calendar quarter of a year. Once this final return is filed, the small business owner's withholding obligations cease.

The process is similar for filing a final FUTA return. The last FUTA return filed by an employer should be marked "final return" and accompanied by a statement indicating where and by whom the employer's records will be kept. If the business has been sold or otherwise transferred, the name of the new owner and the date when the transfer took place should be included in the statement.

> **COMMENT**
>
> The annual tax return for a partnership, corporation, S corporation, limited liability company, or trust includes check boxes near the top front page just below the entity information. For the tax year in which the business ceases to exist, the taxpayers should check the box that indicates this tax return is a final return. If there are Schedule K-1s, the same procedure applies on the Schedule K-1.

Final wage and withholding information. Employers also must issue final wage and withholding information to employees. Generally, an employer required to file a final Form 941 must furnish Forms W-2 to its employees on or before the date required for filing the final Form 941.

Self-employed individuals. Individuals engaged in a trade or business as sole proprietors or partners must pay self-employment tax on net earnings from self-employment. Self-employment tax has two components:

- A 12.4 percent tax on self-employment income for old age, survivors, and disability insurance (OASDI) up to the Social Security wage base; and
- A 2.9 percent tax for Medicare. The Medicare portion is not subject to a cap.

Self-employment tax for sole proprietors with no employees is levied and collected as part of income tax. An individual having net earnings from self-employment of at least $400 in a tax year must file a Schedule SE, Self-Employment Tax, and report self-employment tax, if any, on Form 1040, U.S. Individual Income Tax Return. The sole proprietor can deduct one-half of the self-employment tax as an adjustment to income on Form 1040.

> **COMMENT**
>
> A sole proprietor is not subject to FUTA but the sole proprietorship must pay FUTA for any of the organization's employees.

STUDY QUESTIONS

9. The cutoff amount for employment tax deposits during the lookback period for depositors required to make semiweekly versus monthly deposits is:

   a. $10,000 or more
   b. $25,000 or more
   c. $50,000 or more
   d. $100,000 or more

10. Sole proprietors can deduct _____ of self-employment tax as an adjustment to their income on Form 1040 returns.

   a. One-third
   b. One-half
   c. Two-thirds
   d. Three-quarters

CONCLUSION

The decision to end or leave a small business is very much a personal journey for the owner. The practitioner can accompany him or her along the way. There are many options to consider. This chapter explored some of them and raised some other issues. Every small business is unique and the practitioner who will be most successful is the one who best knows his or her small business owner client and can craft an exit strategy tailored to that client's needs.

CPE NOTE: When you have completed your study and review of chapters 1-3, which comprise this Module, you may wish to take the Quizzer for the Module.

For your convenience, you can also take this Quizzer online at **www.cchtestingcenter.com**.

Alternative Minimum Tax: A Growing Problem

This chapter helps practitioners understand the basic structure and current rules of the alternative minimum tax (AMT), the impact the AMT has on individuals, and the future of the AMT.

LEARNING OBJECTIVES

Upon completion of this chapter you will be able to:

- Understand the historical underpinnings of the AMT;
- Identify credits and other items allowable against potential AMT liability;
- Calculate AMT liability;
- Describe who is impacted the most by the AMT; and
- Recommend certain strategies designed to reduce AMT exposure.

INTRODUCTION

The purpose of the AMT is to prevent taxpayers with substantial economic income from avoiding all tax liability through the use of exclusions, deductions, and credits. The AMT is a separate tax system that parallels the regular tax system. It is imposed on individuals, corporations, and estates or trusts in an amount by which the tentative minimum tax exceeds the regular income tax for the tax year. The AMT applies different tax rates to a broader base of income than under the regular tax system. It also reduces certain deductions and other tax benefits through a system of adjustments and preferences. AMT liability is calculated on these tax forms:

- Form 6251, Alternative Minimum Tax – Individuals for individuals;
- Form 4626, Alternative Minimum Tax- Corporations for corporations; and
- Form 1041, Schedule I, U.S. Income Tax Return for Estates and Trusts for estates and trusts.

Unless Congress acts to repeal or reform the AMT (or to extend temporary relief), millions more individuals could be liable for the AMT starting in 2007.

HISTORY OF THE ALTERNATIVE MINIMUM TAX

Congress designed the AMT nearly 40 years ago to ensure that very wealthy individuals did not evade federal taxes completely. In 1969, the AMT applied to fewer than 200 taxpayers. Today, hundreds of thousands and potentially millions of taxpayers are or may be liable for the AMT. The explosive and controversial growth of the AMT is largely due to Congress' failure to index the AMT for inflation while becoming increasingly dependent on the income that the AMT brings into the federal coffers. Several proposals have been floated in Congress to "reform" the AMT, but so far none has been acted on.

COMMENT

In 2001, the IRS revealed that about 4,500 people with incomes of more than $200,000 still did not pay either the regular income tax or the AMT. Estimates for the current year run close to triple that number.

Alternative minimum taxable income (AMTI) is the individual's regular taxable income increased by certain preference items. Under the Tax Equity and Fiscal Responsibility Act of 1982, a rate of 20 percent was applied to AMTI in excess of an exemption amount of $40,000 for joint filers or $30,000 for single-filing taxpayers. The exemption amounts were not indexed for inflation, even though the regular rates were to be indexed for inflation annually. Nonrefundable credits, other than the foreign tax credit, were not allowed against the AMT. Further, and affecting deductions common to many middle-class individuals in addition to the wealthy, the standard deduction and the deductions for personal exemptions, state and local taxes, and interest on home equity loans were not allowed. On the other side of the equation, incentive stock option gain that was largely exempt from immediate regular tax liability was included in AMTI.

The Tax Reform Act of 1986 increased the AMT tax rate from 20 percent to 21 percent, and the exemption amount was phased out for joint-filing individuals with AMTI in excess of $150,000, or $112,500 for single-filing taxpayers. Deferral preferences were properly adjusted over time, and a minimum tax credit was added. Preferences were added for interest on private activity bonds and for appreciation on charitable contributions. Net operating losses were allowed to offset only 90 percent of AMTI. Similarly, the foreign tax credit could not reduce the tentative minimum tax by more than 90 percent.

Although the 1982 and 1986 Acts set the basic structure of the AMT, they did not signal the end to further fine-tuning. Further changes made in the determination of AMTI for individuals tended to reduce certain preference items that had raised AMTI for certain taxpayers, as well as increase the exemption amounts and the application of certain credits for all individuals. At the same time, however, subsequent fine-tuning also generally raised the tax rate imposed on AMTI for all taxpayers.

The Revenue Reconciliation Act of 1990 repealed the preferences for charitable contributions of appreciated property and percentage depletion on oil and gas wells. The requirement that alternative depreciable lives be used in computing the deduction for the accelerated cost recovery system (ACRS) depreciation was also repealed. Additionally, the amount of the preference for intangible drilling expenses was substantially reduced.

The Omnibus Budget Reconciliation Act of 1990 increased the individual AMT tax rate from 21 percent to 24 percent as the maximum regular tax rate was increased from 28 percent to 31 percent. The rate was increased again by the Omnibus Budget Reconciliation Act of 1993 to 26 (minimum) and 28 percent (maximum) when the maximum regular tax rate was increased from 31 percent to 39.6 percent. The Revenue Reconciliation Act of 1997 changed the AMT capital gain rates to reflect the lower capital gain rates adopted for the regular tax. The Jobs and Growth Tax Reconciliation Act of 2003 revised the AMT rates for dividends to mirror the lower rates of the regular tax.

The Omnibus Budget Reconciliation Act of 1993 increased the AMT exemption amounts to $45,000, or $33,750 for single-filing taxpayers. The AMT exemption amounts were increased to $49,000 and $35,750 for single-filing individuals for 2001 and 2002. In 2003, 2004, and 2005, the amounts were further increased to $58,000 or $40,250 for single-filing individuals. The amounts were even further increased to $62,550 for joint filers or $42,500 for single-filing individuals in 2006.

The Tax Increase Prevention and Reconciliation Act of 2005 allowed the nonrefundable personal credits to offset the AMT on a temporary basis for 2006. The Economic Growth and Tax Relief Reconciliation Act of 2001 (EGTRRA) provided that the then-new child tax credit, the adoption credit, and the saver's credit could offset the AMT. The American Jobs Creation Act of 2004 permitted the foreign tax credit to offset the entire tentative minimum tax. The Tax Relief and Health Care Act of 2006 allowed the minimum tax credit for individuals to be refundable in part.

The Small Business and Work Opportunity Tax Act of 2007 extended the waiver of the AMT to the credit for taxes paid with respect to employee cash tips (the FICA tip credit) and to the work opportunity tax credit (WOTC). The general business limitation rule is now applied to these credits separately and the tentative minimum tax is zero. The effect is to allow both of these credits to be taken against both the regular tax and the AMT.

Fine-tuning of the AMT is expected to continue in 2007, particularly in connection with an extension of the higher exemption amounts for the year, retroactive to January 1, 2007.

THE ALTERNATIVE MINIMUM TAX IN 2007

The AMT is imposed on an individual in an amount by which the tentative minimum tax exceeds the regular income tax for the tax year. The tentative minimum tax is the sum of:

- 26 percent of so much of the taxable excess as does not exceed $175,000 ($87,500 for married couples filing a separate return); and
- 28 percent of the remaining taxable excess.
- The taxable excess is so much of the AMTI as exceeds the exemption amount.

The maximum tax rates on net capital gain and dividends used in computing the regular tax are used in computing the tentative minimum tax.

Exemption Amounts

The exemption amounts for 2007, unless Congress extends the higher 2006 amounts at the eleventh hour, are scheduled to be:

- $45,000 for surviving spouses and married couples filing a joint return;
- $33,750 for other unmarried individuals; and
- $22,500 for married couples filing separate returns.

> **REMINDER**
>
> These amounts are not indexed for inflation. They do not go up unless Congress specifically raises them for any particular year.

Phaseouts. The exemption amounts are phased out by an amount equal to 25 percent of the amount by which the individual's AMTI exceeds:

- $150,000 in the case of surviving spouses and married couples filing jointly;
- $112,500 in the case of other unmarried individuals; and
- $75,000 in the case of married couples filing separately.

This phaseout computation is expected to remain the same regardless of whether Congress extends or tinkers with the 2006 exemption amounts for the 2007 tax year.

> **EXAMPLE**
>
> Anne, a single individual, has AMTI of $150,000. She can claim an exemption amount of only $24,375 and not the full exemption amount because her income exceeds $112,500.

Her exemption amount is determined as follows:

1. Determine the amount by which Anne's AMTI exceeds the threshold amount ($150,000 – $112,500 = $37,500).

2. Multiply the difference by 25 percent ($37,500 × 0.25).

3. The product, $9,375, is subtracted from $33,750, the exemption amount available to Anne as a single individual.

4. This results in the $24,375 exemption available to Anne ($33,750 – $9,375). Anne's AMTI is $125,625 ($150,000 – $24,375).

5. Her AMT liability is $32,662.50 ($125,625 × 0.26).

Because Anne's AMTI does not exceed $175,000, the second rate of 28 percent does not come into play. If her AMTI was $200,000 after the exemption, her AMT liability would be different.

Anne's AMT liability, if her AMTI exceeded $175,000, would be determined as follows:

$175,000 × 0.26 = $45,500

$25,000 × 0.28 = $7,000

$45,500 + $7,000 = $52,500

STUDY QUESTIONS

1. Which of the following acts did **not** increase the AMT tax rate?

a. Tax Reform Act of 1986

b. Omnibus Budget Reconciliation Act of 1990

c. Omnibus Budget Reconciliation Act of 1993

d. Tax Increase Prevention and Reconciliation Act of 2005

2. The phaseout of the AMT exemption amount for unmarried individuals begins at what AMTI level?

a. $75,000

b. $112,500

c. $150,000

d. None of the above is the phaseout threshold for single filers

THE GROWING THREAT

The number of taxpayers affected by the AMT is likely to increase substantially in 2007. The principal reason for this increase is lower AMT exemption levels than in recent years and certain nonrefundable personal credits no longer being allowed against the AMT. Also, the fact that the AMT exemption levels are not indexed for inflation whereas the regular income tax is will enlarge the number of taxpayers affected by the AMT. In other words, if an individual's income barely keeps pace with inflation each year, his or her regular income tax would remain constant while his or her AMT liability would enlarge. This difference is cumulative and, therefore, grows more pronounced with each passing year. Many in Congress agree that growth has reached crisis proportions.

> **PLANNING POINTER**
>
> Congress is expected to consider an AMT "patch" for 2007 (and possibly for 2008) before the start of 2008. A patch is a temporary measure designed to limit the growing impact of the AMT, especially on middle income, two-wage earner families. Congress may allow the nonrefundable personal credits to be used against AMT liability and could enact higher exemption amounts or extend those that applied in 2006. Some equivalent relief is likely.

> **PLANNING POINTER**
>
> AMT patch legislation has reached just about the end of the line. Another patch "extension" for 2008 is possible but, sooner or later, major AMT reform will take place. Planning to defer preference items into 2009 in order to avoid or lower the AMT in 2007 and 2008 might begin to make sense depending on the hoops through which the taxpayer must jump to do so. This strategy is especially relevant to those who just fall into the AMT at this time because reform efforts are certain to aim at getting that particular group out of AMT danger.

The AMT is a huge revenue raiser for the federal government. Estimates are that the tax will bring in $1.2 trillion additional revenue between now and 2015. If the AMT were abolished, as some lawmakers support, the federal government would need to cut spending proportionately or, more likely, find another revenue source including a general tax rate increase under the regular tax.

> **COMMENT**
>
> Senator Charles Grassley (R-Iowa) has told Congress that in repealing or reforming the AMT, offsets should not be found to replace the money collected by the AMT because the AMT was never meant to collect so much revenue.

> **COMMENT**
>
> According to Senate Finance Committee Chairman Max Baucus (D-Montana), 25,000 AMT taxpayers had adjusted gross incomes (AGI) of less than $20,000 in 2005 and 2006. Nearly 200,000 AMT taxpayers made between $75,000 and $100,000. More people making less than $100,000 paid the AMT than people making more than $1 million, he added.

NONREFUNDABLE PERSONAL CREDITS

The nonrefundable personal credits (other than the adoption credit, child credit, and saver's credit) are allowed against the AMT only to the extent that the individual's regular income tax liability exceeds his or her tentative minimum tax without regard to the AMT foreign tax credit. The adoption credit, child credit, and saver's credit are allowed to the full extent of the individual's regular tax and AMT.

ESTATES AND TRUSTS

Estates, trusts, and their beneficiaries are subject to the same AMT rules as are individuals. The exemption amount is $22,500 in the case of an estate or trust. The exemption amount is phased out by an amount equal to 25 percent of the amount by which the taxpayer's AMT exceeds $75,000.

AMTI is determined by applying the regular rules for the allocation of tax items along with the adjustments and preferences. Items can be allocated by determining the trust's or estate's distributable net income (DNI)—taking into account adjustments and preferences, but without regard to the exemption amount—and applying the regular tax rules for the taxation of estates and trusts.

DNI limits estates' and trusts' distributions deduction and beneficiaries' reportable gross income. DNI also determines character of amounts distributed to beneficiaries. DNI is the taxable income of a trust or estate considered to be available for distribution to beneficiaries.

This standard method of using DNI to figure the AMTI of a trust or estate cannot be used if it is inconsistent with any adjustments to the trust's or estate's taxable income in computing DNI.

CORPORATIONS

Corporations are also subject to the AMT, but under a different scheme. The corporate exemption amount is $40,000. The exemption is not completely phased out until AMTI reaches $310,000 (for 2006). The tentative minimum tax for the tax year is 20 percent of so much of the AMTI as exceeds the exemption amount, reduced by the AMT foreign tax credit. The AMTI of any corporation for any tax year is increased by 75 percent of the excess over the AMTI of the adjusted current earnings (ACE) of the corporation. ACE is the AMTI for the tax year determined with the adjustments.

CALCULATING AMT LIABILITY FOR INDIVIDUALS

AMTI is the individual's regular taxable income increased by certain adjustments. In the case of items that involve the timing of deductions, the AMTI treatment negates the deferral of income (or takes back some of the tax breaks) resulting from the regular tax treatment of these items.

Adjustments

Each adjustment that an individual must take into account to compute the AMTI:

- Decreases the amount of a deduction that has been taken for regular tax purposes;
- Prohibits the deduction entirely; or
- Increases the amount of income recognized for AMT purposes (generally as *preference items* that are added back to regular tax income).

Decreasing Deductions

Medical expenses. Medical expenses are deductible only to the extent they exceed 10 percent of the taxpayer's AGI (as opposed to exceeding 7.5 percent under the regular tax system).

Investment interest. The amount allowed as a deduction for investment interest for any tax year cannot exceed the net investment income of the taxpayer for the tax year. The amount disallowed as a deduction for any tax year must be treated as investment interest paid or accrued by the taxpayer in the succeeding tax year.

Investment interest is any interest allowable as a deduction that is paid or accrued on a debt properly allocable to property held for investment. It does not include any qualified residence interest or any interest which is taken into account in computing income or loss from a passive activity of the taxpayer. *Net investment income* is the excess of investment income over investment expenses. Investment income includes gross income from property held for investment, the excess of the net gain attributable to the disposition of property held for investment, and net capital of property held for investment. It also includes qualified dividend income of the taxpayer.

Depreciation. The depreciation deduction allowed for any tangible property other than certain personal property placed in service on or after January 1, 1987, is determined under the alternative depreciation system (ADS). The 150 percent declining-balance method applies to property placed in service on or after January 1, 1999. The 150 percent declining-balance method should be used until the straight-line method must be used. The straight-line method should be used the first tax year for which using the method will yield a larger deduction. The straight-line method must be used for any other property if the depreciation deduction determined with respect to such other property is determined by using the straight-line method for purposes of the regular tax. Depreciation on property acquired after September 10, 2001, and before January 1, 2005 (January 1, 2006, for certain property), which is permitted an additional allowance under the regular tax, is computed without any AMT adjustment.

Mining exploration and development costs. The amount allowable as a deduction in computing the regular tax for costs paid or incurred for each mine or other natural deposit (other than an oil, gas, or geothermal well) is capitalized and amortized ratably over a 10-year period. The taxpayer should begin with the tax year in which the expenditures were made. If a loss is sustained with respect to any property with mining costs, a deduction is permitted for the expenditures for the tax year in which such loss is sustained in an amount equal to the lesser of the amount allowable for the expenditures if they had remained capitalized, or the amount of such expenditures that was not previously amortized.

Pollution control facilities. The deduction for any certified pollution control facility placed in service after January 1, 1987, is calculated under the ADS using longer class lives and the modified accelerated cost recovery system (MACRS) using the straight-line method. The straight-line depreciation method is used for facilities placed in service after December 31, 1998.

Circulation expenditures. *Circulation expenditures* are expenses for maintaining or increasing the circulation of periodicals. The amount allowed as a deduction in computing the regular tax for amounts paid or incurred after December 31, 1986, is capitalized and with respect to circulation expenditures is amortized ratably over a three-year period for the AMT beginning with the tax year in which the expenditures were made. If a loss is sustained to such property, a deduction is permitted for the expenditures for the tax year in which the loss was sustained in an amount equal to the lesser of the amount allowable for the expenditures had they remained capitalized or the amount of such expenditures that was not previously amortized.

Research and experimental expenditures. The amounts allowed as a deduction in computing the regular tax for research and experimental expenses paid or incurred after December 31, 1986, are capitalized and amortized ratably over a 10-year period for the AMT beginning with the taxable year in which the expenditures were made. If a loss is sustained to such property, a deduction is permitted for the expenditures for the tax year in which the loss was sustained in an amount equal to the lesser of the amount allowable for the expenditures if they had remained capitalized or in the amount of such expenditures that was not previously amortized.

Specified long-term contract. Under the AMT, the taxable income from long-term contracts entered into by the taxpayer on or after March 1, 1986, is determined by the percentage of completion method of accounting. The method of accounting does not apply to home construction contracts. For contracts excepted from the percentage of completion method of accounting for regular tax purposes, the simplified procedure for allocating costs is used to determine the percentage of completion under the AMT.

Incentive stock options. AMTI includes any excess of the fair market value of stock acquired through the exercise of an option when a taxpayer's rights in the acquired stock first become transferable or when the rights are no longer subject to a substantial risk of forfeiture over the amount paid for the stock. If the stock is acquired by exercising an incentive stock option and the stock was disposed of in the same year, no AMT adjustment is required.

Mortgage interest. The only eligible mortgage for AMT interest deduction purposes is one whose proceeds were actually used to build, buy, or substantially improve an individual's main or second home. Such interest also includes interest on any mortgage resulting from the refinancing of a taxpayer's main or second home, but only to the extent that the amount of the mortgage resulting from such refinancing does not exceed the amount of the outstanding debt prior to refinancing.

> **COMMENT**
>
> The interest on a mortgage whose proceeds are used to refinance another mortgage is not deductible.

Qualified mortgage interest includes interest that is paid or accrued on a debt that was acquired by the taxpayer before July 1, 1982. Also, the debt must have been secured by property that was the taxpayer's main home or second home. The second home can be used by the taxpayer or his or her family members. Family members include spouses, ancestors, lineal descendants, and brothers and sisters by whole or half blood.

Denial of certain farm losses. No loss of the taxpayer for any tax year due to tax shelter farm activity is permitted. Any loss from a tax shelter farm activity that is disallowed shall be treated as a deduction allocable to such activity in the first succeeding tax year. *Tax shelter farm activity* is any farming syndicate or any other activity consisting of farming that is a passive activity.

Code Sec. 199 Deduction Not Reduced. Effective for tax years beginning after December 31, 2004, qualified taxpayers can claim a deduction equal to the lesser of a phased-in percentage of taxable income (adjusted gross income if the taxpayer is an individual, trust, or estate) or qualified production activities income. The deduction cannot exceed one-half of the *W-2 wages*. For taxpayers other than corporations, the Code Sec. 199 deduction used to determine the regular tax is also used to determine AMTI.

Eliminated Deductions

In computing AMTI, the following deductions are not allowed altogether:

- The standard deduction;
- Personal exemptions;
- Miscellaneous itemized deductions;
- State, local, and foreign real property taxes;
- State and local personal property taxes; and
- State, local, and foreign income taxes.

> **REMINDER**
>
> Miscellaneous itemized deductions include such items as professional dues, unreimbursed job expenses, tax preparation fees, and certain legal expenses.

Preferences (Increases to Regular Taxable Income)

Generally, preferences increase taxable income in arriving at AMTI. The preferences that individuals must take into account to compute the AMTI are described here.

Depletion. *Depletion* is the excess of the deduction for depletion over the adjusted basis of each mineral property (other than oil and gas properties) at the end of the tax year.

> **COMMENT**
>
> This deduction is usually a result of a taxpayer's investment in a passthrough entity such as a partnership. When a taxpayer invests in a passthrough entity, the activity may be considered to be a passive activity.

Intangible drilling costs. These costs are the amount by which excess intangible drilling costs arising in the tax year exceed 65 percent of the net income from oil, gas, and geothermal properties of the taxpayer. This preference does not apply to independent producers. It only applies to taxpayers that are integrated oil companies. However, such companies cannot reduce their AMTI in any tax year by more than 40 percent (30 percent in the case of tax years beginning in 1993).

Tax-exempt interest. This is interest on specified private activity bonds issued after August 7, 1986, reduced by any deduction that would have been allowed if such interest were includible in gross income when calculating the regular tax. Any exempt-interest dividend shall be treated as interest on a private activity bond to the extent of its proportionate share of the interest on such bonds received by the company paying the dividend. Private activity bonds do not include any qualified 501(c)(3) bonds or any refunding bonds if the refunded bond was issued before August 8, 1986.

Accelerated depreciation or amortization. The straight-line method is used to compute depreciation on real property for which accelerated depreciation was determined using pre-1987 rules. A recovery period of 19 years is used for 19-year real property. A recovery period of 15 years is used for low-income housing. For leased personal property (except recovery property), the recovery period amount is that by which the regular tax depreciation using the pre-1987 rules exceed the depreciation permitted by the straight-line method.

Exclusion for gains on sale of certain small business stock. In the case of gain on the sale of certain small business stock, 7 percent of the amount of excluded gain from gross income for the tax year.

> **REMINDER**
>
> Taxpayers must also account for loss limitations unrelated to farm and passive activities.

STUDY QUESTIONS

3. Which of the following nonrefundable personal tax credits is *not* allowed to offset the AMT?

   a. Saver's credit

   b. Child credit

   c. Adoption credit

   d. All of the above exemptions are allowed as offsets

---

4. AMT deductions for mortgage interest upon refinancing:

    a. Are not applicable to adjustable rate mortgages

    b. Apply only to the taxpayer's principal residence, not to second or vacation homes

    c. Include interest on refinancing both a main and second home but only to the extent the debt level is not increased

    d. AMT does not allow any deduction for mortgage interest

---

ALTERNATIVE TAX NET OPERATING LOSS DEDUCTION

The alternative tax net operating loss (NOL) deduction is the net operating loss deduction allowable for the tax year, except that the amount of such deduction for AMT purposes must not exceed the sum of:

1. The lesser of the amount of such deduction attributable to net operating losses, or 90 percent of AMTI determined without regard to such deduction; plus
2. The lesser of the amount of such deduction attributable to the sum of carrybacks of NOLs from tax years ending during 2001 or 2002 and carryovers of net operating losses to tax years ending during 2001 and 2002, or AMTI determined without regard to such deduction reduced by the amount determined under 1 above.

ALTERNATIVE MINIMUM TAX FOREIGN TAX CREDIT

The AMT foreign tax credit is worth special mention because it is a non-refundable credit that **is** permitted to offset the AMT. The regular tax for purposes of computing the AMT is reduced by the regular foreign tax credit in order to avoid a double credit. Generally, the AMT foreign tax credit is determined in the same manner as the regular foreign tax credit, with these differences:

- The amount of the credit is limited to a portion of the taxpayer's gross AMT that is proportionate to the portion of the taxpayer's AMTI that comes from foreign sources. The *gross AMT* is the applicable AMT rate or rates multiplied by the excess of AMTI over the minimum tax-exemption amount. The amount of the regular tax foreign tax credit is limited to a portion of the taxpayer's tax liability that is proportionate to the portion of the taxpayer's taxable income that comes from foreign sources;
- The determination of whether income is high-taxed income for purposes of computing the credit is made on the basis of the 26- and 28-percent AMT rate for individuals, rather than the regular tax rates;

- The AMT foreign tax credit is limited to the amount of the taxpayer's gross AMT liability that exceeds 10 percent of the taxpayer's gross AMT liability computed without reference to the alternative tax NOL deduction and the excess intangible drilling and development costs (IDC) deduction; and

- The AMT foreign tax credit is determined as if dividends from a corporation eligible for the possessions tax credit, or the Puerto Rico economic activity credit, were a separate category of income for purposes of the foreign tax credit rules. However, this rule only applies to the portion of the dividends for which the dividends received deduction is disallowed under the rules for adjusted current earnings. In years before 1995, this rule applies only with respect to dividends from a corporation eligible for the possessions tax credit. It does not apply to dividends from a corporation eligible for the Puerto Rico economic activity credit.

EXAMPLE

Henry's foreign AMTI is $35,000, and the entire AMTI is $140,000. His gross minimum tax is 26 percent of the excess of AMTI over the exemption amount ($140,000 – $33,750), or $27,625. The limitation percentage is $35,000 divided by $140,000, or 25 percent. The AMT foreign credit limitation is 25 percent of $27,625, or $6,906.25.

COMMENT

The rule limiting the amount of the credit does not apply to some corporations for tax years beginning before August 6, 1997.

CALCULATING AMT

A taxpayer must first calculate his or her regular tax and then determine whether preferences and adjustments must be added back to taxable income (or subtracted in some case) to calculate AMTI.

Components

The components of an AMTI computation are structured in this order:

1. ADD: Net operating loss deduction to the regular tax amount
2. ADD OR SUBTRACT: Adjustments
   Adjustments include: medical expenses, investment interest, depreciation, mining exploration and development costs, pollution control facilities, circulation expenditures, research and experimental expendi-

tures, long-term contracts, incentive stock options; mortgage interest, farm shelter losses, standard deductions, personal exemptions, itemized deductions, and tax refunds

3. ADD: Preferences

   Preferences include: depletion, intangible drilling costs, tax-exempt interest, accelerated depreciation or amortization of property, and exclusion for gains on sale of certain small business stock

4. SUBTRACT: Alternative tax net operating loss

Generally, the recalculation of the adjustments and preferences results in amounts that reflect the difference between the regular tax items and the AMT items.

Capital Gain Income

To arrive at the AMT liability, the following calculations on AMTI are necessary:

1. AMTI – Exemption amount = AMT base
2. AMT base × AMT rate = Tentative AMT
3. Tentative AMT – Regular tax = AMT liability

Although the *AMT rate* for purposes of computing tentative AMT in this three-step calculation is generally either the 26 percent or the 28 percent rate, depending on the level of AMTI, the rate as applied to net capital gains (including qualified dividends) is limited to the lower regular net capital gains rate for that portion of AMTI attributable to such net capital gains.

> **COMMENT**
>
> Do not confuse the concept of a "tax preference item" for AMT purposes with the preferred tax rate given to net capital gains under both the regular tax and the AMT. Although capital gain is "preferred," that favored status within the tax code is not reflected in any add-back to income in computing AMTI. On the contrary, net capital gain continues its favored rate status only, as under the regular tax.

The AMT on noncorporate net capital gains (which includes qualified dividend income) cannot exceed the sum of:

1. The AMT on the taxable excess, with the taxable excess reduced by the lesser of either net capital gain or the sum of adjusted net capital gain and unrecaptured Section 1250 gain; plus

2. 5 percent (zero percent starting in 2008) of so much of adjusted net capital gain (or the taxable excess, if less) as does not exceed an amount equal to the excess of the amount of taxable income that may be taxed at a rate below 25 percent over the taxable income reduced by adjusted net capital gain; plus
3. 15 percent of so much of adjusted net capital gain (or the taxable excess, if less) as does not exceed the amount taxed under (2); plus
4. 25 percent of the taxable excess that exceeds the amounts taxed under items 1, 2, and 3 (i.e., to account for unrecaptured Section 1250 gain).

Therefore, for AMT purposes, a noncorporate taxpayer's capital gains (including qualified dividends) are computed in the same manner as for the regular income tax, including netting of gains and losses in separate tax-rate groups.

> **CAUTION**
>
> Although the calculation is the same, the gain or loss amounts may differ from the regular tax amounts because of AMT adjustments and preferences affecting the bases of the capital assets (for example, different bases as the result of depreciation adjustments or a different AMT capital loss carryover).

STUDY QUESTIONS

5. The lesser of the amount for the alternative tax NOL deduction attributable to NOLs or _____ of AMTI determined without considering such deduction is used to ensure that the deduction for alternative tax NOLs does not exceed a certain amount.

   a. 100 percent
   b. 90 percent
   c. 75 percent
   d. 50 percent

6. The final step in calculating AMTI, once the regular tax is calculated and all adjustments and preferences are accounted for, is to:

   a. Subtract the alternative tax NOL deduction
   b. Recalculate the accelerated depreciation or amortization of property
   c. Add tax refunds received for state and local taxes from prior year
   d. None of the above is the final step

TAXPAYERS AFFECTED BY THE ALTERNATIVE MINIMUM TAX

The number of taxpayers affected by the AMT is determined not only directly by the dollar amount of preference items and deductions that are taken but also the AMT's equally direct interaction with the regular tax system. Reductions in regular tax liability, whether from decreases in regular tax rates or from expansions of credits and deductions, will increase the number of taxpayers impacted by the AMT. Similarly, increases in regular tax liability will decrease overall the number of taxpayers impacted by the AMT.

Larger Families

Personal exemptions are allowed against the regular income tax, but not the AMT. Taxpayers with large families have many personal exemptions, which significantly reduce their regular income tax liability relative to AMT liability.

COMMENT

According to the Tax Policy Center, taxpayers with three or more children were almost four times as likely to owe AMT as those with no children in 2006.

Married Taxpayers

Most married couples pay less tax under the regular income tax than they would if they were single. However, under the AMT, tax rates are identical for married and single taxpayers and the exemption amounts, although larger for couples than singles, are not proportionately doubled ($62,550 vs. $42,500 for 2006). Under the regular income tax, the standard deduction for joint filers is twice the amount it is for singles. That benefit is lost completely because the standard deduction is not allowed at all in computing AMTI.

COMMENT

The Tax Policy Center predicts married couples will be 15 times more likely to owe AMT than singles in 2007 because of these differences but also because they tend to have children (qualifying for the dependency exemption only under the regular tax) and higher household incomes (on which the AMT exemption may be phased out).

> **REMINDER**
>
> The 2006 exemption levels were:
> - $62,550 if taxpayer was married filing jointly or as a surviving spouse;
> - $42,500 if taxpayer was single or a head of household; and
> - $31,275 if taxpayer was married filing separately.

Upper Middle-Class Taxpayers

In 2006 (the latest year in which firm figures were available at the production of this course), the available AMT exemption amounts were reduced by 25 percent of the amount by which an individual's taxable income for AMT purposes (AMTI) exceeded:
- $150,000 for joint filers and surviving spouses;
- $112,500 for single-filing taxpayers; and
- $75,000 for a married couple filing separate returns.

The AMT exemption amounts are eliminated entirely if AMTI exceeds:
- $400,200 for joint filers;
- $282,500 for single individuals and heads of households; and
- $200,100 for married taxpayers filing separately.

The 2007 exemption levels (unless Congress should raise them) are:
- $45,000 if the taxpayer is married filing jointly or as a surviving spouse;
- $33,750 if taxpayer is single or a head of household; and
- $22,500 if taxpayer is married filing separately.

Middle-Income Taxpayers

Middle-income taxpayers are increasingly affected by the AMT. By 2011, a higher percentage of taxpayers with incomes between $50,000 and $100,000 will be subject to the AMT than for taxpayers with incomes exceeding $500,000, the President's Advisory Commission on Tax Reform projected. By 2015, more than three-quarters of taxpayers with incomes between $50,000 and $1 million will be subject to the AMT.

Taxpayers with Substantial Medical Expenses

Taxpayers may deduct medical expenses in excess of 7.5 percent of AGI under the regular income tax, but the threshold is 10 percent of AGI under the AMT. Therefore, taxpayers with both large incomes and large medical expenses are likely to be subject to the AMT.

Taxpayers in Jurisdictions Having High Taxes

State and local taxes are deductible under the regular income tax, but not the AMT. Thus, high state and local taxes reduce regular tax liability, increasing the likelihood that a taxpayer will owe AMT.

Taxpayers with Legal Fees

Under the regular tax system, filers may deduct legal fees incurred in cases that generate taxable damages, such as punitive damages or damages for nonphysical injuries, as miscellaneous itemized deductions to the extent that they exceed 2 percent of AGI. However, miscellaneous deductions are not allowed under the AMT. As a result, a taxpayer with substantial legal fees should have much less taxable income under the regular tax than under the AMT.

> **COMMENT**
>
> If the legal fees are larger than the damage award, the taxpayer can actually owe more AMT than his or her net gain from the lawsuit.

Taxpayers Exercising Incentive Stock Options

The exercise of incentive stock options generally creates income that is immediately taxable under the AMT, but that is not taxable under the regular income tax until the stock is actually sold. Individuals must include in AMTI the excess of the fair market value of the stock over the purchase price of the stock on the date of exercise. If the stock is ultimately sold at a profit, the AMT paid earlier can be taken as a credit against the regular income tax owed. If the stock price falls, the taxpayer can end up with a substantial AMT liability even though he or she never realized any income.

Taxpayers Having Personal Credits

Under present law, for tax years 2007 and thereafter, nonrefundable personal credits with certain exceptions may not reduce regular tax liability below the tentative minimum tax. Thus, a taxpayer may be affected by the AMT without technically having an AMT liability if the taxpayer's regular tax exceeds the tentative minimum tax by an amount that is less than the credits. In this case, the taxpayer may reduce his or her regular tax liability to the tentative minimum tax amount but cannot use the full amount of credits because they cannot be used to reduce tax liability below that of the tentative minimum tax.

> **COMMENT**
>
> The Joint Committee on Taxation estimates that in tax year 2007 nearly 5.7 million taxpayers with AGIs between $75,000 and $100,000 will be affected by the AMT and experience AMT liabilities or lost credits totaling $6.3 billion.

STUDY QUESTIONS

7. Which of the following is **not** a reason the Tax Policy Center predicts married couples will be 15 times more likely to owe AMT than single taxpayers for 2007?

   a. Married taxpayers tend to have higher incomes than single taxpayers.

   b. Married taxpayers often have children with their accompanying dependency and itemized deductions under the regular tax that are not allowed as AMT deductions.

   c. AMT tax rates are identical for married and single taxpayers.

   d. All of the above are reasons for the higher likelihood of AMT liability for married taxpayers.

8. Why are taxpayers in high-tax jurisdictions more likely to be subject to the AMT?

   a. The AMT is more closely aligned with most state and local tax rates than is the regular income tax structure.

   b. People living in high-tax jurisdictions tend to have more discretionary income of types taxed by AMT.

   c. State and local taxes are deductible under the regular income tax but not AMT.

   d. Taxpayers in high-tax jurisdictions are no more likely to incur an AMT liability than taxpayers in low-tax jurisdictions.

STRATEGIES FOR MINIMIZING ALTERNATIVE MINIMUM TAX LIABILITY

AMT tax strategies primarily have two threads:
- Timing of income and deductions; and
- Avoidance of certain deductions and preferences.

Accelerating or deferring income or deductions for regular tax purposes may have an impact on the amount of AMT paid, either looking at a current year or at an average of several years. For those individuals who are near the threshold of the AMT, pushing income or deductions in or out of one year into the next may help qualify the taxpayer for regular tax treatment one year while subjecting him or her to lower AMT the next. In addition, as Congress gets closer to enacting true AMT reform in either 2008 or 2009, timing income or deductions to either benefit or escape from those new rules might prove strategically beneficial.

Making a decision to avoid certain deductions and preferences is a strategy that requires an evaluation of the economic benefits compared to the tax benefits. These benefits can be personal, business, or investment related. In any of those cases, an expenditure or investment without the full regular tax benefits connected with it may not be worth incurring; from an economic viewpoint, the taxpayer's money might better be spent elsewhere.

Itemized Deductions

Individuals subject to the AMT commonly benefit by timing their tax items, deferring certain items and accelerating others. One way to take advantage of the rate differentials between an AMT year and a regular tax year is to accelerate items of income into the AMT year and postpone deductions into the regular tax year. This strategy may result in an overall tax savings.

A taxpayer who is not subject to the AMT each year should remember that certain itemized deductions, such as charitable contributions, reduce AMTI. Therefore, a taxpayer should attempt to maximize these allowable deductions in any tax year in which he or she faces the AMT. However, certain other itemized deductions, such as miscellaneous itemized deductions, do not reduce AMTI; therefore, the taxpayer should delay such deductions until he or she is subject to the regular tax.

Additionally, a taxpayer should delay payment of tax preference items, such as state and local income taxes, property taxes, medical expenses, and miscellaneous expenses until a regular tax year.

> **CAUTION**
>
> The delay is advantageous provided it does not impair credit status or business standing, or cause the taxpayer to incur late charges.

Stock Options

The taxpayer should avoid exercising incentive stock options in the year in which he or she is subject to the AMT. The excess of the stock's fair market value at the time of exercise over the option price is an item of tax preference even though such excess is not subject to regular income tax.

Capital Gains

If large long-term capital gains will affect the AMT, the taxpayer should delay the asset sale until after year-end or consider spreading the gain over a number of years by using an installment sale. An installment sale, however, should only be used if it would limit the years the taxpayer's income is affected by the AMT. If the gain is large, the installment sale may cause many tax periods to become vulnerable to the AMT.

> **COMMENT**
>
> Although the maximum rate of AMT on net capital gains is limited to 15 percent as it is for regular tax purposes, capital gains may increase overall adjusted gross income and, consequently, affect the marginal AMT tax rate, as well as the phaseout of the AMT exemption amount among other benefits allowed to any particular taxpayer.

Certain Deductions

Taxpayers may take steps in connection with deductions that include tax preference items subject to the AMT to reduce their tax liability. For instance, taxpayers can undertake to eliminate certain tax preferences. In other words, certain deductions—including the accelerated depreciation deduction on real property, as well as expensed research and development costs and expensed mining exploration and development costs—are tax preference items only to the extent that they exceed an otherwise allowable deduction. By deducting a lower, nonaccelerated amount for regular tax purposes, a taxpayer can exclude these items from his or her AMT computation.

Depreciation

For property placed in service after December 31, 1998, the AMT adjustment for the MACRS depreciation allowance claimed on certain property depreciated under MACRS using the straight-line method was eliminated. Accordingly, taxpayers no longer are required to compute a separate AMT adjustment for MACRS residential rental and nonresidential real property and any other MACRS property using the straight-line or 150-percent declining-balance method for regular tax purposes. However, other amounts of accelerated depreciation remain limited for AMT purposes.

OPTIONS FOR REFORMING THE AMT

Left unchecked, the AMT will continue to reach more and more middle-income taxpayers. Estimates vary of how many. According to the Congressional Budget Office, the number could reach 30 million by 2010.

Projected Future Effects of the AMT on Individuals

Tax Years	Millions of Tax Returns Subject to AMT	Billions of Dollars of AMT Revenue
2007	20	$41
2008	25	$60
2009	25	$75
2010	30	$90

Source: Congressional Budget Office, Revenue and Tax Policy Brief (No.4), April 15, 2004.

Congress

Senate Finance Committee Chairman Max Baucus (D-Montana) and ranking member Charles Grassley (R-Iowa) have introduced S. 55, legislation that would repeal the AMT effective for tax years after 2006 retroactive to January 2007. Various other members of Congress have introduced bills that would reduce the AMT tax rate, increase and index the basic AMT exemption, allow personal tax credits to offset AMT liability, and allow state and local property taxes to be deducted from the AMT tax base.

The House and Senate adopted S. Con. Res. 21, the president's FY 2008 budget resolution, on May 17, 2007. The resolution calls for a one-year patch for the AMT. The Administration's proposal would increase the basic AMT exemption to $65,350 for joint returns and to $43,900 for unmarried taxpayers. It would also allow personal tax credits to offset AMT liability in full. These changes would be effective for 2007.

The Small Business and Work Opportunity Tax Act of 2007 permits the work opportunity tax credit and the credit for taxes paid with respect to employee tips to offset AMT liability permanently. In other words, the tentative minimum tax is considered to be zero for purposes of determining the tax liability limitation with respect to such credits. The Small Business and Work Opportunity Tax Act of 2007 applies to credits determined in tax years beginning on or before January 1, 2007.

Prior to enactment of this Act, business tax credits generally could not total more than the excess of the taxpayer's income tax liability over the tentative minimum tax or, if greater, 25 percent of the regular tax liability in excess of $25,000. Credits in excess of the limitation were carried back one year and carried over for up to 20 years. Consequently, business tax credits generally could not offset AMT liability.

Cost of Repeal

There are many options available to replace federal revenue if the AMT is repealed. In a June 2007 statement, the Director of the Tax Policy Center provided options to the Senate Finance Committee for fixing the AMT.

According to the Center, Congress could repeal the AMT outright if the following changes to the regular tax were made:

- Repeal the state and local regular tax deduction and reduce regular income tax rates by 2 percent;
- Increase regular income tax rates in the 25 percent and higher brackets by 15 percent; or
- Increase regular income tax rates in the 25 percent and higher brackets by 12 percent and repeal the 2003 regular tax cuts for capital gains and qualified dividends.

Another recommendation of the Tax Policy Center included combining complete AMT repeal with a 4 percent tax on AGI in excess of $200,000 for married couples filing jointly or $100,000 for other tax filers. This would sharply reduce the number of high-income tax filers who pay no federal income tax, according to the center, ironically better succeeding where the AMT has failed. That option apparently would be close to revenue-neutral over the 2007–2017 budget period. Through 2010, even with the 4 percent add-on tax, the top effective tax rates on ordinary income and capital gains could remain below 39.6 percent and 20 percent levels, respectively, for individual taxpayers, the center added.

Partial Repeal

Tax Policy Center. The Tax Policy Center submitted ways to reform the AMT as opposed to outright repeal. The Center advocated for reform that would shield middle- and upper-middle-income taxpayers from the effects of the AMT. The simplest reform would be to extend the exemption amounts for 2007 and index the AMT for inflation.

The center further explained that a more comprehensive reform would encompass allowing AMT to incorporate the standard deduction, dependent exemptions, state and local tax deductions, and the deductions for miscellaneous expenses and medical expenses. The center predicted that all of these items would reduce the number of AMT taxpayers in 2007 and would spare nearly all taxpayers with incomes below $200,000 from the AMT. Additionally, the minimum tax rates could be reduced, the phaseout of the minimum tax exemption could be eliminated, and all nonrefundable personal credits could be allowed to offset the AMT, according to the center.

American Enterprise Institute. The American Enterprise Institute has presented a reform plan that would eliminate or cap deductions and exclusions, and then use the revenues gained to reduce marginal tax rates. The first measure to be eliminated would be the state and local tax deduction, and the special treatment of state and municipal interest payments, the institute announced. Next, according to the institute, the mortgage interest deduction would be capped at $100,000. Institute spokespersons have noted that this would provide a gain in revenue that could be used to further reduce marginal rates. Subsequent measures, such as repealing the health insurance exemption, child tax credit, and social security benefit exemptions, would also have an enormous impact, the institute's representatives added.

STUDY QUESTIONS

9. A strategy for taking advantage of rate differentials between an AMT year and a regular tax year to create an overall tax savings is to _____ items into the AMT year and _____ into the regular tax year.

   a. Accelerate income; postpone miscellaneous itemized deductions
   b. Accelerate income; postpone charitable contributions
   c. Accelerate preference items; postpone income
   d. Postpone state and local tax payments; accelerate income

10. The Tax Policy Center suggested a revenue-neutral method for financing complete AMT repeal that:

    a. Adds a 4 percent tax for adjusted gross incomes exceeding $200,000 for joint filers and $100,000 for other filers
    b. Raises tax rates for all but the 10 percent bracket filers
    c. Caps the mortgage interest deduction at $100,000 and repeals exemptions currently allowed under the regular income tax structure
    d. Replaces the AMT with a 20 percent flat tax for all filing statuses

CONCLUSION

The complexity of the AMT is mainly due to its divergences from the regular tax system. The tax is expanding its reach and affecting more and more taxpayers. The growing number of taxpayers subjected to this "parallel" tax system is beginning to perceive the AMT as unfair. With all the flaws inherent in the AMT that are becoming apparent, legislative action is likely, but it is uncertain how far Congress will go.

Many challenges to repealing or reforming the AMT have appeared, and only time will determine what will happen as debate over the issue continues. In the meantime, taxpayers must live with the system as it stands at present. They must consider the impact of the AMT in virtually all tax planning for the regular income tax or such planning will be compromised. Familiarity with the AMT has become critical for taxpayers and their practitioners in making informed decisions about savings, education, retirement, and other important matters. Until the AMT is "reformed," it will continue to intrude into the bottomline tax liability of an increasing number of taxpayers.

MODULE 2 — CHAPTER 5

Family Limited Partnerships

This chapter provides an overview of the family limited partnership (FLP), including formation and operational issues, use as an estate planning and asset protection tool, and the tax and nontax advantages and disadvantages of this popular entity.

LEARNING OBJECTIVES

Upon completion of this chapter, you will be able to:
- Describe the key attributes of the FLP;
- Understand how the FLP operates as a significant wealth preservation, estate planning, and asset protection vehicle;
- Evaluate tax and nontax advantages and disadvantages of FLPs;
- Review applicable federal estate, income, and gift tax law;
- Recognize and be able to plan around IRS challenges to the FLP; and
- Be prepared to implement FLP best practices and planning tips.

INTRODUCTION

The family limited partnership has long been recognized as a popular and effective wealth preservation, estate planning, and asset protection tool. A properly structured, funded, and operated FLP can successfully minimize estate, gift, and income tax liability, transfer family wealth from one generation to the next, and protect assets from creditors. An improperly structured and managed FLP, however, will invite IRS attention and scrutiny. In recent years, the IRS has waged an aggressive assault on FLPs in light of their significant tax minimization features. Nevertheless, FLPs remain viable wealth preservation and asset protection tools when properly structured and administered. Although the IRS continues to attack FLPs, it is generally the overly abusive or disrespected FLP scheme that becomes entangled in IRS litigation. But a properly formed, funded, and operated FLP that has a valid nontax purpose for its formation will be respected for federal transfer tax purposes.

FLP STRUCTURE

A *family limited partnership* is simply a limited partnership formed by family members. As with a traditional limited partnership, an FLP consists of at least two partners: a general partner and a limited partner. A *general partner* controls the operation, management, and investment decisions of the partnership, and bears unlimited liability for the partnership's debt and other liabilities. A general partner must own a minimum 1 percent interest in the partnership. The general partner who may only own a 1 percent partnership interest in the FLP, however, will nevertheless be able to control and manage 100 percent of the FLP assets. Moreover, as with traditional limited partnerships, a corporation, limited liability company (LLC), S corporation (S corp), or trust may act as general partner of an FLP, thereby reducing a controlling family member's exposure to personal liability.

A *limited partner*, on the other hand, is prohibited from participating in the management or operation of the FLP and has no voting rights. Limited partners cannot make investment or management decisions, remove partnership assets, make distributions, or force liquidation of the partnership. Due to the limited partner's inability to participate in management or control operation of the FLP, a limited partner's liability is generally limited to the amount of his or her capital contribution.

As with traditional partnerships, the FLP is not a taxable entity. Instead, partners in an FLP report their distributive share of partnership income, loss, and deductions on their individual income tax return. Partnerships file Form 1065, U.S. Partnership Return of Income, to report income and expenses. The partnership passes the information to the individual partners on Schedule K-1, Form 1065. The partners report the information and pay any taxes due on their respective Form 1040s. Thus, any income or loss flows through to the partners and is reported on their individual tax returns. Because partners are not employees of the partnership, no withholding is taken out of their distributions to pay income and self-employment taxes on their Forms 1040.

FLP FORMATION

In the typical FLP context, parents (or grandparents) contribute the majority of the FLP's initial assets in exchange for both general and limited partnership interests. Assets such as the family business, real estate interests, cash, marketable securities, and other assets, including those expected to appreciate, can be contributed to an FLP. Assets transferred to the FLP are not subject to tax and therefore an FLP can be funded tax-free.

Partnership Interests

In exchange for their initial contribution, the senior family member usually receives a small general partnership interest (typically 1 or 2 percent) and a large limited partnership interest (the remaining 98 or 99 percent), thus initially serving in both the general and limited partner capacities. Subsequently, the senior family member will transfer or gift the limited partnership interests to his or her children and/or grandchildren, but retain the general partnership interest. Retaining the general partnership interest enables the senior family member to maintain control over assets while allowing his or her children, as limited partners, to become owners of (nonvoting) economic interests in the partnership. The ability of taxpayers in the older generation (who have originally built the family wealth and are the main, if not only, contributors to the FLP) to transfer their wealth but keep control of the assets is one of the most attractive attributes of the FLP entity. It is important to note that the older generation donor is gifting an *interest* in the partnership, not the partnership *assets*.

Partnership Agreement

For an ordinary partnership to be recognized under state law, the partners are not required to enter into a partnership using a written agreement. However, it is highly recommended that, especially for tax purposes, partners in an FLP create and sign a written partnership agreement that specifically enumerates, among other items, the partners' rights and responsibilities, the FLP's term, and includes key provisions expressly stating the family's nontax or business reasons for forming the FLP. A typical limited partnership agreement will include, among other items, the partnership's:

- Purpose;
- Term;
- Percentages of interest;
- Capital;
- Allocation of profits, losses, and tax items;
- Distributions;
- Liabilities;
- Management; and
- Terms for dissolution, liquidation, and termination.

Purpose. The most important provision to be addressed in an FLP agreement is the partnership's purpose clause. Intense scrutiny by the IRS, recent case developments, and practical business planning strongly necessitate the creation of a well-drafted partnership agreement and a detailed explanation of the nontax and business purposes of the FLP. Most courts now require FLPs to have a legitimate and significant nontax or other business purpose, other than federal tax savings, for the formation of, and transfer of assets to, the entity. The FLP that can show its formation was motivated by legitimate nontax or other business concerns will be more successful in thwarting IRS attacks and continuing to take advantage of the significant tax benefits associated with these entities. Valid nontax reasons for establishing an FLP include:

- Creating, preserving, and increasing family wealth;
- Providing a mechanism for continuity of management of family assets, including active involvement by younger family members;
- Avoiding fractionalization of family assets;
- Lowering administrative costs and investment fees through centralized, coordinated, and active management of family assets;
- Protecting assets from the claims of creditors;
- Keeping assets and wealth within the family by restricting nonfamily members' rights to acquire interests (including provisions for retaining interests in the event of divorce); and
- Facilitating post-mortem transfers.

Transfer restrictions. The limited partnership agreement should outline the transfer rights (and restrictions) of both limited and general partners, as well as whether and how substitute partners may be admitted to the FLP. In the FLP context, provisions on transfer rights are typically highly restrictive, both to keep ownership of assets within the family unit and to create discounts for lack of marketability and lack of control in valuing limited partnership interests for transfer tax purposes. Once the agreement is completed and signed by all partners, and a certificate of limited partnership is filed with the Secretary of State, the assets should be transferred to the partnership and all legal formalities followed.

Funding. The timing of transfers and type of assets contributed to an FLP are important issues that require consideration, especially in light of recent court decisions. First, transfers of partnership interests to the younger generation should not be made before assets have been transferred to the FLP. Under current case law (discussed later), the transfer of assets to an FLP after transfer of limited partnership interests to family members constitutes an indirect gift of the full value of the underlying assets, subject to federal gift tax provisions.

Investment management tool. Principally, FLPs are used as an investment management tool, rather than as a family business management device per se. The types of assets typically transferred to FLPs include the family business, real estate investment properties such as condominiums and other rental properties, cash, stock, and other marketable securities. Because of the varied types of assets that can be transferred into an FLP, the entity is a preferable structure for managing many family assets, not just the family business. An FLP is a distinctly advantageous investment management device because it:

- Provides significant estate, gift, and income tax minimization;
- Shields assets from creditors as well as ex-spouses;
- Provides exclusive, coordinated, and centralized management of all family assets;
- Avoids fractionalization of family assets and provides simplification of ownership transfers;
- Allows pooling of investments for increased organization and efficiency, enhancing future investment opportunities, and reduces investment management fees and expenses; and
- Provides continuity of asset management.

STUDY QUESTIONS

1. No withholding is subtracted from FLP partners' distributions because:
   a. Partners are expected to file quarterly estimated tax statements rendering their distributive share of partnership income tax
   b. Assets are held by the partnership and thus family members are not taxed on the FLP holdings
   c. Nonemployee partners are not subject to the tax withholding rules applied to employees of the partnership
   d. The FLP is not a taxable entity

2. The major benefit of the FLP structure is to:
   a. Enable members of the younger generation (the general partner's beneficiaries or heirs) to assume voting rights in matters of the family's investments
   b. Enable the wealth-building member of the older generation to transfer wealth but keep control of the partnership's assets
   c. Establish a partnership without the formality of creating a written partnership agreement
   d. Balance the percentages of rights to the partnership's assets among members of both the older and younger generations of partners

NONTAX BENEFITS

An FLP provides considerable nontax benefits that may suit family goals regardless of the tax savings available. The nontax or business purposes for forming FLPs are critical to obtaining anticipated tax savings in light of recent case law. FLPs provide the nontax benefits described here.

Consolidation of Management

An FLP can be used to consolidate ownership and management of the family business and/or multiple family assets and investments into a single entity. Instead of maintaining separate brokerage accounts or trusts for each child, the FLP holds one brokerage account and the children (or trusts for the children) own partnership interests. Consolidating investments and family assets into a single FLP can reduce investment fees, as well as accounting and management expenses.

Generational Planning and Control

A senior family member may be able to retain control over management of property they contributed to the FLP by retaining the general partnership interest, even if the majority of the equity value has been transferred to the younger generation. This permits the older generation to maintain control over the asset base it has built while allowing the younger generation to enter the family business and assume an equity position.

Operational Unity

An FLP provides the family business with operational unity, despite giving away interests in the business to different family members.

Gifting

Parents may find it difficult to gift undivided interests in certain assets to children or grandchildren. An FLP offers maximum flexibility because partnership interests are readily divisible into fractional shares that can be transferred by gift, bequest, or intrafamily sale. For example, a senior family member can transfer partnership interests in the family business to his or her children without breaking up business and investment assets. FLP interests are also easily transferred on the partnership's books. Instead of having to notify the investment firm or firms through which the FLP is invested—and selecting which portfolio assets to move—the partnership interests in the portfolio can be shifted in the FLP's records.

Transfer Restrictions

An FLP agreement can restrict the ability of partners to transfer their interests to others, significantly nonfamily members, thereby keeping the assets in the family and preventing recipients in the younger generation from potentially spending down their interests. For example, in the event of a divorce in which a limited partner ceases to be a family member, the partnership documents can require that the interest be transferred back to the FLP at the fair market value, keeping assets within the family. Alternatively, transfer restrictions can provide that any transfer of an FLP interest must be approved by all existing partners before the transferee can obtain partnership rights. Limited partnership interests in an entity controlled and managed by the family of an ex-spouse are not likely viewed as appealing assets during divorce proceedings.

Creditor Protection

An FLP can protect family assets against claims of a limited partner's creditors. Because a limited partner has incredibly circumscribed rights, limited partnership interests are not desirable to creditors. A creditor who seizes a limited partnership interest will be required to pay income tax on his or her share of FLP earnings. If an FLP has earned income, but the general partner does not declare a distribution, each general and limited partner must nevertheless report his or her distributive share of the partnership's earnings on an individual income tax return, in the year received by the partnership. Moreover, limited partnership shares are difficult to seize because they are not publicly traded. And although creditors can reach the personal assets of a general partner, if the general partnership interest is owned by an LLC or S corp, the personal assets of the individual member or shareholder may be protected from the claims of the partnership's creditors.

Simplified Estate Administration

The FLP owner's personal representative will exercise control over the assets as per the partnership agreement upon their death, simplifying estate administration. Also, because assets are owned by the FLP, and not the individual partners, only a decedent-partner's FLP interest is subject to probate. Further, if a decedent owns out-of-state real property, ancillary probate in states where the property is located may be avoided if the properties are owned by the FLP.

Real Property Benefits

An FLP permits the distribution of the owner's estate among family members without the need to liquidate or fractionalize assets, which is a significant benefit where the estate's assets are real estate.

STUDY QUESTIONS

3. The benefit of operational unity afforded by an FLP means that:
   a. The family businesses have no management change when the partnership is formed.
   b. The family businesses experience no immediate division of ownership or fractionalization of assets when the FLP is formed.
   c. Members of the younger generation of family gradually assume voting rights without gaining actual operating control of the businesses.
   d. None of the above is the primary benefit of operational unity.

4. Protection against assets being withdrawn from the FLP in case of a family member's divorce is achieved through:
   a. A partnership agreement clause requiring interests to be transferred back to the family if a partner ceases to be a family member
   b. A partnership agreement clause preventing a relative by marriage from acquiring a limited partner's majority voting rights in the FLP
   c. Transferring the partnership's total tax liability to the former in-law subsequent to the divorce
   d. A majority vote of members of the partnership to ban the former in-law from holding a partnership interest and requiring partnership buy-back of that individual's partnership assets

TRANSFER TAX BENEFITS

Gift Tax

The gift tax applies to transfers by gift of any property. A *gift* is made if property (including money) or the use of or income from property is given, without the expectation of receiving something of equal value in return. The transfer of limited partnership interests to family members are gifts, subject to gift tax, *unless* the limited partner gives full and adequate consideration in exchange for the partnership interest. Partners can also receive interests by sale, installment sale, or bona-fide self-canceling installment note (so-called installment gifts), personal services contribution, or any combination thereof. Because the transfer of a limited partnership interest in an FLP is considered a gift, unless proven otherwise, proper planning and consideration will markedly reduce the associated transfer taxes.

The federal lifetime and annual gift tax exclusions are powerful tools, not only for reducing gift tax but for income and estate taxes as well. In the context of gifting FLP limited partnership interests, members of the older generation are able to use their lifetime and annual gift tax exclusions to minimize transfer taxes when the members gift shares to children or grandchildren.

Moreover, the annual and lifetime gift tax exclusions work in conjunction with certain valuation discounts (discussed in further detail below) that may be taken upon the transfer of FLP minority interests by using the discounts to draw down less of the transferor's credit amount when making gifts of FLP minority interests. Thus, *minority discounts* and *lack of marketability discounts* (allowable reductions in the value of the gift because it is a minority interest) permit greater leverage of the annual exclusion and the unified credit. Once the FLP has been established and funded, limited partnership interests may be transferred at a discounted rate by means of a gift-giving program using lifetime and annual gift tax exclusions.

Annual gift tax exclusion. Code Sec. 2503(b) allows an annual exclusion for gifts of a present interest in property. IRS rulings provide that gifts of limited partnership interests in FLPs qualify as gifts of present interests for purposes of the annual gift tax exclusion. The lifetime gift tax exclusion applies to transfers made during life and at death. However, for the annual gift tax exclusion to apply, the gift of a limited partnership interest must qualify as a present interest within the plain meaning of Code Sec. 2503(b)(1). That is, the donee must receive an unrestricted right to the immediate use, possession, or enjoyment of the property. For 2007, the annual gift tax exclusion operates to exclude from gift tax the first $12,000 worth of gifts per donee. For married individuals, *gift splitting* permits both spouses to separately gift up to $12,000 per donee, per year. In effect, a married couple can gift $24,000 to each donee, per year, without triggering gift tax liability.

Lifetime gift tax exclusion. For years 2007, 2008, and 2009, the lifetime gift tax exclusion is $1 million. The lifetime gift tax exclusion operates to exempt from gift tax the first $1 million in value of all taxable gifts that exceed the $12,000 per year, per donee annual gift tax exclusion amount. Note that since 2004, the estate tax exclusion has been separate from the gift tax exclusion and is no longer "unified." The estate tax credit shelters $2 million in 2007 and 2008, and $3.5 million in 2009.

EGTRRA. Under the Economic Growth and Tax Relief Reconciliation Act (EGTRRA), the gift tax is imposed on lifetime transfers and the estate tax is imposed on transfers at death. In 2010, the estate tax is officially scheduled to end for one year, but the gift tax will continue. Many in Washington, however, see Congress revising the terms of the estate and gift taxes in compromise legislation before the rules for post-2009 go into effect. EG-TRRA repealed the estate tax for individuals dying in 2010 but left the gift tax in place. Under EGTRRA, the credit against the lifetime gift tax will continue to exempt $1 million from tax through 2009, whereas the credit against the estate tax will increase from $2 million to $3.5 million during the same period. In 2010 and beyond, the gift tax calculation will also take on a new formula, based on a new rate schedule, minus amounts allowable as credits in preceding years. Therefore, despite the federal estate tax "repeal," there remains a need for transfer tax planning.

Discounts

One of the most attractive features of an FLP involves the valuation discounts attendant to the transfer of limited partnership interests. Because a limited partnership interest cannot be sold or otherwise converted into cash, and lacks management, control, and voting rights, tax law discounts the value of such limited partnership interests. Due to the illiquid nature of the assets involved, limited partnership interests are worth substantially less for transfer tax purposes than the underlying pro-rata, fair market value (FMV) of the assets held by the FLP. As a result, the IRS may allow discounts for, among other things, lack of control and lack of marketability on the transfer of limited interests in an FLP. The combined discounts can substantially reduce a taxable estate and the value of the transfer, typically between 20 and 40 percent.

Valuation methods. To determine the FMV of a limited partnership interest in an FLP, a professional appraiser may use one of a number of valuation methods, such as the net asset value of the FLP, the net income generated by the FLP's assets, or both. Once the limited partnership's value is determined, the appraiser then applies the lack of control discount and the lack of marketability discount. In determining the appropriate valuation of FLP interests, appraisers consider a number of factors, including specific provisions of the partnership agreement (such as liquidation provisions), the type of assets held by the FLP, and the FLP's dividend-paying capacity.

Lack of control discount. The lack of control discount (or minority interest discount) takes into account the fact that the holder of a limited partnership interest lacks:

- Management or operation role or rights;
- Ability to liquidate the business, reach the underlying assets of the FLP, or compel distributions; and
- Possesses limited voting rights.

Because of the lack of control, limited partnership interests are valued much lower than the liquidation value of the underlying assets. In effect, limited partnership interests can be transferred at low transfer tax costs.

Lack of marketability discount. A minority interest in an FLP may be far less marketable, or liquid, than an interest in the underlying assets of the business. Further, provisions in the FLP's operating agreement may limit the partner's ability to transfer his or her interest in the entity. The lack of marketability discount takes into consideration the fact that the owner of an interest in a nonpublicly traded entity will have a more difficult time finding a willing buyer of that interest, than would the interest holder of a publicly traded company. That is, there is no ready-made "market" for limited shares in a family partnership.

> **EXAMPLE**
>
> Tom forms an FLP by contributing assets with an aggregate FMV of $3 million. If Tom later makes a gift of a 1 percent limited partnership interest to each of his three children as part of an annual gift giving program, the pro-rata portion of the FLP's underlying assets attributable to each of the 1 percent membership interests is $30,000. However, because of the lack of management control and lack of marketability of those gifted interests, a qualified business appraiser determines that the children's respective interests are worth 25 percent less than their liquidation value. Applying a 25 percent discount, each child's limited partnership interest is worth only $22,000 for gift tax purposes. This amount is less than the $24,000 annual gift tax exclusion allowed to Tom and his spouse under the gift splitting rules. Therefore, the transfers are not subject to transfer tax at all.

IRS challenges. Discounts applied in the valuation of FLP interests are frequently challenged by the IRS. Courts examine not only the amount of the discount but also the method of valuation. Thus, employing the expertise of a professional appraiser is essential to deriving and defending the discounts taken for FLP interests. Moreover, excessive valuation discounts will invite IRS scrutiny. Typically, the combined discounts should fall within the 20 to 40 percent range. Further, the IRS also carefully scrutinizes FLPs that claim substantial discounts in cases where readily tradable assets such as marketable securities are transferred to the entity, because there is a ready market for such securities or stock.

STUDY QUESTIONS

5. Unlike the changes it made to the estate tax, EGTRRA:

   a. Left the gift tax in place, with its portion of the unified credit separate from the estate tax credit since 2004

   b. Left the gift tax in place for annual gifting but lowered its lifetime gift tax exclusion

   c. Changed the exclusion amounts identically for the gift and estate taxes

   d. Did not refer to the gift tax

6. Which of the following actions is **not** a reason the IRS may choose to challenge the valuation of FLP interests?

   a. A professional appraiser who finds no comparable entities for sale or publicly traded in conducting the FLP appraisal

   b. Substantial lack of marketability claims for FLP assets consisting of publicly traded stock

   c. Combined lack of control and lack of marketability discounts of 50 percent

   d. All of the above motivate IRS valuation challenges

Estate Tax

The estate tax is based on all property transferred at the time of the estate holder's death. The *taxable estate* is the value of the gross estate, less applicable deductions. The *gross estate* is the FMV of all assets owned by the decedent on the date of death, including all property, real or personal, tangible or intangible, wherever situated.

For returns filed for 2006, 2007, or 2008, $2 million can be excluded from federal estate tax. As mentioned, in 2009, $3.5 million may be excluded from the reach of the estate tax.

Any partnership interest owned at death by a general partner of an FLP is includible in the general partner's estate. If done properly, lifetime transfers of limited partnership interests to family members will reduce the taxable estate of senior family members. In this scenario, the senior family member transfers the value of the asset to his or her children, removing it from the estate for federal estate tax purposes, while the senior member (general partner) retains control over the FLP assets.

The estate tax will be officially repealed for decedents dying after December 31, 2009. Although the estate tax is scheduled to be temporarily repealed in 2010, it currently is scheduled to return in 2011 with an exemption of only $1 million unless Congress makes the repeal permanent, or it may do away with the one-year repeal before it takes effect in 2010.

Under EGTRRA, the estates of individuals who die in 2010 will pay no estate tax, but the estates of those dying in 2011 or beyond could pay up to a 55 percent rate on estates of more than $3 million. Planning is also complicated by the gift tax, which remains in place. Few believe that we will reach 2010 without having Congress revise these rates and amounts.

FLP discounts also reduce the value of the assets subject to estate tax. For example, if a decedent dies while owning a business of marketable securities, estate tax applies to the full FMV of the assets. However, if the decedent does not own the asset outright but rather owns an interest in an FLP that owns the asset, the value of the asset is discounted due to the lack of control over the asset and lack of marketability.

EXAMPLE

Assume Tom created an FLP by funding it with $2 million in real estate that he expected to appreciate significantly. Tom took back a 1 percent general partner interest and a 99 percent interest in the FLP's assets as a limited partner. Tom gifts a 70 percent limited partnership interest to his daughter, Sophie. If the FLP were to liquidate, Sophie would receive $1.4 million, or 70 percent of the value of the FLP. Due to the minority discount and lack of marketability discount, Sophie's limited partnership interests are worth 30 percent less than their liquidation value, according to a qualified business appraiser. Applying a 30 percent discount, Sophie's limited partnership interests are worth $980,000 for gift tax purposes. The transfer will use up $980,000 of Tom's $1 million lifetime gift tax exclusion. Ultimately, Tom was able to transfer assets valuing $420,000 (discount amount) without estate tax or gift tax. Moreover, any future appreciation on the transferred assets is removed from Tom's estate and escapes estate tax upon Tom's death.

Income Tax

FLPs offer several income tax advantages, including single-level (i.e., individual) taxation, nonrecognition of FLP contributions, and the flexibility to make special allocations of profits, losses, and deductions.

Single-level tax. For federal income tax purposes, FLPs are generally taxed as a partnership with one level of taxation at the partner level. Corporations, on the other hand, are taxed once at the corporate level and also at the shareholder level.

Pass-through entity. An FLP is not a taxable entity. Partnership income, loss, deductions, and credits of the partnership simply "pass through" to the individual partners, who report their share of the partnership's income, or losses, on their individual income tax returns. This facilitates income shifting from members of the high-bracket older generation to lower-bracket children. Further, because partners are not employees of the partnership, no withholding tax is deducted from their distributions to pay self-employment taxes or the income tax due on their share of partnership income reported on their Forms 1040. Quarterly estimated tax payments on that income, however, may be required.

Nonrecognition of gain. Generally, gain or loss is not recognized when appreciated property is contributed to a partnership in exchange for a partnership interest. Code Sec. 721(a). Thus, appreciated property can be transferred to an FLP without tax consequence to the partnership or partners. However, the nonrecognition rule of Code Sec. 721(a) is subject to the "investment company exception" of Code Sec. 721(b), discussed in detail below. Essentially, the nonrecognition rule will not apply, and gain (but not loss) will be recognized on the transfer of appreciated assets to an FLP that would qualify as an "investment company" (within the meaning of Code Sec. 351) if the partnership were incorporated (Reg. § 1.351-1(c)(1). An FLP will constitute an investment company if, after the contribution of appreciated property to the partnership, more than 80 percent of the value of the FLP's assets (excluding cash and nonconvertible debt obligations):

- Are held for investment;
- Are stocks or securities (marketable or not) interests in regulated investment companies, or real estate investment trusts; and
- When transferred, result in diversification of the transferor's interests in the contributed property.

Special allocations of profits, losses, and deductions. An FLP that holds an operating business is able to allocate profits, losses, and deductions among its partners. Unlike an S corp, which does not allow for special allocations of profits, losses, and deductions, an FLP may allocate a disproportionate share of profits, losses, and deductions of the partnership to one or more partners as long as the allocation has a *substantial economic effect* between the partners, as required under Code Sec. 704.

STUDY QUESTIONS

> **7.** In what calendar year will an estate be subject to the least amount of estate tax?
>
> **a.** 2007
> **b.** 2008
> **c.** 2009
> **d.** 2010

---

8. Because an FLP is a passthrough entity, it offers the major income tax advantage of:

   a. No liability for making estimated tax payments

   b. Partners' ability to use the FLP as an investment company without recognition of gain from appreciation or corporate-level taxation

   c. Income shifting from older-generation partners to lower-bracket children

   d. All of the above are major tax advantages of FLPs

DISADVANTAGES OF THE FLP

Despite their significant tax and nontax benefits, FLPs do have certain disadvantages, described here.

Cost

Legal fees for establishing an FLP can range from several thousand dollars to tens of thousands of dollars, depending on the size and complexity of the business, assets, and the estate plan. Appraisal fees increase costs.

Loss of Stepped-Up Basis

Although transfer taxes can be significantly reduced by using an FLP, the donee, as limited partner, will likely get a much lower basis in the transferred assets (and therefore higher potential capital gain) by taking the assets with a Code Sec. 1015 carryover basis rather than a Code Sec. 1014 stepped-up basis based on the date-of-death or alternate valuation date. Thus, transfer tax advantages must be weighed against possible income tax disadvantages.

Investment Company Issue

Although the general rule is that neither gain nor loss is recognized when property is contributed to an FLP in exchange for a partnership interest, the investment company rule of Code Sec. 721(b) provides an important exception. Code Sec. 721(b) is intended to prevent a partnership from being used as a vehicle for portfolio diversification. Under Code Sec. 721(b), contribution of appreciated property to an FLP will result in a taxable event if, after the funding, the FLP qualifies as an *investment company* within the meaning of Code Sec. 351.

Integrity

Under Code Sec. 704(e), unless younger family members have a legitimate capital interest in the partnership, their interests in the FLP will be disregarded for income tax purposes and partnership income will be taxed solely to the donors. (Note that under the "kiddie tax" rules, family members younger than age 24 may find partnership income taxed at their parents' rate anyway).

Swing Vote Issue

The IRS takes into account possession of a *swing vote* as an enhancement to the value of a partnership interest. In IRS Technical Advice Memorandum 9436005, the Service analyzed gift transfers of interests in a closely held entity that resulted in ownership interests of 30 percent held by each of the donor's three children and 5 percent interests held by the donor and the donor's spouse. In this situation, family members could possibly combine their interests to create what amounts to a swing vote having the ability to influence management, control, and income distribution. In addition to creating a governance issue, this analysis can raise the gift tax value of each FLP interest.

STUDY QUESTIONS

9. All of the following typically are disadvantages of FLPs *except:*

   a. Swing votes of combined interest that influence business operations of the FLP

   b. Assets transferred to an FLP are no longer under the complete control of the individual owner and are not valued as highly because the marketability of such an asset within the partnership is impaired.

   c. The kiddie tax rules apply to partnership income, which tax younger members' income at their parents' rate

   d. High legal fees may be charged for creating the partnership

10. Code Sec. 721(b) is structured to do which of the following?

    a. Stop income shifting

    b. Prevent an FLP from being used as a portfolio diversification vehicle

    c. Prohibit younger family members from having their FLP interests disregarded for income tax purposes

    d. None of the above

IRS ATTACKS ON FLPS

As the FLP garnered greater recognition as a tax-saving tool, IRS frustration intensified. In the last decade, the IRS has launched an aggressive offensive against FLPs. Initially, the IRS met with little success in the courts despite the myriad theories used to attack FLPs, the majority crafted to recapture the full fair market value of the *assets* transferred to the FLP. IRS arguments have included the following:

- Sham transaction theories, including the substance over form;
- Step transaction and economic substance doctrines;
- Transfer restriction provisions of Code Sec. 2703;
- "Applicable restrictions" of Code Sec. 2704; and
- Gift-on-formation arguments.

In litigation tried between 2000 and 2004, the courts rejected these arguments, heralding a series of taxpayer victories. However, some of these previous arguments have reemerged as successful IRS weapons against FLPs. In light of these developments, it is imperative to review and understand the IRS's previous arguments that, although earlier dismissed by the courts, may generally be reemerging.

Previously Failed IRS Arguments

Code Sec. 2703(a). Under Code Sec. 2703(a), the IRS argued that any transfer restrictions in an FLP's partnership agreement should be disregarded in valuing the assets for federal estate and gift tax purposes. Code Sec. 2703(a) provides that for the purposes of the estate, gift, and generation-skipping transfer tax, the value of any property transferred shall be determined without regard to any restrictions on the right to sell or use the property. The IRS asserted that because the partnership agreement imposes restrictions on a limited partner's right to sell or use the underlying assets, the restrictions should be ignored under Code Sec. 2703(a). The courts rejected this argument. In *E. Church* (DC-TX, 2000-1 USTC ¶60,369 (Jan. 18, 2000), aff'd per curiam, CA-5 (unpublished opinion), 2001-2 USTC ¶60,415, 268 F3d 1063), the Fifth Circuit reasoned that Code Sec. 2703(a) did not apply because the transfer was of FLP interests, not partnership assets.

Gift on creation. Courts have offered various reasons for rejecting the IRS's argument that the very formation of an FLP constitutes a gift. The IRS argued that because assets were transferred to the FLP in exchange for a limited partnership interest valued at a discount—and thus the value of the assets transferred into the FLP exceeded the value of the limited partnership interest—the reduction of the contributing partner's net worth constituted a gift. Courts have rejected the IRS's argument for various reasons. In *Church*, for example, the Fifth Circuit held there was no gift on creation because the partner's interest was proportionate to the partner's contribution to the FLP. In R. *Gulig* (CA-5, 2002-2 USTC ¶60,441, 293 F3d 279 (June 17, 2002)), the court reached the same decision but rejected the IRS's argument in part because the transferor did not give up control over the assets contributed to the FLP.

Code Sec. 2704(b). Code Sec. 2704(b) provides that, within the FLP context, if there is a transfer of an interest in an FLP to a member of the transferor's family, and the transferor and family members hold, immediately before the transfer, control of the FLP, any *applicable restriction* is to be disregarded in valuing the interest. A restriction on liquidation is not an applicable restriction if it is not more restrictive than limitations on liquidations under state law. Courts have rejected Code Sec. 2704(b) arguments. For example, in *B.P. Kerr* (CA-5, 2002-1 USTC ¶60,440, 292 F3d 490 (June 10, 2002)) and *I.F. Knight* (115 TC 506, Dec. 54,136, 115 TC No. 36 (Nov. 30, 2000)), the courts reasoned that an FLP agreement's provisions that place restrictions on a partner's right to withdraw from the FLP, or transfer his or her interest, do not constitute "applicable restrictions" on the ability of the FLP to liquidate. The courts further reasoned that the provisions limiting the partner's right to withdraw from an FLP are not more restrictive than limitations that would generally apply under state law.

Substance over form doctrine. The IRS has used the substance over form doctrine to look beyond the form of the transaction and to treat the transaction according to the taxpayer's *actual purpose* in creating the entity. The IRS has applied this analysis to look through an FLP with no "business purpose" other than the transfer of wealth to family members at a discount.

In the FLP context, the IRS asserts the actual substance of the transaction was not that of a functioning partnership, but instead an outright gift of FLP property to other family members. Thus, the IRS argued that the partnership form should be ignored and the gifts should be valued at the full fair market value of the underlying assets. In *Church* and the *Strangi* line of cases, courts rebuked the substance over form argument. However, the *business purpose* facet of the substance over form doctrine has been incorporated into other IRS arguments, discussed below, that have been successfully employed to defeat FLP discounts.

Step transaction doctrine. The *step transaction doctrine* examines whether separate transactions should be collapsed into a single transaction for tax purposes. Generally, the IRS argued that when formation and funding of an FLP occurred close in time to the transferor's death, the transfer of partnership interests and testamentary transfers should be viewed as a single testamentary transaction. According to the IRS, creation of the FLP and subsequent gifts of limited partnership interests have no purpose other than to avoid estate and gift tax.

STUDY QUESTIONS

11. Rulings in the **Kerr** and **Knight** cases did not uphold the IRS applicable restrictions argument under Code Sec. 2704(b) because:

   a. Restrictions on the ability of a partner to withdraw from an FLP do not constitute "applicable restrictions" on the ability of the FLP to liquidate.

   b. Partnership agreement terms restricting withdrawals of partners or transfers of partnership interests were not more restrictive than general state limitations for liquidation of partnerships.

   c. The parties never agreed to the restrictions, which were not specified in the partnership agreement.

   d. None of the choices is the reasoning for the rulings against the IRS.

12. The examination by the IRS and courts of the taxpayer's actual purpose in conducting an FLP transaction is part of the:

   a. Gift on creation theory

   b. Substance over form doctrine

   c. Applicable restrictions argument

   d. Step transaction doctrine

Code Sec. 2036(a): Retained Interests

The IRS has experienced some success in its battle against overly aggressive FLPs using the Code Sec. 2036(a) retained interest provision. Code Sec. 2036(a) is designed to prevent an individual from circumventing estate tax by transferring title to assets while continuing to retain control, use, or enjoyment of the property, unless the transfer qualifies as a bona fide sale for adequate and full consideration.

Code Sec. 2036(a) provides that the full value of property transferred to an FLP will be included in the donor's taxable estate if prior to death, the donor retained either of the following:

- The possession, use, or enjoyment of the assets; or
- The right to designate persons who shall possess or enjoy the assets.

The transferor retains *possession or enjoyment* of property if he or she retains a substantial present economic benefit (as opposed to a contingent or speculative benefit that may or may not be realized). Code Sec. 2036(a) will apply where there is an express or implied understanding among the parties that the donor will retain the use, possession, or enjoyment of the property, even if the retained interest is not a legally enforceable right. Code Sec. 2036(a), however, provides an exception to inclusion in the decedent's estate if the transfer qualifies as a "bona-fide sale for adequate and full consideration in money or money's worth." To qualify for the exception, there must be both:

- A bona fide sale; and
- Adequate and full consideration.

Adequate and full consideration. Generally, when assets are transferred into an FLP in exchange for a proportionate interest in the partnership, and the formalities of the partnership entity are respected, the *adequate and full consideration* requirement will be satisfied. In determining whether the adequate and full consideration element has been met, courts examine the following circumstances:

- How proportionate the interests credited to each partner were to the FMV of the assets each partner contributed to the FLP;
- Whether the assets contributed by each partner to the FLP were properly credited to the respective capital accounts of the partners; and
- Whether the partners were entitled to distributions from the FLP in amounts equal to their respective capital accounts (*D. A. Kimbell,* CA-5, 2004-1 USTC ¶60,486, 371 F3d 257 (May 20, 2004)).

Further, the exchange of assets for FLP interests must be roughly proportionate so the transfer does not deplete the estate.

Bona fide sale exception. To satisfy the *bona fide sale* prong, courts look to whether the transferor actually parts with his or her interest in the assets transferred and the FLP actually parts with the interest issued in exchange (*Kimbell,* CA-5, May 20, 2004*).* Note that *sale* as used in this situation means "an arm's length transaction." Income taxes generally are not due upon such "sale." However, many courts also have begun to look at whether there is a "substantial and nontax or other business purpose" for the FLP's formation.

Economic substance revived. Despite courts' previous rejection of the IRS's economic substance argument, the doctrine resurfaced in the 2004 *Kimbell* case, as the crux of the Fifth Circuit's bona fide sale analysis. Since *Kimbell,* courts (at least the Tax Court, and Third and Fifth Circuit Courts) have looked to whether the facts and circumstances reveal a "substantial business or other nontax purpose" for forming the FLP. The nontax reason for forming the partnership must have been a significant factor and must be established by objective evidence.

Arm's-length transaction. Courts, however, have approached the "bona fide sale" exception as also requiring an "arm's length transaction." Courts have concluded that an arm's-length transaction can occur within the FLP context despite the fact that such a transaction involves the presence of family members on both sides of the transaction.

Case-law limits on Code Sec. 2036(a). Despite the IRS's recent successes employing the Code Sec. 2036(a) retained-interest argument, the FLP remains a viable estate planning and wealth preservation tool. Court rulings have consistently been tied closely to the specific facts of each case, and cases the IRS has won commonly involve egregious fact patterns and abusive FLP schemes. Thus, it is the improperly formed, operated, and ultimately disrespected and abusive FLP that will find itself battling the IRS. The following summaries of case law not only exemplify the commonalities of Code Sec. 2036(a) cases, but also provide insight on how *not* to operate and manage an FLP.

Strangi. The *Strangi* line of cases has been the most discussed of the body of FLP cases. Practitioners initially believed the court's decision spelled the end for FLPs. The *Strangi* case is filled with bad facts and—like many of the other Code Sec. 2036(a) cases won by the IRS—is a lesson on how not to form and operate an FLP.

In *A. Strangi* (CA-5, 2005-2 USTC ¶60,506, 417 F3d 468 (July 15, 2005)), the Fifth Circuit determined that an implied agreement existed wherein Mr. Strangi would retain possession or enjoyment of the assets he transferred to his FLP. Therefore, the full value of the underlying assets was included in his estate for tax purposes. In reaching its determination, the court found it significant that:

- Mr. Strangi was virtually on his deathbed when his son-in-law, acting under a power of attorney, transferred approximately 98 percent of Mr. Strangi's net worth to the FLP, including his home, in exchange for a 99 percent limited partnership interest;
- The remaining 1 percent interest was held by a corporate general partner, Stranco, in which Mr. Strangi owned a 47 percent interest, and members of his family owned the remaining 53 percent;
- Mr. Strangi lacked sufficient liquid assets to provide for his basic living expenses, medical care, or other liabilities after his assets were transferred to the FLP;
- The FLP made a number of distributions to Mr. Strangi before and after his death to pay for various personal expenses, including more than $3 million to pay estate and inheritance taxes and $40,000 to pay funeral and estate administration expenses;
- Mr. Strangi continued to reside in the home that he transferred to the FLP;

- The FLP accrued rent on its books, but it was not paid until more than two years after Mr. Strangi's death; and
- The FLP never engaged in the conduct of any active business or made any investments.

The court further determined that the transfer did not qualify as a bona fide sale. In determining whether the bona fide sale exception applied, the court referred to the "legitimate and substantial nontax or business purpose" language of *Kimbell*. While the Strangi estate asserted several nontax purposes for the FLP's formation, the court found none of the reasons credible.

Erickson. In *H.E. Erickson* (93 TCM 1175, Dec. 56,919(M), TC Memo 2007-107), the Tax Court held the entire value of property transferred by decedent to an FLP two months before her death was includible in the decedent's gross estate under Code Sec. 2036(a)(1). The court determined that decedent implicitly retained enjoyment of the assets transferred to the FLP and the bona fide sale exception did not apply because the FLP's formation lacked a legitimate and substantial nontax purpose.

The decedent's daughter, acting as the decedent's power of attorney (as well as cotrustee of a credit shelter trust created for the decedent's benefit under her predeceased husband's will), formed an FLP when decedent's health was significantly declining. It was not until two months after the FLP's formation, and only days before decedent's death, that the daughter finally transferred the decedent's assets to the FLP, despite partnership agreement provisions requiring funding upon formation. After the decedent's death, the FLP had to provide the estate with money to meet its liabilities.

The Tax Court determined that an implied agreement existed among the parties that the decedent would retain the right to possess and enjoy the assets transferred to the FLP. In reaching this determination, the court found it important that:

- There was a significant delay in transferring the assets to the FLP;
- The FLP provided decedent's estate with money to meet its liabilities;
- The estate received distributions when no other partner did; and
- The partnership had little practical effect during decedent's life.

In determining that the transfer did not qualify as a bona fide sale for full and adequate consideration, the court pointed to the facts that:

- The FLP was a collection of passive assets;
- There was a substantial delay in funding the FLP;
- The FLP was effectively formed unilaterally with the same daughter on every side of, and controlling, the transaction;
- The estate was financially dependent on the FLP; and

- The decedent's age and health at the time of formation indicate the transfers were made to avoid estate tax liability.

Although the court acknowledged that each partner contributed assets to the FLP in exchange for a partnership interest, the court stated that the existence of legitimate transfers of value does not mandate a conclusion that the bona fide sale exception is met. The transaction must have a legitimate and significant nontax purpose as well as adequate and full consideration, the court held.

IRS losses on Code Sec. 2036(a). Two FLP cases in which it was determined that the bona fide sale exception *did* apply both involved circumstances where the courts found that the FLP was created for a legitimate and substantial nontax or other business purpose (*E.S. Stone,* 86 TCM 551, Dec. 55,341(M), TC Memo 2003-309, and *Kimbell,* cited earlier). As a result of these two taxpayer victories, other taxpayers and their advisors have tried to model characteristics of their FLPs based on the facts and circumstances of these two cases to ward against a successful IRS attack.

Stone. In *Stone,* the Tax Court ruled that the bona fide sale exception applied and assets transferred to the FLP were not includible in the decedent's gross estate. The transfer of assets to five FLPs by a deceased couple constituted a bona fide sale for adequate and full consideration because:
- The donors' capital accounts reflected the fair market value of the contributed assets;
- Distributions were based on the relative capital accounts of the partners;
- The donees/children actively participated in the management of FLP property after formation; and
- The donors retained sufficient assets to maintain their accustomed standard of living.

Additionally, the FLPs had economic substance in that:
- They were operated as joint enterprises for profit;
- The family respected the FLP as a separate entity;
- There was no commingling of assets; and
- The donors, not their children, were the ultimate decision-makers as to which of their assets to transfer to the FLPs.

Kimbell. *Kimbell* was the first case that applied Code Sec. 2036(a) to the structure of the FLP, as opposed to placing the sole focus on the decedent's continued personal use or enjoyment of property. Shortly before her death, the decedent's trust transferred approximately $2.5 million in cash, oil and gas working interests and royalty interests, securities, notes, and other assets in exchange for a 99 percent limited partnership interest. As a result of other transfers, the decedent's interest in the FLP totaled 99.5 percent. An LLC operated and formed by the decedent's son contributed approximately $25,000 in cash for a 1 percent pro-rata general partnership interest. The decedent retained $450,000 in assets outside of the LLC and FLP to cover personal expenses. The LLC, as general partner, managed the FLP and had exclusive authority to make distributions. The decedent died still holding the limited partnership interest. The Fifth Circuit held that the bona fide sale exception did apply because there was a "substantial business or other nontax business purpose" for the FLP's formation. The Court held that the transfer qualified as a bona fide sale for adequate and full consideration.

First, the transfer was made for adequate and full consideration because:

- The decedent received a partnership interest proportionate to the assets she contributed to the FLP;
- The assets decedent transferred were properly credited to her partnership account; and
- The partnership agreement required distributions to the partners according to their capital account balances.

Second, the bona-fide sale prong was satisfied because:

- Sufficient assets were retained by decedent outside the FLP;
- Formalities were respected;
- The FLP was actively managed; and
- There were credible, nontax business reasons for the FLP that fit the family's needs.

Kimbell does not necessarily provide guidance to individuals who gift away limited FLP interests to family members but retain a general partnership interest and continue to manage or control the FLP. To protect against a possible Code Sec. 2036 attack, the donor should never retain a general partnership interest in the FLP. Ideally, the general partnership interest should be held by an S corporation or an LLC.

STUDY QUESTION

13. Which of the following reasons was *not* used to determine that Mr. Strangi retained possession or enjoyment of his FLP assets?

a. Mr. Strangi overpaid rent for residing in FLP property in the months preceding his death to help fund the FLP.

b. Mr. Strangi retained insufficient liquid assets outside the partnership to provide for his personal expenses, for which the FLP made distributions.

c. The FLP never conducted active business or made investments.

d. Estate administration expenses were paid by the FLP.

Indirect Gift Trap

The IRS has also successfully asserted that assets transferred to an FLP after gifts of limited partnership interests are made constitute indirect gifts of the FLP's underlying assets and thus are subject to federal gift tax. The IRS has, and may likely continue to have, success in offering this argument. Under current case law, transfers of assets to an FLP *after* transfers of limited partnership interests are made to family members may constitute indirect gifts, subject to federal gift tax. In *J.C. Shepherd* (CA-11, 2002-1 USTC ¶60,431, 283 F3d 1258 (Feb. 28, 2002)), the Eleventh Circuit determined that the taxpayer made an indirect gift to his children when he created an FLP on August 1, 1991, transferring two 25 percent interests in the FLP to his children. Yet, the taxpayer did not fund the FLP until August 30, 1991, when he conveyed an interest in land and later bank stock to the FLP. The Eleventh Circuit upheld the Tax Court's determination that the actual gift was of land and valued the gift as such. In *M. Senda* (CA-8, 2006-1 USTC ¶60,515, 433 F3d 1044 (Jan. 6, 2006)), the Eighth Circuit followed suit. The taxpayer formed the FLP in 1996 but did not fund the partnership until 1998.

Gift Tax Exclusion Trap

Code Sec. 2503(b) allows an annual exclusion for gifts of *present* interests in property. To qualify for the annual gift tax exclusion, the donee must receive immediate economic enjoyment of the gift. A *present interest* is an unrestricted right to the immediate use, possession, or enjoyment of the property or its income. In *C.M. Hackl* (CA-7, 2003-2 USTC ¶60,465, 335 F3d 664 (July 11, 2003)), the Seventh Circuit held that gifts of member interests in a family LLC did not qualify for the annual gift tax exclusion because they were gifts of future interests. The restrictions on transferability of the shares revealed that the shares were of no immediate, substantial economic value. In *Hackl* a married couple created an LLC, funded with their contributions of tree farms, cash, and securities. The tree farms were intended to be a long-term venture. The Hackls made gifted interests to their children and grandchildren, expecting the transfers to be largely free of gift tax by using their Code Sec. 2503(b) annual gift tax exclusion amounts. Under the operating agreement members had no right to withdraw or receive their capital contributions from the LLC, sell their shares, or receive distributions except on dissolution. Further, only Mr. Hackl had authority to dissolve the company. Although *Hackl* involved a family LLC, the court's reasoning is equally applicable to FLPs.

PLANNING TIPS FOR FLPS

Based on this chapter's discussion of the Code Sec. 2036(a) case law and the IRS position on FLPs, this checklist of planning tips summarizes the "do's and don'ts:"

- Avoid "deathbed transfers" and establish the FLP while the owner is still in good health;
- Have and document the (legitimate) business or other nontax purposes for the FLP's formation;
- Form and operate the FLP in accordance with all legal formalities;
- Do not make overly aggressive valuation discounts and use a professional valuation expert;
- Transfer FLP interests to members in proportion to the value of assets or services they contribute to the FLP;
- Document the FMV value of each partner's respective contribution to the FLP in his or her capital account;
- Follow partnership accounting rules;
- Do not commingle personal and partnership assets;
- Do not transfer the donor's principal residence to the FLP unless the donor vacates the home;
- Have the donor avoid personal use of FLP assets and if assets are used personally, pay (and not just accrue) FMV rent;
- Do not make loans from the FLP to the donors;
- Place title to the transferred assets in the name of the partnership;
- Avoid making gifts of FLP interests before assets are transferred to the partnership;
- Make distributions on a pro-rata basis to all partners, not solely the donor;
- Actively manage FLP assets after the property is transferred;
- Do not specially allocate income from specific assets contributed by particular partners/members to those respective partners/members (i.e., ensure sharing of net income from all assets);
- Avoid transferring only passive assets to the FLP;
- Ensure the donor retains sufficient assets and income outside the FLP to meet living and other expenses and to satisfy personal debts;
- Ensure the donor does not retain any right to designate who will possess or enjoy FLP assets;
- Require each family member of the FLP be represented by separate legal counsel during the formation process;
- Avoid unilateral creation and seek input from, and negotiate with, other family members/partners concerning FLP formation, structure, funding, and operational issues to avoid the appearance that the FLP's creation was a mere "testamentary" substitute;

- Ensure each limited partner retains no control through voting rights, the ability to remove the general partner(s), or rights to amend the FLP agreement; and
- Create and respect separate FLP bank accounts.

STUDY QUESTIONS

14. A major reason that the Hackls failed to gift transfers of interests without incurring gift tax liability was:

  a. The donees received future interests, and excludible gifts must provide immediate economic enjoyment for donees.

  b. The recipients of the gifts were not considered immediate family members.

  c. Members of the LLC retained the right to withdraw or receive their capital contributions from the LLC or to sell their shares.

  d. Members received regular distributions from the LLC.

15. Which of the following is *not* a planning tip recommended for establishing a viable FLP?

  a. Avoid gifting FLP interests before assets are transferred to the partnership.

  b. Transfer interests to members in proportion to the value of assets or services they contributed to the partnership.

  c. Partners should only be allocated income from the assets that they contributed.

  d. Develop and document a legitimate nontax purpose for forming the partnership.

CONCLUSION

It is instrumental that an FLP be properly funded, operated, and managed. Although FLPs can offer tremendous tax benefits, as well as nontax and asset management advantages, proper planning, adherence to IRS guidelines, and strict compliance with state law is key.

MODULE 2 — CHAPTER 6

Passive Activity Loss Limitations

The passive activity loss rules generally limit the ability of taxpayers to shelter income with deductions and credits from business activities to which they lack a physical connection through sufficient personal efforts. The passive activity loss rules allow deductions and credits generated from a passive activity to only offset income that is related to such activity.

Congress first enacted these rules in the Tax Reform Act of 1986 to prevent the growing abuse of loss creation to offset wage and other "actively" produced income. Congress has been fine-tuning the passive activity loss rules ever since, both with large carve-out areas such as rental real estate and with other, special interest provisions affecting areas such as oil and gas and the alternative minimum tax. Only recently, H.R. 2691 was introduced to allow a partial exemption from passive activity loss limitations for qualified wind facilities; and H.R. 5420 would exempt historic-structures rehabilitation credits.

LEARNING OBJECTIVES

Upon completion of this chapter, you will be able to:

- Distinguish passive losses from ordinary losses;
- Recognize sources of passive activity income;
- Determine when taxpayers have materially participated in an activity;
- Differentiate when rental activity is and is not subject to passive activity loss rules;
- Understand how the passive activity rules interact with trusts;
- Explain the advantages of using a business form regarding passive activity loss rules;
- Determine when taxpayers may group passive activities and why; and
- Understand how the alternative minimum tax (AMT) interacts with the passive activity loss rules.

OVERVIEW

The strategic importance of the passive activity loss rules is twofold:

- Passive activity losses are only useful in offsetting passive activity income; without passive activity income they must be carried forward to subsequent tax years; and

- Passive activity income may be realized tax free in effect if there are sufficient passive activity losses, whether current or carryforward, to cover that income.

Although the passive activity loss rules contain many nuances, some basic principles run throughout. Keep these in mind to have a place on which to hang all the details presented throughout this course:

- Individuals, trusts and estates, personal service corporations, and closely held C corporations may only deduct passive activity losses from passive activity income. Likewise, passive activity credits may only be applied to taxes on passive income;
- A *passive activity* is a trade or business activity in which taxpayer does not materially participate;
- *Rental activity* is a passive activity without regard to taxpayer's material participation, except for real estate professionals and certain taxpayers primarily providing services and short-term rentals. Natural persons with less than $150,000 in adjusted gross income who are actively participating in rental real estate activity may offset a limited amount of rental income (up to $25,000 each year) against nonpassive income; and
- Deductions and credits that are disallowed under passive activity rules may be carried forward and used as passive activity deductions and credits in succeeding years. Remaining passive activity deductions are deductible against nonpassive income when the taxpayer disposes of the passive activity's assets.

PASSIVE ACTIVITIES

The restriction on deducting passive activity losses applies to loss deductions taxpayers would normally otherwise claim as business expenses. Code Sec. 162 allows taxpayers to deduct ordinary and necessary business expenses in carrying on a trade or business. Code Sec. 212 likewise allows individuals to deduct ordinary and necessary expenses for the production of income. Because of the potential for widespread abuse within the operation of these two Code provisions, however, the passive activity rules of Code Sec. 469 were enacted as a "companion" to them.

Basically, the passive activity rules limit a taxpayer's ability to deduct losses otherwise allowed under Code Sec. 162 or 212 that are generated from activities in which he or she does not materially participate. The rules limit loss deductions by allowing losses from passive activities to only offset income from the same passive activities. Under Code Sec. 469(b), suspended losses must be carried over into subsequent tax years.

Participation

The passive activity rules restrict the use of losses from the conduct of a trade or business if the taxpayer does not materially participate in that activity. There are two types of participation:
- Material participation, which generally applies to business activities; and
- Active participation, applicable to rental real estate activities.

Rental Activity

Congress has carved out a special niche in the passive activity loss rules for rental activity. Losses from a rental activity are generally considered passive activity losses, regardless of a taxpayer's level of participation in the activity.

Intent of the rental activity treatment. Congress created this special treatment for rental activity for two reasons:
- Income received from rental activities is not subject to the self-employment tax under Code Sec. 1402(a)(1); and
- The material participation requirement would not be a sufficient indicator of whether taxpayers involved in rental activity deserved to receive the business expense deduction.

Exceptions. To the otherwise-ironclad rule that rental income always produces passive activity income that may be offset only by related deductions and credits, three limited exceptions have been created:
- Rental losses in which a real estate professional materially participates as a real estate professional;
- Rental of a dwelling unit also used for personal purposes during the year for not more than 14 days or 10 percent of the period the home was rented; and
- Rental real estate losses up to $25,000 may be deducted by a natural person whose modified adjusted gross income is less than $100,000. The taxpayer must actively participate, own at least 10 percent of the property, and not be a limited partner. The $25,000 exception is phased out at the rate of $0.50 for every $1 of modified adjusted gross income above $100,000 (effectively terminating at $150,000).

Other Activities

As with many other areas of the tax laws, Congress has carved out more than one exception. In addition to the exceptions for activities by real estate professionals, the following two activities are not considered passive activities and losses stemming from them are not restricted by Code Sec. 469(a):
- Holding interests in oil or gas wells held directly by the taxpayer or through a flowthrough entity; and
- Trading personal property on behalf of others with an interest in the activity.

> **COMMENT**
>
> In addition to carve-out exceptions to the passive activity rules based on activity, certain types of income are excluded from the reach of the passive activity rules, as described later for income.

STUDY QUESTIONS

1. _____ is a term applied especially to rental real estate activities in determining passive activity loss.
   a. Active participation
   b. Nonpassive substantial participation
   c. Passive substantial participation
   d. None of the above applies

2. Which of the following is **not** an exception to the rule that rental income produces passive activity income that can be offset only by related deductions and credits?
   a. Rental real estate losses of less than $25,000 by an active participant having a modified AGI of less than $100,000
   b. Rental of a personal-use dwelling unit rented for not more than 14 days a year or 10 percent of the days rented
   c. A real estate professional with material participation in the rental incurring rental losses
   d. All of the above are exceptions

PASSIVE ACTIVITY INCOME

A determination of passive activity income is important because deductions and credits generated on account of the activity responsible for generating passive activity income can only offset that passive activity income. To prevent taxpayers from using passive losses to offset their unrelated income, the passive activity loss rules of Code Sec. 469 restrict the deduction of passive activity losses to the amount of the individual taxpayer's passive activity income from that activity. This is reported for most passive activity on lines 3a and 3b of Form 8582, Passive Activity Loss Income.

Any net passive activity income (passive activity income minus passive activity loss) for an activity—as is the case of any amount of income—however, may be offset by those deductions or credits generally available to reduce any amount of ordinary income, regardless of whether it is "passive."

The passive activity deductions in excess of passive activity gross income (passive activity losses) in a particular year are carried forward indefinitely and deducted from passive gross income in subsequent years. The disallowed passive activity loss for a year is allocated among all of the taxpayer's activities that produced the loss. The allocation determines the treatment of disallowed losses when an activity ceases to be a passive activity to the taxpayer and the proper application of loss limitations under other Code sections that may apply after the passive activity limitations.

Likewise, a taxpayer's passive activity credit is only applied against a taxpayer's tax liability allocable to his or her passive activities. If credits attributable to passive activities exceed the liabilities for those activities, the excess (disallowed) passive activity credit must be allocated to each of the taxpayer's credits arising from a passive activity for the tax year of the disallowance. Any disallowed credit is treated as a credit from the activity to which it is allocated for the taxpayer's immediately succeeding tax year.

STUDY QUESTION

> **3.** Credits attributable to passive activities that exceed the liabilities for those activities are:
>   **a.** Grouped together and carried forward indefinitely
>   **b.** Are allocated to each of the taxpayer's credits arising from passive activities for the tax year of disallowance
>   **c.** Are not treated as a credit from the activity to which they are allocated
>   **d.** None of the above is applicable to excess credits

What Is Passive Activity Income?

Passive activity income stems from activities in which the taxpayer:
- Does not materially participate;
- Rents property;
- Holds only a limited partnership interest; or
- Obtains gain from the disposition of an interest in a passive activity or property used in a passive activity.

From a broad-view perspective, passive activity income is determined in one of two ways:
- Looking at the income source; or
- Looking at the extent to which the person receiving the income has been active in its generation.

Looking at the Income Source

The Code itself does a good job of listing those activities that are *not* to be governed by the passive activity loss rules at all or in modified form. Congress has carved out significant exceptions to the definition of passive activity income. These special categories include:

- Portfolio income (interest, dividends, royalties, and annuities);
- Personal service income;
- Income from adjustments due to Code Sec. 481 accounting method changes;
- Income or gain from investments of working capital;
- Income from an oil or gas property;
- Income from intangible property significantly created by the taxpayer; and
- Cancellation of debt income, if the debt is not allocated to passive activities under interest expense allocation rules.

> **COMMENT**
>
> Portfolio-type income derived in the ordinary course of a trade or business may be passive activity gross income if it is derived from a passive activity.

> **COMMENT**
>
> The exceptions to passive activity income do not always produce a better result for the taxpayer. Income under these exceptions cannot be offset by losses or deductions related to passive losses. However, on the flip side, expenses incurred to generate this type of excluded income that exceed the income may offset unrelated income, subject to other limiting Code provisions in certain cases (for example, net capital losses).

Gain on multiple-use property. As already mentioned, passive activity income also includes gain from the disposition of an interest in a passive activity or property used in a passive activity. To ensure that the passive activity loss/passive activity gain connection remains, gain realized from the disposition of property used for both passive and nonpassive activities must be allocated between the two activities. This allocation must reasonably reflect the property's multiple uses during the 12 months immediately preceding the disposition.

Once again, there is an exception! Taxpayers do not have to worry about multiple-use allocation if their interest in the property is no greater than the lesser of $10,000 or 10 percent of the fair market value of all property used in the activity immediately before disposition of the property. In this case, all the gain will be treated as passive activity income and may be offset by passive activity losses (in addition to other deductions, as the case may be).

Gain on substantially appreciated property. Gain from the disposition of property used in a nonpassive activity whose fair market value exceeds 120 percent of its adjusted basis is also not considered passive activity income. However, as an exception to the exception, that gain may be treated as passive gross income if the taxpayer used the property in a passive activity for at least 20 percent of the time the taxpayer held an interest in it or for the entire 24-month period before the disposition.

> **REMINDER**
>
> The rule for substantially appreciated property only applies to the portion of the gain from the disposition determined to be passive activity by the allocation rules for multiple-use property mentioned above for property used for more than one purpose during the 12-month period before the property's disposition.

> **EXAMPLE**
>
> Abby acquires a building on January 1, 2007, and sells it for $1 million on April 1, 2009. The building's value substantially appreciated in the interim. Abby used the building for a trade or business in which Abby materially participated until January 1, 2009, and then began leasing it to tenants until its sale. Because Abby used the building for both passive and nonpassive activities during the 12-month period before the sale date, the allocation rules would require that the gain be allocated between them. The building was used for 3 out of the 12 months in a passive activity, so the multiple-use rules would require 25 percent of the gain to be treated as passive income, whereas 75 percent would be treated as nonpassive.
>
> However, the entire amount is not treated as passive income from the sale of substantially appreciated property because the 3-month period of passive activity use did not endure for 20 percent of the time Abby possessed the property and the passive activity was not in effect for the entire 24-month period before the disposition.

Property held for investment. Even if the taxpayer used substantially appreciated property in a passive activity for either of the required amounts of time, gain from the disposition of substantially appreciated property may yet be treated as nonpassive portfolio income. Interest in property held through a C corporation or similar entity is considered to be held as an investment, and gain from its disposition is considered nonpassive portfolio income. Gain from the disposition of interest in property held for investment for more than 50 percent of the time the taxpayer held the interest in nonpassive activities is also considered portfolio income.

> **REMINDER**
>
> Similar to substantially appreciated property, the rules for property held for investment only apply to the portion of the gain from the disposition determined to be passive activity gain when the property was used for both passive and nonpassive purposes within the 12 months preceding the disposition.

Property converted to inventory. Taxpayers who hold property for one purpose and later sell it as inventory of their trade or business may be able to apply a special rule in treating the gain as passive activity income. Taxpayers should disregard treatment of the property as inventory and treat it as originally held if, prior to the disposition, it was not held as property for sale in the ordinary course of business for 80 percent of the time the taxpayer possessed it and was not originally acquired for the main purpose of selling to customers in the ordinary course of business.

> **EXAMPLE**
>
> Allison purchased equipment to be rented out as part of her construction equipment rental business. She leased the equipment for four years before Allison became a construction equipment retailer. Afterward, Allison placed the equipment on the market for sale. After a total of five years of possession, she sold the equipment for $100,000. Allison should not treat the gain from the sale of the equipment as attributable to inventory; she must treat it as gain from rental activity, a passive activity. The property was acquired for the purpose of renting, not selling, in the ordinary course of business and was not held for the purpose of selling for 80 percent of the time that Allison possessed it.

Looking at the Income Recipient

Taxpayers subject to the passive loss limitation include individuals, trusts, estates, personal service corporations, and closely held C corporations. The rules do not apply to S corporations and partnerships but do apply to their respective shareholders and partners. The rules apply to personal service corporations and closely held C corporations on a consolidated basis.

In addition to defining passive activity income as income derived from certain types of business or investment activities or assets, it is also defined from the perspective of the taxpayer's activities—that is, whether the taxpayer is active or passive in a particular business enterprise. In fact, in most cases, an active ongoing business can produce nonpassive income for some taxpayers and passive activity income for others, depending upon how active each taxpayer has been in the business.

Is the taxpayer active enough in a business to be considered to have sufficiently "earned" that business income, at least for passive activity loss purposes? If so, he or she does not realize passive activity income from it. If not, his or her income from the business is passive activity income.

For tax purposes, the determination of whether the taxpayer is sufficiently inactive in the business in order for his or her income from it to be considered passive activity income depends upon whether the taxpayer "materially participates" in the business. *Material participation* is the term of art by far most used and most litigated in the area of passive activity losses.

STUDY QUESTIONS

---

4. Which of the following is **not** a special category of income that is excepted from passive activity loss rules at all or in modified form?

   a. Income or gain from investing working capital

   b. Income from intangible property that was significantly created by the taxpayer

   c. All cancellation of debt that is not allocated to passive activities

   d. All of the above are exceptions

5. The special passive loss rule for property converted to inventory requires taxpayers to treat gain from sale of property as passive activity gain if:

   a. The property was not held for sale to customers for 60 percent of the time in the ordinary course of business.

   b. The property was originally acquired for the main purpose of sale to customers in the ordinary course of business.

   c. The purchaser acquired the property with the intent of leasing it long-term.

   d. None of the above is the requirement for property converted to inventory.

MATERIAL PARTICIPATION

A taxpayer must "materially participate" in a trade or business to avoid income from that business being considered passive activity income. This requirement is Congress's first defense against tax-shelter planners, promoters, and participants. It also poses the first and often the biggest trap into which taxpayers fall.

A taxpayer materially participates in an activity under Code Sec. 469(g) if he or she is involved in the operations of the activity on a regular, continuous, and substantial basis. Any work done by an individual in connection with an activity in which the individual owns an interest (other than an interest owned through a C corporation) at the time the work is done is deemed to be participation. The participation of the taxpayer's spouse is taken into account in determining whether a taxpayer materially participates in an activity. Material participation is determined separately for each tax year.

Material participation in an activity depends generally on the facts and circumstances surrounding the taxpayer's involvement. Safe harbor provisions, however, automatically treat a taxpayer as materially participating if he or she spends a minimum number of hours participating in an activity in a current year or a prior year, as outlined next.

Seven Tests for Material Participation

A taxpayer is automatically treated as materially participating in an activity for a tax year if he or she meets one of seven tests. The first four tests look to a set number of hours of participation in the tax year. The next two tests look to material participation in prior tax years. The final test looks to the facts and circumstances about the taxpayer's relationship with the concern.

500 minimum hours test. The individual participates in the activity for more than 500 hours during the year.

> **EXAMPLE**
>
> Sam, who works at his leasing office facility on and off over the year, averages about 10 hours each week. He is deemed to materially participate.

Substantially all participation test. The individual's participation in the activity for the tax year constitutes substantially all of the participation in such activity of all participating individuals (including individuals who are not owners of interests in the activity) for the year.

> **EXAMPLE**
>
> Sam, who works at his leasing office facility on and off over the year, averages about 1.5 hours each week. Aside from his brother who put in 5 hours total during one busy weekend, Sam is the only worker. He is deemed to materially participate.

Equal participation test. The individual participates in the activity for more than 100 hours during the tax year, and his or her participation in the activity for the tax year is not less than the participation in the activity of any other participating individual (including individuals who are not owners of interests in the activity) for such year.

> **EXAMPLE**
>
> Sam works at his leasing office facility on and off over the year for a total of 110 hours. His brother worked 100 hours and his only other employee worked 90 hours. He is deemed to materially participate.

Aggregated participation test. The activity is a significant participation activity for the tax year, and the individual's aggregate participation in all significant participation activities during the year exceeds 500 hours.

A *significant participation activity* is one in which the taxpayer participates for more than 100 hours during the year; the activity is a business; and the business must be otherwise considered a passive activity with respect to that individual under any other of the seven tests. The business cannot be a rental or investment activity.

> **EXAMPLE**
>
> Sam, employed full-time as an accountant, also owns interests in a restaurant and a shoe store, each having several full-time employees. Sam works in the restaurant for 400 hours and in the shoe store for 150 hours during the tax year. Sam would fail all tests if he could not aggregate participation in the restaurant and shoe store activities. Because both are significant participation activities (more than 100 hours each), he can aggregate them and pass the 500 hours for presumed material participation.

Five-out-of-ten-years' participation test. The individual materially participated in the activity for any 5 tax years (whether or not consecutive) during the 10 tax years that immediately precede the taxable year).

> **EXAMPLE**
>
> Sam is considered to materially participate under the equal participation test, during 2000 through 2004. His ownership interest and this five-year stretch alone will entitle Sam to use any passive activity losses from his leasing business against any income he realizes during 2005 through 2010.

Three-year personal service activity test. Individuals are more inclined by the IRS to be considered to have materially participated if the activity is personal service activity. Under the three-year personal service activity test, the individual is considered to have materially participated in any year if he or she materially participated in the activity for any three tax years preceding the tax year, regardless of whether they were consecutive.

> **EXAMPLE**
>
> Sam owns an engineering firm and materially participates in the firm under any of the other six tests in 2001, 2003, and 2007. Assuming the firm continues, he is deemed to materially participate in any year after 2007, too.

A *personal service activity* is defined under the Code Sec. 469 regs as the performance of personal services in a trade or business in which capital is not a material income-producing factor. It includes fields such as health, law, engineering, architecture, accounting, actuarial science, performing arts, or consulting.

All facts and circumstances (catch-all) test. As a last resort, the individual may argue that, based on all of the facts and circumstances, he or she has materially participated in the activity on a regular, continuous, and substantial basis during the year.

Under this test, individuals are deemed to have materially participated in the activity if all the facts and circumstances show participation on a regular, continuous, and substantial basis during such year.

With regard to management activities, IRS regulations also require that taxpayers participate in the activity for at least 100 hours; that persons other than the taxpayer who manage the business not receive any compensation; and that the hours of management conducted by other individuals do not exceed those hours of management conducted by the taxpayer.

STUDY QUESTIONS

6. For the equal participation test of material participation, the individual not only must participate in the activity for at least 100 hours during the tax year but also:
   a. He or she must have materially participated in the activity for any 5 out of the past 10 tax years.
   b. His or her participation must be not less than that of any other participating individual, even those who are not owners.
   c. He or she must conduct a personal service activity.
   d. His or her spouse's hours of participation are not taken into account for the minimum participation required.

7. Income and losses from a business are considered nonpassive if the sum of the taxpayer's time in all significant participation activities totals at least _____ for the year.
   a. 100 hours
   b. 500 hours
   c. One calendar quarter
   d. Nine months of work weeks

Qualifying Participation

For "participation" to count toward material participation, the taxpayer's efforts must be directed toward the kind of work customarily performed by the owner of a similar trade or business, not purely "make work" performed to avoid the disallowance of losses under Code Sec. 469. Work the taxpayer performs in his or her capacity as an investor does not count toward fulfilling the requirement. Nonqualifying investor activity includes studying and reviewing financial statements, preparing or compiling financial analysis of the activity for the taxpayer's individual use, and monitoring the finances or operations of the activity while not acting as a manager.

Taxpayers are not allowed to consider commuting time used to travel to a trade or business site in the hourly requirements for material participation. According to the Tax Court, "Commuting is an inherently personal activity and as such does not constitute 'work' in connection with a trade or business" (*Truskowsky*, T.C. Summary Op. 2003-103).

Travel time constitutes neither services nor participation in the activity and is not integral to the operations of an activity in most cases.

Limited partnership interests. In general, limited partners are not deemed to materially participate in partnership activities. As a result, a limited partner's share of partnership income is usually passive income. However, if the individual passes the 500 minimum hours test, five-out-of-ten years' participation test, or three-year personal service activity test, income from the limited partnership interest will no longer be considered passive activity income and resulting losses may be deducted. In addition, general partners or acting general partners may hold limited partnership interests, yet still materially participate in the partnership under any one of the seven tests.

EXAMPLE

Adam owns all of the stock of a C corporation. The corporation is the general partner and Adam is the limited partner in a partnership. The partnership has a single activity, a restaurant, which is a trade or business activity. During the tax year, Adam works for an average of 30 hours per week in connection with the partnership's restaurant activity. Because Adam participates in the restaurant activity during such year for more than 500 hours, he meets the 500 minimum hours test. Therefore, Adam is treated as materially participating in the activity of the restaurant for the taxable year, even though he retains a limited partnership interest.

Imputed interests. Closely held C corporations and personal service corporations are treated as materially participating in an activity if shareholders owning 50 percent or more of the outstanding stock materially participate in the activity. Closely held C corporations can also satisfy the material participation standard under an alternative rule based on the participation of full-time employees in the activity.

Substantiating Material Participation

Taxpayers may use *any reasonable means* to show they materially participate in an activity. This includes, but is not limited to, identification of the performance of services over a period of time and the approximate number of hours spent performing such services through use of appointment books, calendars, or narrative summaries. Under Temp. Reg. § 1.469-5T(f)(4), contemporaneous daily time reports and logs are not necessary if participation is established by other reasonable means.

To spot taxpayers who do not materially participate in an activity, the IRS instructs its auditors to look for the following indicators:

- The taxpayer is not compensated in return for services;
- The taxpayer maintains a residence hundreds of miles away from the activity;
- The taxpayer has a Form W-2 job requiring 40 plus hours a week for which he or she receives material compensation;
- The taxpayer has numerous other investments, rentals, business activities, or hobbies that absorb significant amounts of time;
- There is a paid on-site management/foreman/supervisor and/or employees who provide day-to-day oversight and care of the operations;
- The taxpayer is elderly or has health issues;
- The majority of hours claimed are for work that does not materially impact operations; or
- Business operations would continue uninterrupted if the taxpayer did not perform the services claimed.

To prove material participation despite any of these indicators requires the taxpayer to prove he or she participated for an adequate amount of time and that the character of that participation meets all requirements. Documentation, including contemporaneous time-and-activity logs, is critical for the taxpayer to carry his or her burden of proof. Determination of these facts is the focus of a substantial amount of litigation.

STUDY QUESTIONS

8. Which of the following is **not** required in order for a limited partner's share of partnership income to be considered nonpassive?

   a. He or she must document the time spent with the partnership.

   b. He or she must materially participate in the partnership.

   c. He or she must satisfy the 500 minimum hours, previous years' participation, or personal service activity test.

   d. All of the above are required.

9. The *any reasonable means* standard for substantiating material participation allows all of the following **except:**

   a. Employing daily time reports and logs

   b. Identification of the performance of services over a period of time

   c. Use of appointment books, calendars, or narrative summaries about services performed

   d. All of the above are allowed to substantiate material participation

RENTAL ACTIVITY

Rentals are generally considered a *per se* passive activity under Code Sec. 469(c)(2). The rules under Reg. 1.469-1T(e)(3) for treating rental activity as *per se* passive are widely encompassing. For the blanket passive activity rule to apply, the taxpayer must simply rent tangible property to others and in return receive income principally for use of that property. Nevertheless, there are six narrow exceptions:

- The seven-day exception;
- The thirty-day exception;
- The personal service exception;
- The incidental exception;
- The business hours exception; and
- The providing-property exception.

If a rental activity is not considered *per se* passive because of one of these six exceptions, the taxpayer still must prove "material participation" to avoid rental income being considered passive activity income. Without one of the six *per se* exceptions, however, no extent of material participation will matter.

There are also a subset of special rules under the special rules for rental activity that have been carved out to offer relief from the rules if one is a real estate professional. Finally, Congress has created a $25,000 exemption from the passive activity rules for rental income received by certain middle-income individual taxpayers.

Six Exceptions to *Per Se* Passive Rental Income

Seven-day exception. Rental activity is not a *per se* passive activity if the average period of use by the customer is fewer than seven days, an example being short-term use of a hotel room.

> **COMMENT**
>
> The IRS calculates the average period of customer use by dividing the total number of days in all rental periods by the number of rentals during the tax year.

> **COMMENT**
>
> For multiple classes of property, the average period of customer use for each class is multiplied by the gross rental income from that class of property over the activity's total gross rental income. Each amount is added up for the total average period of customer use.

Thirty-day exception. If customers use the property for an average period of 30 or fewer days and significant personal services are performed by or on behalf of the owner of the property in making the property available to the customer, the rental activity is not considered *per se* passive, an example being a year-round vacation rental property.

Personal service exception. Taxpayers who perform extraordinary personal services to make the property available to the customer—for example, hospitals and nursing homes—avoid *per se* passive activity classification regardless of the average rental period.

Incidental exception. In this case, the rental of the property is incidental to a nonrental activity.

> **EXAMPLE**
>
> Lodging provided to an employee or the employee's spouse or dependents is incidental to the activity in which the employee performs services if the lodging is furnished for the employer's convenience.

Business hours exception. Making property available during defined business hours for nonexclusive use by various customers avoids classification as *per se* passive activity. To be considered nonexclusive use, the taxpayer must not grant a particular customer exclusive use of the property during the time the customer is using it; such as by renting a car or chartering an airplane (***Kenville***, DC N.D., 97-2 USTC ¶50,936). Reg. § 1.469-1T(3) (viii), Example 10, notes that leasing a golf course to multiple customers, for different periods, yet all at the same time is considered nonexclusive use. Other examples include health clubs and spas.

Providing-property exception. A *per se* passive activity does not occur if the taxpayer is compensated for providing property for use in an activity conducted by a partnership, S corporation, or joint venture in which the taxpayer owns an interest.

Material Participation in Rental Activity

Once a taxpayer overcomes the burden of proving the rental activity is not a *per se* passive activity, the taxpayer must show that he or she materially participated in the rental activity. If this requirement is met (see the criteria for material participation, reviewed earlier in this course), the taxpayer may deduct the losses.

EXAMPLE

The taxpayer-wife manager of legal support services, supervises staff, and meets the legal needs of her fellow attorneys on a daily basis. She will be deemed to have materially participated in the business and the losses from the business will be considered nonpassive (*Assaf*, T.C. Memo. 2005-14, CCH Dec. 55,915(M)).

CAUTION

Even if a taxpayer overcomes the burden of the *per se* classification of rental activity for condominiums, vacation cottages, time-shares, hotels, motels, and bed & breakfasts, and proves he or she materially participated in the rental activity, the IRS may still disallow loss deductions under Code Sec. 280A(d)(1) if the taxpayer uses the vacation residence as a personal residence for more than 14 days or 10 percent of the days during which it is rented.

Reg. § 1.469-9(e)(1) treats each of a taxpayer's interests in real estate property as a separate real estate rental activity. Unless the taxpayer elects to group all of its real estate properties as a single real estate activity under Reg. § 1.469-9(g), material participation must be shown for each individual property (grouping activities is discussed later in this course).

Real Estate Professionals

Congress has created special rules to offer relief from these limitations for real estate professionals. Rental real estate activity is not considered a *per se* passive activity if conducted by a "real estate professional."

To qualify as a *real estate professional,* the individual taxpayer must show that more than one-half of the personal services he or she performed in a trade or business during the tax year were in the real estate business. Activities that fulfill this requirement include:

- Development or redevelopment of property;
- Construction or reconstruction;
- Acquisition or conversion;
- Rental;
- Management or operation;
- Leasing; and
- Brokerage activities.

Additionally, real estate professionals must have performed more than 750 hours of services during the tax year in that real property trade or business. Once deemed a real estate professional, the taxpayer must still show that he or she materially participated in the activity to prove the losses were not the result of passive activity.

CAUTION

The IRS instructs its auditors to carefully scrutinize returns to ensure that the time requirements for real estate professional status are met. To prove material participation, taxpayers may use any reasonable means under Reg. § 1.469-5T(f)(4), but that means must include proof of services performed and hours attributable to those services. In particular, the IRS will closely compare the time a taxpayer spends in his or her main occupation with the time claimed to have been spent on a real estate rental activity.

CAUTION

Activities by the taxpayer's spouse may assist the taxpayer in meeting the material participation requirement for passive activity loss deductions. However, the IRS will only consider whether each spouse individually meets the time requirements in determining whether a taxpayer is considered a real estate professional.

$25,000 Active Participation Allowance

As discussed previously, natural persons may deduct passive activity losses up to $25,000 under Code Sec. 469(i) for rental real estate activities in which they actively participate and if they have modified adjusted gross incomes of less than $100,000. To be entitled to this special de minimis treatment, the taxpayer also must have at least a 10 percent interest in the activity throughout the year and not have an interest as a limited partner. Real estate rental activities in which a taxpayer actively participates are reported on lines 1a, 1b, and 1c of Form 8582.

COMMENT

Many vacation homes are rented for seven or fewer days. The IRS treats these activities as businesses and not as rentals. The $25,000 rental real estate allowance and the active participation standard do not apply. Net losses from these activities are passive unless the taxpayer materially participates in the property rental process.

Phaseout. The $25,000 active participation allowance is phased out for higher-income taxpayers. The $25,000 allowance is reduced by 50 percent of the amount by which their adjusted gross income exceeds $100,000.

EXAMPLE

In *Hammond,* the Tax Court prohibited a taxpayer couple from offsetting losses stemming from their rental activity because it was passive income. Additionally, the court completely disallowed the exception for active participation because 50 percent of the amount by which the taxpayers' adjusted gross income exceeded $100,000 was greater than the $25,000. That is, the taxpayers' adjusted gross income was greater than $150,000 (*Hammond* T.C. Summary Op. 2004-156),

---

Active participation standard. The active participation standard is less strenuous than the material participation standard. According to Congress, the active participation standard can be satisfied without regular, continuous, and substantial involvement in operations, as long as the taxpayer participates. This includes the making of management decisions or arranging for others to provide services, in a "significant and bona fide sense." Management decisions that meet the active participation requirement include approving new tenants, deciding on rental terms, approving capital or repair expenditures, and other similar decisions.

This limit is complicated further when certain housing deductions and credits are taken into consideration. Under Code Sec. 469(i)(6)(B), no active participation is required for:

- The commercial revitalization deduction under Code Sec. 1400I;
- The rehabilitation credit under Code Sec. 47; or
- The low-income housing credit under Code Sec. 42.

> **COMMENT**
>
> Commercial revitalization deductions are computed and reported on lines 2a, 2b, and 2c of Form 8582. The rehabilitation and low-income housing credits for property placed into service after 1989 are reported and computed on lines 3a, 3b, and 3c of Form 8582-CR.

To claim the rehabilitation credit under Code Sec. 47 the deduction-equivalent of the credit counts toward the $25,000 allowance limit. However, the deduction-equivalent amount is reduced by 50 percent of the amount by which the taxpayer's adjusted gross income exceeds $200,000.

> **COMMENT**
>
> Under Code Sec. 469(j)(5), a *deduction-equivalent* is the amount, which taken as a deduction, would reduce the taxpayer's tax liability by an amount equal to the effect of the rehabilitation or low-income housing credit.

In addition, taxpayers may make deductions under the commercial revitalization deduction of Code Sec. 1400I and claim the low-income housing credit under Code Sec. 42 without limit. However, the commercial revitalization deduction and the deduction-equivalent of the low-income housing credit must also both meet the $25,000 limit.

Ordering rules. When taxpayers claim more than one of these deductions or credits, Code Sec. 469(i)(3) imposes ordering rules on taxpayers to determine what losses are deductible. The allowance is applied in the following order:
1. Losses not attributable to commercial revitalization deductions;
2. Losses attributable to commercial revitalization deductions;
3. Credits attributable to credits other than rehabilitation and low-income housing credits;
4. Credits attributable to the rehabilitation credit; and
5. Credits attributable to the low-income housing credit.

The "Self-Rental" Rule

Reg. § 1.469-2(f)(6) maintains that a taxpayer's gross rental activity income for the tax year received from renting property is not treated as passive activity income if the taxpayer rents out the property for use in a trade or business activity in which the taxpayer materially participates. However this does not allow the taxpayer to claim what are still considered passive activity losses on those rental activities.

> **COMMENT**
>
> If the taxpayer rents real property to the business, it cannot be rented incidental to development activity under Reg. § 1.469-2(f)(5).

Under this rule, however, taxpayers who self-rent assets may not group the activity with rental of any other property; even with other self-rented property.

Taxpayers also cannot use gains derived from self-rental activity to offset losses recognized from unrelated passive activities.

> **EXAMPLE**
>
> The Court of Appeals for the Ninth Circuit recently found that preventing self-rental activity losses from offsetting unrelated passive activity income was in line with Congress's intention of "preventing the sheltering of positive income sources through the use of tax losses derived from passive business activities" (*Beecher*, CA-9, 2007-1 USTC ¶50,379). This was true even though the taxpayer had a bona fide business purpose and did not structure any transaction for tax purposes.

TRUST AND ESTATE ISSUES

Trusts are generally covered by the passive activity loss rules under Code Sec. 469(a)(2). However, grantor trusts as defined in Code Sec. 671 are excluded from the passive activity rules under Reg. § 1.469-1T(b)(2). For grantor trusts, material participation is determined at the grantor level, rather than at the trust level. The IRS instructs its auditors that grantor trusts are not recognized as separately taxable entities and should be ignored entirely, while looking to the activities of the grantor in determining whether the passive activity loss rules should apply.

Unfortunately, little IRS guidance is available on how the passive activity rules affect prohibited losses claimed by nongrantor trusts. The IRS has reserved Reg. § 1.469-8 for applying the passive activity loss rules to trusts, estates, and their beneficiaries and Reg. § 1.469-5T(g) for defining material participation of trusts and estates.

Material Participation

A recent Technical Advice Memorandum clarified the IRS's position on determining whether a testamentary trust has materially participated in a business activity. In the view of IRS Chief Counsel, a testamentary trust is considered to have materially participated in an activity if its fiduciaries meet the requirements for material participation (Technical Advice

Memorandum 200733023). Although this clarification is helpful, it is not official guidance.

This memorandum was contrary to a 2003 federal district court decision that deemed a trust to have materially participated in an activity (*The Mattie K. Carter Trust*, DC Texas, 2003-1 USTC ¶50,418). The federal district court for the Northern District of Texas confronted a situation involving a nongrantor trust holding a working cattle ranch that was also used for oil and gas interests. The district court allowed the loss deduction, because "common sense" dictated that the participation of the trust in the ranch operations involved looking to the activities of the employees working on the ranch to further its business. The court was persuaded by the taxpayer's argument that a trust, similar to a C corporation, had to have a living person act on its behalf:

> The Trust, however, is very similar to a closely held C corporation. The Trustee, like the board of directors of a C corporation, has the fiduciary obligation to the beneficiaries of the Trust for the benefit of such beneficiaries. Moreover, the Trust, like a C corporation, is a legal entity and is subject to entity-level U.S. federal income taxes. In addition, and most importantly, as a legal entity, the Trust, like a C corporation, can act only through its fiduciaries, employees and agents. Therefore, the Trust is most analogous to a closely held C corporation.

The IRS, on the other hand, rejected this interpretation, declaring that because businesses cannot *not* look to the owner's employees to satisfy the material participation requirement, neither should trusts.

COMMENT

Further support of this pro-taxpayer position is found in the legislative history of Code Sec. 469, Senate Committee Report to P.L. 99-514 (1986), S. Rep. No. 99-313. That report maintained that an estate or trust has materially participated in an activity if the executor or fiduciary has materially participated in the activity.

Rental Real Estate

Trusts may not take advantage of the $25,000 active participation allowance for real estate activities because they are not individuals, even if an individual acts on its behalf. However, under Code Sec. 495(i)(4), a decedent's estate may take advantage of the active participation allowance for two years if the decedent actively participated in the real estate rental activity, excluding the amount allowable to a surviving spouse.

Distributions

Under Code Sec. 469(j)(12), if an asset from a passive activity is distributed to a beneficiary by a trust (or an estate), a pro-rata share of the activities' net losses, if any, are added to the basis of the asset immediately before the transfer. That adjustment will tend to reduce the passive activity income realized by the beneficiary from any gain on the assets' eventual sale.

STUDY QUESTION

10. For rental real estate, a decedent's estate may take advantage of the $25,000 active participation allowance for two years if:

  a. The beneficiaries of the estate continue management of the real estate rentals without interruption.
  b. The decedent actively participated in the real estate rental activity.
  c. The real estate ownership was part of a GRAT.
  d. All of the above are requirements for claiming the allowance.

PERSONAL SERVICE CORPORATIONS AND CLOSELY HELD C CORPORATIONS

In addition to applying to outright ownership interests and interests as a general partner, the passive loss rules also apply to interests in personal service corporations and, in some circumstances, to closely held C corporations themselves. The passive loss rules generally do not apply to large C corporations unless they are closely held or are personal service corporations.

Material Participation

Taxpayers with interests in closely held C corporations or personal service corporations materially participate in an activity if one or more of the shareholders who hold 50 percent of the outstanding stock of the corporation materially participates in the activity. Thus, in this limited circumstance, it is possible for an individual taxpayer to meet the material participation requirement through the activity of others.

COMMENT

Closely held C corporations that do not qualify as personal service corporations are considered to have materially participated in an activity when they have a certain number of full-time employees involved in the activity under Code Sec. 465(c)(7)(C).

> **REMINDER**
>
> A closely held corporation, as used here, is defined under Code Sec. 542(a)(2) as a corporation with 50 percent of its outstanding stock owned by no more than five individuals.

Offset. A closely held C corporation may offset passive losses by the "net active income" of a closely held C corporation under Code Sec. 469(e)(2). The net active income of the corporation is:

- Income not attributable to passive activity;
- Portfolio income; or
- Income-producing property held for investment in the normal course of business.

Real Estate Advantage

Closely held C corporations and personal service corporations are treated as materially participating in an activity if shareholders owning 50 percent or more of the outstanding stock materially participate in the activity. Closely held C corporations can also satisfy the material participation standard under an alternative rule based on the participation of full-time employees in the activity.

As a result, to avoid the *per se* passive activity rule on income from real estate rentals, Code Sec. 469(c)(7) allows closely held C corporations renting real property to show that 50 percent of their gross receipts were derived from real property trades or businesses in which the corporation materially participates. This is a significant improvement over the one-half of all trades and 750 hours of service rules that apply to real estate individuals.

STUDY QUESTIONS

11. Closely held C corporations that are not personal service corporations are considered to have materially participated in an activity when:

- **a.** One or more shareholders holds at least 76 percent of the outstanding stock and materially participates in the activity
- **b.** Its principal employee-owners materially participate in at least 50 hours of the activity during the tax year
- **c.** The majority shareholder actively participates in the activity to any extent
- **d.** A certain number of full-time employees are involved in the activity under Code Sec. 465(c)(7)(C)

> **12.** A closely held C corporation that rents real property avoids the *per se* passive activity income rule if:
>
> **a.** 25 percent of the corporation's gross receipts involved real property trades or businesses in which the corporation materially participates
>
> **b.** 75 percent of the corporation's net receipts involved real property trades or businesses in which the corporation materially participates
>
> **c.** Half of all trades and 750 hours of service per year constitute material participation by employee-shareholders
>
> **d.** 50 percent of its gross receipts are derived from real property trades or businesses in which the corporation materially participates

ELECTION TO GROUP PASSIVE ACTIVITIES

An important threshold consideration in dealing with the passive activity loss rules is the question of what constitutes a single activity of the taxpayer. This is because, although taxpayers may deduct passive activity losses against passive gains within a single activity, classification of a taxpayer's passive activities into multiple activities prevents the deduction of net passive loss from one particular activity against net passive gain from a separate activity. Identification of a taxpayer's activities is determined by the facts and circumstances. Being allowed to group activities can be pivotal in determining the amount of passive income available to offset passive losses, as well as in assessing the extent to which a taxpayer materially participates in an activity.

Whether activities must be considered individually or may be combined into one activity depends on whether they constitute an appropriate economic unit for passive loss purposes.

One or more trade or business activities, or rental activities, may be treated as a single activity if the activities constitute an appropriate economic unit for the measurement of gain or loss for purposes of the passive loss rules. Whether activities constitute an appropriate economic unit, and therefore may be treated as a single activity, depends upon "all the relevant facts and circumstances" (discussed below).

In addition, other "grouping" restrictions apply to:

- The combination of activities of passthrough entities and corporations;
- The combination of business and rental activities; and
- Tax-avoidance combinations.

As an enforcement measure for the grouping rules, a taxpayer who groups more than one business activity must notify the IRS of the grouping by attaching an election statement to his or her income tax return; no other notification is permitted.

> **COMMENT**
>
> The election to group passive activities cannot be made on an amended return or during an audit.

"Relevant Facts and Circumstances"

Reg. § 1.469-4(c)(2) allows taxpayers to use "any reasonable method of applying the relevant facts and circumstances" in deciding whether to group activities.

As guidance, the IRS provides that the following factors are given the greatest weight in determining whether activities are from an appropriate economic unit:

- Similarities and differences between the types of trades or businesses;
- The extent of common control;
- The extent of common ownership;
- Geographical location; and
- Interdependencies between activities.

> **CAUTION**
>
> Once a taxpayer has chosen a method of grouping the activities, the activities may not be regrouped in subsequent tax years unless a "material change in the facts and circumstances" has occurred.

> **EXAMPLE**
>
> Alberto owns a bakery and a movie theater in a mall in Baltimore and a bakery and movie theater in Philadelphia. Alberto does not materially participate in any of the businesses, which create both passive activity losses and income. Under the regulations, Alberto could combine gains and losses from the bakery and the movie theater in Baltimore, as this grouping is based on geographical location. A similar group would be appropriate for the bakery and the movie theater Philadelphia. He could also group gains and losses from the bakeries and form a separate group that combines gains and losses from both movie theaters.
>
> Alberto could also group gains and losses from all of the activities together, because all the activities have common ownership. Once Alberto decides on a grouping, however, he must maintain this grouping for all subsequent tax years unless a material change in the businesses' circumstances requiring a change to the grouping occurs.

Material Participation

Electing to group related activities into a single activity makes it easier for taxpayers to meet the tests for material participation. Meeting the requirements for grouping activities reduces the taxpayer's burden to show material participation because, rather than having to prove material participation for each individual activity, the taxpayer only has to prove material participation for all activities within the group as a whole.

Rental Activities

A rental activity generally cannot generally be grouped with a trade or business. However, a rental activity may be grouped with a trade or business if either is insubstantial in relation to the other or the owner has the same proportionate interest in the rental as in the business.

EXAMPLE

A taxpayer leased equipment to an S corporation of which he was the majority owner. The Tax Court found that taxpayer's leasing activity, a passive activity, could be grouped with the S corp's business (*Schumacher*, T.C. Summary Op. 2003-96). The taxpayer's rental activity was "insubstantial" in relation to the activities of the S corp. The taxpayer created and operated the leasing activity solely for the benefit of the S corp and spent little time conducting its affairs as compared to the activities of the S corp. Additionally, the purpose of the leasing activity was to enhance the ability of the S corp to do business and did not provide an income stream independently from the S corp.

Insubstantial activity. The meaning of *insubstantial* is unclear because the IRS has refused to define the term in official guidance. The IRS received comments asking for clarification when it issued final regs under 1.469-4 in T.D. 8565. The IRS determined:

> Because the regulations already adopt a facts and circumstances test that looks at all of the pertinent factors [for grouping], it is not necessary to specify that the term *insubstantial* refers to factors other than gross income. In addition, to avoid complex and mechanical rules, the final regulations do not adopt a bright-line or safe-harbor gross revenue test.

Courts, however, have taken a crack at defining it. For example, in one particular case, the IRS conceded that a married couple's rental activities and management activities were an appropriate economic unit under Reg. § 1.469-4. However, the IRS argued that facts that made the two activities an appropriate economic unit could not be used to sustain a finding that one activity was "insubstantial" in relation to the other. The court rejected this argument, with the judge remarking: "We have difficulty imaging a scenario where two activities are so interdependent that they form an appropriate economic unit, yet are not 'essential' to each other in a way that the government's definition would allow them to be considered 'insubstantial'" (Indianapolis Div., DC Ind., 2000-1USTC ¶50,372).

Rental real estate. Each of a qualifying taxpayer's interests in rental real estate must be treated as a separate activity unless the taxpayer elects to treat all interests in rental real estate as a single activity. That election is permitted only if two requirements are met:

- More than one-half of the personal services performed in trades or businesses by the taxpayer during the tax year must be performed in real property trades or businesses in which the taxpayer materially participates; and
- The taxpayer must perform more than 750 hours of services during the taxable year in real property trades or businesses in which the taxpayer materially participates.

Limited Partnership Interests

Taxpayers owning limited partnerships may group the following activities with another activity only if it is in the same line of business:

- Holding, producing, or distributing motion picture films or videotapes;
- Farming;
- Leasing Code Sec. 1245 property;
- Exploring for, or exploiting, oil and gas resources; and
- Exploring for, or exploiting, geothermal deposits.

IRS Recharacterization

In addition to denying grouping for not being formed around an appropriate economic unit, the IRS, under Reg. § 1.469-4(f), can regroup a taxpayer's passive activities if any of them does not form an appropriate economic unit and the principal purpose of the taxpayer's grouping choice was to avoid the Code Sec. 469 restriction on passive activity losses.

EXAMPLE

Five physicians form a partnership, in which none of them materially participates, to acquire several pieces of X-ray equipment. Although each individual owns a medical practice, the equipment is bought at a volume discount to be shared by all. The physicians pick a general partner and each receives a limited partnership interest in exchange for the equipment provided to the partnership. The physicians receive service from the partnership in proportion to their interests and pay for those services at fees set as though the physician were dealing with a third party.

The physicians do not group their limited partnership income with income from their individual medical practices. Some of them had passive losses from investing in a tax shelter, whereas others had passive real estate investment losses. Instead, they offset income from the partnership against these passive activity losses.

This grouping is incorrect. The IRS will likely regroup the limited partnership gains and losses with those from the taxpayers' individual medical practices because the activities are interdependent and are in similar lines of business. Allowing the physicians to offset the gains from the partnership with the passive losses from the tax shelter and real estate investments is against the purpose of Code Sec. 469 and the IRS could assert Code Sec. 6662 accuracy penalties when appropriate.

DISPOSITION OF INTEREST

The passive loss limitation is lifted when a taxpayer disposes of his or her entire interest in a passive activity in a fully taxable transaction. Suspended passive activity losses attributable to the activity and losses recognized on the disposition may then be deducted from active and portfolio income. Likewise, if the passive activity itself is terminated, all remaining net passive losses from that activity become deductible.

EXAMPLE

Andrew acquires an interest in a partnership that engages in the passive activities and accumulates losses for several years. Although the partnership cannot recognize the losses due to a lack of passive activity income, Andrew may recognize the loss as nonpassive upon liquidation of his interest.

Three requirements apply to the special disposition-of-interest rule:
- The taxpayer must dispose of its entire interest in the activity;
- The disposition must be in the form of a fully taxable transaction; and
- The taxpayer must not be related to the party acquiring the interest under Code Sec. 267(b) or as between a partner and partnership—a transaction that is forbidden by Code Sec. 707(b)(1).

Taxpayers who sell their interests to related parties retain the passive activity losses under Code Sec. 469(g)(1)(B) until the related party sells the interest to an unrelated party. For purposes of this rule, sales between trusts or estates and their beneficiaries are considered to be between related parties.

When taxpayers elect to group activities together, all activities generally must be sold to recognize all losses from the disposition of interest in a passive activity. Taxpayers seeking to take advantage of Code Sec. 469(g) by deducting all current and suspended passive activity losses are best advised not to elect to group their activities. If they partially dispose of the properties, for example by only selling 1 out of 10 grouped properties, passive activity losses generally will be limited to the amount of passive activity gain they recognize from the disposition. Nevertheless, a taxpayer who disposes of a substantial part of an activity may treat that part as a separate activity for purposes of freeing passive losses if he or she can establish with reasonable certainty the share of losses and credits that are allocable to the disposed portion.

STUDY QUESTION

---

13. A taxpayer who wishes to group multiple passive business activities notifies the IRS of the election by:

    a. Attaching an election statement to the income tax return

    b. Filing an amended return noting the election with "Grouping Passive Activities" on the top of page 1

    c. Declaring the election on the next period's income tax return or, if an audit is ongoing, by notifying the examiner in writing

    d. None of the above is the acceptable means of notification

---

ALTERNATIVE MINIMUM TAX

Application of Passive Activity Rules to the AMT

The passive activity rules were enacted to combat specific tax-sheltered arrangements, but the alternative minimum tax (AMT) was established to combat tax abuse by broadly restricting the amount of special adjustments and preferences "wealthy" taxpayers could claim on their returns. The passive activity loss rules are applied in special ways to compute AMT liability, as compared to their usage for regular income tax liability.

Computing AMTI

In computing alternative minimum taxable income (AMTI), passive activity losses are disallowed for taxpayers other than C corporations to the extent they exceed passive activity income. This AMT treatment mirrors that under the regular tax. Outstanding aggregate passive activity losses must be carried forward into subsequent tax years and are allowed as a deduction against future income from the passive activity for the year in which the taxpayer disposes of the interest in the activity.

However, the passive activity rules for AMT change from regular tax treatment when one recomputes an individual's regular tax liability to reflect adjustments for tax preferences. For purposes of computing a taxpayer's AMTI, IRS Announcement 88-45 reminds taxpayers that adjustments related to a passive activity, such as the depreciation deduction, will often reduce the amount of passive activity loss the taxpayer would have been allowed to deduct for his or her regular tax liability.

> **EXAMPLE**
>
> Angela materially participates in real estate rental activity and is allowed to deduct $15,000 worth of otherwise passive activity loss. Because the AMT applies, Angela is required to recompute her depreciation deductions for the leased property, thus decreasing her passive activity income loss deduction by $10,000. Her final allowable passive activity income loss deduction under the AMT is $5,000.

Some calculations of AMTI may even turn a passive activity loss into a net gain!

> **EXAMPLE**
>
> Aaron materially participates in real estate rental activity and is allowed to deduct $5,000 worth of otherwise passive activity loss. Because the AMT applies, Aaron is required to recompute his depreciation deduction for the leased property, thus decreasing his passive activity income loss deduction by $10,000. This creates a net gain of $5,000 for purposes of calculating Aaron's AMTI.

> **COMMENT**
>
> In Announcement 88-45, the IRS stated that once taxpayers have made these adjustments to their passive activity losses for purposes of the AMTI, they do not have to again make them on Form 6251, Alternative Minimum Tax – Individuals; that would lead to duplicative adjustments.

Insolvent taxpayers. For insolvent taxpayers, the treatment for AMT purposes is different from that for the regular tax. Although calculation of AMTI requires adjustments to regular income tax liability that may reduce passive activity losses, the AMT rules under Code Sec. 58(c)(1)(A) offset these adjustments by the amount of insolvency a taxpayer possesses at the end of the year. This offset is equal to the amount by which the taxpayer's liabilities exceed the fair market value of his or her assets.

> **EXAMPLE**
>
> Taxpayer Anne has assets with a fair market value of $300,000 and liabilities of $330,000. Anne has a passive activity loss of $50,000 and no passive income for the year. This amount is suspended for regular tax purposes. However, Anne may take a passive activity loss deduction of $30,000 in calculating AMTI because this is the amount by which her liability exceeds the fair market value of the assets.

Qualified residence interest. Under Code Sec. 469(j)(7), qualified residence interest is not considered passive activity loss. However, only *qualified housing interest*—a narrower term—is disregarded from the computation of AMTI under Code Sec. 58(b)(3). This is defined as the qualified residence interest paid during the tax year on indebtedness to acquire, construct, or improve the principal residence of the taxpayer, according to Code Sec. 56(e)(1).

> **EXAMPLE**
>
> Alec owns a condominium in the city and a house in the suburbs. Although the house is Alec's primary residence, the condominium is his secondary residence. Alec is subject to the AMT. Alec's regular income tax liability is recomputed to reflect the interest deduction on the condominium. Only the qualified housing interest for Alec's primary residence—the house in the suburbs—is disregarded for AMTI purposes.

STUDY QUESTIONS

> **14.** What is the major effect of the passive activity rules on AMT liability?
>
> **a.** AMT preference item adjustments to passive activities often reduce the amount of passive activity losses otherwise deductible under the regular tax system
>
> **b.** AMT liability is usually lowered by allowing the same offsets as under the regular tax system
>
> **c.** Aggregate passive activity losses may be carried forward for longer periods for AMT liability calculations than under the regular tax system
>
> **d.** None of the above is the primary effect

15. Qualified housing interest for AMTI calculations:

   a. Is deductible at a higher percentage for AMT than under the regular tax system

   b. Excludes deductions for interest paid on any mortgage not for the taxpayer's primary residence

   c. Excludes interest on indebtedness for home improvements on the taxpayer's primary residence

   d. None of the above applies to qualified housing interest

CONCLUSION

Passive activity loss rules limit ordinary taxpayers' ability to shelter their personal income using deductions and credits from activities in which they have little or no involvement. The rules only allow use of deductions and credits to offset passive income related to the activity, unless the taxpayer can prove that he or she participated materially. Special exceptions alleviate the material participation requirement for certain rental activities, trusts and estates, and businesses. In addition, for activities in which taxpayers do not materially participate, the rules prevent the grouping of passive losses to offset unrelated passive income. Taxpayers should take heed of these rules, as well as their application to the alternative minimum income tax regime.

CPE NOTE: When you have completed your study and review of chapters 4-6, which comprise this Module, you may wish to take the Quizzer for the Module.

For your convenience, you can also take this Quizzer online at **www. cchtestingcenter.com.**

MODULE 3: NEW TAX LAW/IRS — CHAPTER 7

IRS Audit Process

The IRS's goal is compliance with the tax laws. The agency seeks to balance service and enforcement to achieve its mission, with the pendulum swinging recently toward enforcement. Congress and the public are particularly concerned about the *tax gap*, the amount of tax that goes unpaid and uncollected each year, now estimated at $345 billion based on figures from 2001.

The sources of the tax gap are many—corporations, unincorporated businesses, nonbusiness income and deductions, employment taxes, and nonfilers, among others. Some people do not comply with the tax laws out of ignorance, but most noncompliance statistically is the result of willful cheating (or at least taking tax positions that are aggressive beyond the bounds of reasonableness).

To demonstrate its diligence and increase the reach of its compliance efforts, the IRS has been stepping up its enforcement efforts in a variety of directions, as well as making more of an effort to publicize them for their deterrent effect.

LEARNING OBJECTIVES

Upon completion of this chapter, you will be able to:

- Describe the progress that the IRS is making in strengthening enforcement;
- Explain the goals of the National Research Program;
- Discuss the IRS's general approach to audits;
- Describe the audit activities of each of the IRS's four operating divisions;
- Discuss the appeals process as it now operates; and
- Discuss the alternative dispute resolution programs maintained by the Office of Appeals.

INTRODUCTION

Increased enforcement, evidenced by urging agents to work harder and smarter, has been the IRS's mantra for the past several years. Stung by stories of how white-shoed tax-shelter advisors and investors had been pulling the wool over the IRS's eyes at a toll of billions of dollars and how a large group of small businesses had secreted billions one dollar at a time, the IRS's reputation as a competent tax authority had suffered greatly. The IRS's reaction was to step up enforcement efforts, in both old and new ways.

This chapter provides an overview of IRS audit programs, in some cases looking at the "big picture," in others, scrutinizing the activities of particular IRS offices. The IRS continues to tout the deterrent effect of its enforcement activities and points to the growth in its audits. At the same time, the IRS stresses "soft" taxpayer contacts, alternative dispute resolution, and joint audit processes. Clearly, this is not your father's IRS.

ENFORCEMENT AND AUDIT STATISTICS

In the last few years, the IRS has been touting its gains in audit coverage and other measures of enforcement, but the statistics reveal that gains are small—or even nonexistent—compared to IRS enforcement actions from the late 1990s. Reasons for these statistics date back to 1998, when Congress passed the IRS Reform and Restructuring Act of 1998 (RRA 98). After Congressional hearings that accused the IRS of thuggery in auditing individuals and seizing their property, Congress decided it was time to rein in IRS enforcement and require that the agency be devoted to taxpayer service. The IRS enforcement budget was slashed. IRS personnel were shifted from enforcement to taxpayer service. IRS audit coverage in every major category declined, and the number of IRS liens (attachments) and seizures of taxpayer property dropped severely.

Although the new focus on taxpayer service was long overdue, the decline in enforcement reflected a naïve belief that the U.S. tax system was wholly self-enforcing. Once Congress realized it had tilted the balance too far in the other direction, it held another round of hearings that focused on abusive tax shelters and other egregious instances of tax noncompliance. Since 2002, the IRS has shifted gears.

Former IRS Commissioner Mark Everson devised a new formula for the IRS that recognized the need for both taxpayer service and enforcement of the tax laws:

Service + Enforcement = Compliance

The IRS acknowledged that tougher enforcement not only has direct benefits but also creates a greater climate of compliance. Acting IRS Commissioner Kevin Brown, taking the helm at the IRS in the spring of 2007, estimated that there was a 3:1 return on investment from audits and enforcement. The IRS enforcement budget has slowly increased in recent years, whereas taxpayer service has been maintained.

At the end of fiscal year 2006, Everson announced that enforcement revenue had increased from $47.3 billion in FY 2005 to a record $48.7 billion in FY 2006. This included $28.2 billion from collection, $17.2 billion from examinations, and $3.3 billion from document matching. Everson noted that the 2005 statistics were above-normal trends because of $2 billion collected from the abusive Son of BOSS tax shelter. Enforcement revenue has increased every year since FY 1999, when it was $32.9 billion.

STUDY QUESTIONS

1. Which occurred as a result of Congressional hearings critical of the IRS following enactment of RRA 98?

   a. IRS personnel were shifted from service functions to enforcement.

   b. The IRS enforcement budget increased to launch more taxpayer-friendly services.

   c. IRS liens increased but seizures of taxpayer property leveled off.

   d. The focus of the IRS was changed from enforcement to taxpayer service.

2. Which describes the trend for the IRS enforcement budget in recent years?

   a. Funds for enforcement have slowly increased and taxpayer service levels have remained level.

   b. Funds for enforcement have remained level as taxpayer service has increased.

   c. Enforcement funding decreased, diverting funding to taxpayer service.

   d. Both enforcement and taxpayer service funding have increased dramatically since 2001.

PRESSURE TO CLOSE AUDITS

In January 2007, the *New York Times* reported that pressure to close audits of big corporations was costing the government billions of dollars. The *Times* said that the reason for the losses was that auditors were limited to issues agreed upon at the beginning of the audit and could not pursue other issues that arose. At one hearing before Congress, then IRS Commissioner Mark Everson denied that there was any pressure to close audits prematurely. At the same time, the Large and Mid-Size Business (LMSB) Division had indicated concern with a backlog of audits and a desire to improve the "currency" of the audit process. It touted its new audit process involving a meeting between the IRS and the taxpayer to agree on contested issues.

LMSB Commissioner Deborah Nolan reiterated Everson's statements at an April 2007 conference. She expressed confidence in agents' and managers' audit decisions. "We are prepared to resolve issues with taxpayers that work in a collaborative way and are transparent with us," Nolan indicated.

Questions have been raised about whether the Limited Issue Focused Examination (LIFE) process or any other LMSB program is preventing IRS examiners from pursuing questionable corporate claims. Congress indicated it will hold hearings, but it has not yet acted.

Pressure to close audits also is being applied to examinations of small businesses. Not only has the IRS found that statistically spending more than the "average" time on an audit produces significantly diminishing returns that could be better spent on another business audit, but that records are more difficult to find on both sides when an audit takes place several years, or more, after the tax year under examination.

WAGE AND INVESTMENT INCOME DIVISION AUDITS

Audits of Individuals

The following table summarizes percentage increases in audits of individuals in 2006 as opposed to 2005 according to the taxpayers' income levels.

IRS Audits of Individuals in Fiscal Years 2005 and 2006			
2006 Income	**Audits in 2005**	**Audits in 2006**	**Increase of Audits (%)**
$1 million+	12,800	17,000	33 (approximately)
$100,000+	219,200	257,800	18
<$100,000	996,100	1.035 million	4

Audits of the wealthiest taxpayers (earnings of $1 million or more) covered 6 percent of taxpayers in this category in 2006. This is a new category for tracking enforcement. In audits of individuals with income exceeding $100,000, the overall coverage of this category amounted to 1.67 percent, a steady increase from a low point of 0.79 percent in FY 2001 but still well below the 2.74 percent rate for FY 1997. Audits of taxpayers with incomes of less than $100,000 increased by 4 percent to 1.035 million, yielding overall coverage of 0.9 percent, a steady increase from FY 2000, but a decline from the FY 1997 coverage of 1.19 percent.

Face-to-face audits of individuals increased by more than 20 percent for FY 2006, from 247,000 to 303,000. Almost 30 percent of audits were face-to-face, conducted by revenue agents, whereas 70 percent were correspondence audits. Audits of all individual returns increased 6 percent, from 1.21 million to 1.29 million returns, the highest number since FY 1998.

COMMENT

IRS Chief Counsel Don Korb commented in October 2006 that contacts with taxpayers—which he has dubbed "touches" rather than traditional audits—are key to compliance. A correspondence audit would be an IRS contact. These contacts can change, encourage, or deter various behaviors, Korb indicated.

Background of the National Research Program

The National Research Program (NRP) is a comprehensive study to measure reporting compliance of individual taxpayers. Another research study undertaken by the same NRP staff is focusing on S corporations. The NRP was inaugurated in 2002 and looked at 46,000 individual returns from 2001. Because of the intrusiveness associated with the IRS's previous Taxpayer Compliance Measurement Program (TCMP), the IRS worked to lessen the burden on taxpayers from the audits conducted as part of this new program. The TCMP was last conducted in 1988, so the IRS desperately needed updated information on taxpayer behavior and compliance.

The IRS estimated that data from the NRP would enable it to reduce no-change audits of accurate returns by at least 15,000 returns a year. The IRS said that the number of no-change audits had increased steadily from less than 21 percent in 1993 to more than 27 percent in 2000. The new data would also enable the IRS to build better compliance programs to more effectively catch tax cheating and ensure that taxpayers pay their fair share of taxes. The IRS incorporated information from the 2001 study into new discriminant formulas for selecting individual income tax returns to be audited. The results from these audits will show the IRS how effectively it has used the study data.

Following are highlights from the 2001 audit statistics:

- Face-to-face audits were conducted for 40,000 of the 46,000 returns, but unlike TCMP audits, the audits were not line-by-line. The IRS used information from third-party reporting and from other sources it could obtain without having to contact taxpayers;
- Correspondence audits numbered 2,600 of overall returns;
- Another 2,600 were no-contact audits; and
- About 1,500 returns were calibration audits in which every line was checked, without requiring line-by-line substantiation by taxpayers.

In performing the study, the IRS used a stratified random sample, dividing tax returns into such categories as wage earners, self-employed individuals, and farmers; the categories included subsamples of individuals at different income levels.

The NRP also focused on filing compliance and payment compliance. For filing compliance, the IRS estimated the individual income tax that was not timely paid that is related to returns that were not timely filed. For payment compliance, the IRS measured the percentage of individual income tax on timely filed returns that was paid timely. IRS records were used to produce these measurements.

In 2007, the IRS announced it would update the 2001 NRP study of individuals by looking at 13,000 tax returns each year, beginning with 2006 returns. Over a three-year period, this process would give the IRS a meaningful sample of 39,000 returns. By continuing the study each year, the IRS would avoid falling behind in collecting the information needed for audit selection. The study began in October 2007, and information from the 2006 study should be available by late 2008 or early 2009, considered a blazing fast turnaround of data for this type of survey.

STUDY QUESTIONS

3. For which annual income level did the **percentage** of individual taxpayers audited by the Wage and Investment Income Division increase the most in 2006?
   a. $25 million or more
   b. $1 million or more
   c. $100,000 or more
   d. Less than $100,000

4. The National Research Program compliance study has used all of the following types of audit techniques **except:**
   a. Line-by-line audits
   b. Face-to-face audits
   c. Information from the 2001 NRP study
   d. All of the above choices are being used by the NRP study

SMALL BUSINESS AND SELF-EMPLOYED DIVISION AUDITS

Unincorporated *Schedule C businesses* have only a 50 percent compliance rate, according to the latest congressionally commissioned tax gap study. Such businesses account for more than $100 billion of unpaid taxes. Not surprisingly, audit focus on these small businesses will become intense over the next several years as the IRS tries to show Congress that it is serious about collecting this large shortfall and is competent to do so.

Despite the fact that the IRS realized immediately after the tax gap report that small Schedule C businesses pose a huge compliance problem, it is hard for audit selection procedures to turn on a dime. The following table summarizes changes in audit rates for small business and self-employed taxpayers.

Comparative Audit Rates for Taxpayers Filing Schedule C			
Gross Receipts	**FY 2004 Audit Rate**	**FY 2005 Audit Rate**	**FY 2006 Audit Rate**
$100,000+	1.86 percent	3.65 percent	3.90 percent
$25,000–$99,000	1.47 percent	2.10 percent	2.10 percent
<$24,999	3.15 percent	3.68 percent	3.80 percent

Small businesses should expect much more scrutiny during the next several years.

COMMENT

Schedule C businesses have been the subject of recent presidential proposals to increase information reporting by third parties, such as credit card companies, which would be required to report payments made to unincorporated businesses. Some observers see information reporting and mandatory withholding as a more effective way to control noncompliance. Even former Commissioner Everson has admitted, "We are not going to audit our way out of the tax gap." Small business organizations, however, are up in arms over the prospects of more information reporting and withholding, arguing that such measures are costly for a business to undertake. They argue that the majority of businesses are compliant and should not be required to shoulder this additional expense.

Audits of C Corporations

Audits of C corporations leveled off from FY 2005 to FY 2006, but the percentages were well below FY 1997 levels. For small corporations (assets of less than $10 million), coverage in FY 2006 was 0.80 percent, a slight increase from the FY 2005 rate of 0.79 percent but a fraction of the 2.22 percent level for FY 1997.

Audits of Passthrough Entities

Audits of all partnerships and S corporations increased more than 20 percent. Despite this growth, the overall FY 2006 audit coverage of passthrough entities was only 0.37 percent, well off the audit coverage before RRA 98.

COMMENT

The second phase of the IRS's National Research Program is focusing on S corporations.

Broadening the Scope of the National Research Program

The NRP methodology initially undertaken to investigate patterns of noncompliance among individuals is now starting to be applied to other taxes and taxpayers. The IRS has been studying S corporation returns, looking at 5,000 returns from 2003 and 2004 and expecting to finish the study in 2008. The study will be used to redefine the tax gap estimates of individual income tax because of the flowthrough of income and expenses from S corps to their shareholders.

> **COMMENT**
>
> As time passes, patterns of noncompliance change. "Like credit scoring, the IRS wants newer models for its audit selection factors. It wants to incorporate any changes in behavior and changes in the tax law," stated Mark Mazur, IRS Director of Research, Analysis, and Statistics. With the new program, the IRS will be able to update its information more regularly, Mazur said.

TAX-EXEMPT AND GOVERNMENT ENTITIES DIVISION AUDITS

The TE/GE Division has become a "hot spot" in tax audits due to abuses recently uncovered within this area of focus. Tax-exempt entities must toe the line, following stringent rules to deserve that significant benefit. Recent audits have discovered that many entities have not been following the rules, either in form or in practice. Taxable entities that find that they are competing with tax-exempts in certain business ventures also have made it known that equity demands a high level of review of tax exempts.

Audit Stats

Audits of tax-exempt organizations increased by more than 40 percent in FY 2006, from 4,900 to 7,000, although this number was well below the pre-RRA 98 level of 10,000 audits.

The TE/GE Division comprises three units:

- Exempt Organizations;
- Government Entities, including tax-exempt bonds; and
- Employee Plans.

Exempt Organizations

After the Pension Protection Act of 2006 enacted many provisions affecting tax-exempt organizations, the IRS Exempt Organization (EO) unit indicated it would provide guidance, education, and outreach in the following areas: donor-advised funds; supporting organizations, credit counseling, the new annual postcard notification requirement for small organizations

(ones having revenues of less than $25,000), and new disclosure require-
ments for sharing information with states.

The law also imposed new requirements to curb abuses of noncash
donations concerning:

- Open space and façade easements;
- Recapture of benefits from exempt-use property that is not used for
  an exempt purpose, including penalties against anyone knowingly and
  falsely identifying property as exempt-use property;
- Contributions of fractional interests in tangible personal property; and
- Abusive tax-shelter transactions.

The IRS is also aware of continued noncompliance with the 2004 reporting
requirements for noncash contributions of more than $500 and will respond
more quickly and thoroughly when it detects noncompliance.

New Projects

The EO unit of TE/GE has been aggressive in its plans for policing certain tax
exempt activities during the upcoming year. These plans are described here.

Gaming. EO will look at activities conducted by organizations in 10 different states, noting that each state regulates and enforces charitable gaming
differently. Gaming organizations have a high level of noncompliance for
paying employment taxes, filing Form 990, and reporting unrelated business
income. EO will also test a gaming risk model by auditing 50 organizations
projected to have a high rate of noncompliance.

Employment taxes. EO will initiate a project using data from the Combined Annual Wage Reporting system administered with the Social Security
Administration to identify noncompliance. Risk-modeling will also be used
to select cases for audit.

Telephone excise tax refund. The project will include guidance, education, examples, and audits for proper filing of Form 990-T.

Community foundations. EO will conduct a compliance project of community foundations, which traditionally were small charitable trusts but
have grown significantly in number, size, and complexity. There will be
follow-up on organizations with compliance issues.

College and university UBIT (unrelated business income tax) project.

EO will develop a project to review the calculation of unrelated business
income and the allocation of income and expenses within large university
systems. The project will roll out to the field in 2008.

Critical Initiatives

EO also plans to scrutinize organizations involved in a number of issues, discussed here.

Prohibition on political activity by charities. EO will follow up to verify the compliance of organizations previously examined. Planning to contact more than 300 organizations that may have violated the rules in 2004 and 2005, the EO unit will review state information to identify potential violators for 2006. EO will continue to monitor state election databases and follow up for future violations. The IRS also began to monitor political contributions by charities to candidates and political organizations. The IRS selected 100 referrals for audit for 2006 and identified 269 cases of direct political contributions.

Credit counseling. EO will examine organizations whose response or failure to respond to compliance checks suggests noncompliance.

Executive compensation. Following publication of its report in March 2007, EO continues to work cases involving:
- Compensation of more than $250,000;
- Loans exceeding $100,000 to officers, directors, trustees, and key employees; and
- Excess benefit transactions.

Form 990 expands reporting to loans to/from highly compensated employees and disqualified persons. Pressured by Congress and the media, IRS scrutiny of abuses in this area—especially insider loans— is expected to increase.

Hospitals. EO sent 500 compliance check letters and questionnaires to tax-exempt hospitals to learn how they qualify for exempt status under the community benefit standard. After analyzing the data, the EO unit will consider examinations and additional compliance check activity. On revised Form 990, the IRS asked about community benefit, billing and collection practices, and management companies and joint ventures. The agency continues to be concerned about whether there are sufficient differences between tax-exempt and for-profit hospitals to justify exempt status.

Down-payment assistance organizations. The IRS found that so-called charities were being used to funnel down-payment assistance from sellers to buyers through circular financing arrangements. EO will conduct examinations of such organizations, issue a report, and consider further compliance measures. EO has also denied tax-exempt status to more than 50 organizations that were providing seller-financed assistance.

Donor-advised funds. EO will conduct audits and cooperate with Treasury and IRS Chief Counsel on a report for Congress. EO's concern is that the funds are used for the private benefit of donors or to avoid rules that apply to private foundations.

Abusive transactions. EO will identify and follow up on charities involved in these transactions and is designing a new form to report involvement.

Draft Form 990. EO released a redesigned draft Form 990 in June 2007. It aims to require the form for the 2008 tax year, to be filed in 2009. The revised form asks for new information in a number of areas and will provide better information to the IRS on the activities of charities and other exempt organizations. The form will require additional information about executive compensation, political activities, fundraising (including gaming), hospitals, tax-exempt bonds by or for the benefit of exempt organizations, foreign activities, and noncash charitable contributions. The last category demonstrated the IRS's concern about contributions that were overvalued on the organization's balance sheet.

Voluntary Compliance Program. EO is considering the use of a self-correction program for exempt organizations. The VCP was proposed by the IRS's Advisory Committee on Tax Exempt and Government Entities. The committee members found that many small organizations failed to file returns. This was a particular problem because an organization's exempt status is revoked if it fails to file a notice or return for three consecutive years, as enacted by the Pension Protection Act of 2006. The committee recommended that organizations be allowed to file delinquent returns for the last three years. The committee also encouraged a vigorous outreach effort by the IRS.

Bonds. The EO Compliance Area and the Tax-Exempt Bonds (TEB) office have collaborated on a joint compliance project to gather information about compliance involving tax-exempt bond proceeds used by Code Sec. 501(c)(3) exempt organizations. EO will collect the information and TEB will analyze the post-issuance compliance practices of charities. TEB may then recommend actions such as education, record retention, or audits. The concern within EO is that the federal tax exemption for interest earned on qualifying state, municipal, hospital, and community development bonds has been mischanneled to enhance the use of a charity for private benefit. Not only does this overreaching affect the developers and promoters, however; the investors in these financial instruments in extreme cases may find themselves without the benefits of tax-exempt interest and, therefore, holding instruments worth far less than their purported value.

Tax-Exempt Bonds

Identification and pursuit of abusive transactions continues to be the focus of the TEB office, a separate unit within TE/GE. TEB estimates there are $40 to 50 billion worth of abusive bond transactions outstanding.

During the coming year, TEB officials will focus on arbitrage-motivated transactions, including the use of swaps and other derivative contracts to divert rebatable arbitrage. This is TEB's highest compliance risk and enforcement focus. TEB will look at abusive transactions involving long investment periods or large investment amounts. These transactions will be given priority, and all appropriate penalties and sanctions will be applied. Many schemes have switched from the investment to the bond yield side. A growing trend centers around manipulating bond insurance and credit enhancements that go into the bond yield.

TEB will make referrals to the IRS Office of Professional Responsibility, IRS Criminal Investigation, the Securities and Exchange Commission, and other agencies regarding "abusive transactions and their promoters." The IRS will examine the liability of advisors and promoters for Code Sec. 6700 penalties. The "lack of diligence by market professionals" will also be scrutinized.

Employee Plans Enforcement

TE/GE's Employee Plans (EP) unit has these priorities for its examination program:

- Expand compliance contacts;
- Conduct more research and analysis; and
- Devote resources to focused examinations.

Research and analysis efforts, such as the National Research Program, are designed to reduce the no-change audits conducted by EP on plans that have few or no problems or issues. EP is using focused exams to narrow the scope of its exams based on a market segment's characteristics and expanding coverage of the segment. EP says it will not expand the exam beyond the initial focus if the examining agent finds "good credibility,...no surprises from the initial interview, and...the internal controls to be good." EP has used this approach since 2005.

EPCU. EP's examination program established an Employee Plans Compliance Unit (EPCU) to provide "soft" contacts with plans that may present problems or questionable items. The idea for the unit was that a telephone or mail contact would be sufficient and that a field exam would not be necessary, reducing the burden on taxpayers and saving agency resources. The EPCU resolves issues without the necessity for a full-scope examination of the books and records of the employee plan in question. As of mid-2007, the EPCU had performed more than 4,700 compliance checks, contacting nearly 4,200 taxpayers since the unit's launch in 2005.

The EPCU uses data analysis to evaluate and select projects. The EPCU initially focused on:

- Waivers and underfunding cases;
- Form 5330, Excise Taxes Related to Employee Benefit Plans; and
- Follow-up to the EPCRS (Employee Plans Compliance Resolution System), the system for correcting plan noncompliance implemented in Rev. Proc. 2006-27.

Letters were issued to plan sponsors to determine whether the funding requirement has been met for the year, including filing a completed Form 5330. Evaluations were also conducted to detect fraud on the Form 5500, prohibited transactions for 401(k) plans, party-in-interest transactions coordinated with the Department of Labor, and master and prototype plans.

Although EP does not have a general compliance program for small business retirement plans, it is investigating compliance levels among such plans, including SEPs (simplified employee pension plans), SARSEPs, and SIMPLE IRA plans.

SEPs and SARSEPs. A *salary reduction simplified employee pension plan (SARSEP)* is a simplified employee pension (SEP) plan set up before 1997 that permits contributions to be made through employee salary reductions. Under a SEP, employers make contributions to traditional individual retirement arrangements (IRAs) set up for employees.

SIMPLE IRAs. Under a *savings incentive match plan for employees (SIMPLE)* IRA plan, employees and employers make contributions to traditional individual retirement arrangements.

The EP website displays general information about small plans, the life cycle of a small retirement plan, and ways to correct plan errors. In 2006, EP issued 200,000 letters to sponsors of SIMPLE IRA plans, offering relief for certain noncompliance actions. The EPCU will conduct a follow-up on a sample of the 200,000 to verify compliance with the terms of the letter.

STUDY QUESTIONS

---

5. Which **gross receipts bracket** of Schedule C-filing taxpayers saw the greatest percentage increase in audits by SB/SE Division examiners in FY 2006?

   a. $1 million and more
   b. $100,000–$999,999
   c. $25,000–$99,000
   d. $24,999 and less

---

6. The Small Business and Self-Employed Division audit rates for small C corporations reveal that:

   a. The corporations were subject to a 2.22 percent audit level in FY 2006, up from 0.80 percent in FY 1997.

   b. Audits of C corporations for FY 2006 exceeded 1997 levels.

   c. Audit levels in 2005 were slightly less than in FY 2006.

   d. Audit rates in fiscal year 2005 were higher than either 1997 or 2006 for C corporations.

7. Which of the following is **not** a new project of the EO unit for the upcoming year?

   a. Employee Plans Compliance Unit

   b. Combined Annual Wage Reporting system data

   c. Compliance project for community foundations

   d. UBIT project for colleges and universities

LARGE AND MID-SIZE BUSINESS DIVISION AUDITS

Audits of C Corporations

The rate of audits of large C corporations leveled off, with coverage levels well below FY 1997 levels and numbers slightly below FY 2005. For large corporations, coverage was 18.6 percent in FY 2006, compared to 24.3 percent for FY 1997, and levels declined slightly, from 10,829 to 10,591 returns. Audits of the largest corporations (those having $250 million or more in assets) dropped from 4,859 to 4,289, and coverage declined from 44.1 percent to 35.3 percent.

> **COMMENT**
>
> Audits of large corporations will be less of a factor as the IRS expands its Compliance Assurance Process, which will scrutinize corporate activities before returns are filed. The IRS will also use limited focus examinations to increase coverage.

LMSB Issue Resolution Programs

The LMSB Division is particularly concerned about the lengthy audit process for a large corporation. For some taxpayers, audits take an average of five years to complete. For the most complex taxpayers, audits can take up to seven years on average.

To shorten the audit process, LMSB has devised a number of innovative programs. Some of these involve planning the audit and working more closely with the taxpayer; others involve LMSB's management of its own resources. These programs include:

- The Compliance Assurance Process (CAP);
- The Joint Audit Planning Process;
- Limited Issue Focused Examinations (LIFE);
- Industry Issue Focus (IIF);
- Prefiling Agreements (PFAs); and
- Various programs with the Office of Appeals.

> **COMMENT**
>
> Taxpayers falling into one of the other IRS divisions should not ignore audit-related developments emanating from LMSB. LMSB traditionally has been a testing ground for various programs that, if successful, subsequently work themselves into the audit procedures and culture of the other IRS divisions.

Compliance Assurance Process. The goal of CAP is to identify and resolve issues before the taxpayer files a tax return, reducing the need for exams as well as taxpayer uncertainty once the return is filed. The IRS and the taxpayer cooperate to look at key events and transactions early in the tax year and resolve uncertainties before the return's filing date. The aim of CAP is to resolve issues in a shorter time period, not to raise a greater amount of tax.

An IRS account coordinator is assigned to each taxpayer participant and determines issues that could arise, based in part on the taxpayer's audit history. The taxpayer and the account coordinator enter into a memorandum of understanding that covers objectives, disclosure to the IRS, and communication. The account coordinator reviews completed business transactions with the taxpayer. The program requires significant resources from both sides.

Agreed-on issues are entered into an issue resolution agreement, then combined into a final closing agreement. If all identified issues in the memorandum of understanding (MOU) have been resolved, the IRS will confirm in writing that it will accept the return as long as certain conditions are met. If some issues are unresolved, the IRS will confirm its acceptance of the return for the agreed-on issues. The IRS will review the return within 90 days of filing. Any unresolved issues can still be taken to Appeals.

Joint Audit Planning Process. This is a post-return filing program that also relies on extensive cooperation between the IRS and the taxpayer. It was devised by the IRS and the Tax Executives Institute. The process requires that both sides be accountable and committed to keeping the examination moving, focusing on audit efficiency to get and stay current.

The IRS and the taxpayer discuss the purpose and scope of information document requests (IDRs) and establish a timeline for requesting and producing documents.

The IRS proposes the scope of the audit but provides a draft to the taxpayer and will consider feedback. The audit team will consider Limited Issue Focused Examinations (described next) and statistical sampling. The IRS and the taxpayer can enter into materiality agreements at the outset to eliminate insignificant items. The audit team cannot add, drop, or substitute issues without the taxpayer's knowledge.

> **COMMENT**
>
> Taxpayers generally have found that the more current the years under examination and the shorter the exam cycle, the more cost effective is the audit process.

Limited Issue Focused Examinations (LIFE). By using risk analysis and materiality considerations, LIFE should help the IRS focus on fewer issues than would be examined in a traditional, full-scope examination. LIFE is most suitable when there are few significant or material identifiable issues and when the taxpayer shows a spirit of cooperation with the IRS. The IRS prefers to have a history of audits with the company but says that companies in their first audit should still be eligible for LIFE.

The IRS reviews the taxpayer's past behavior and examination results, obtains information about the taxpayer's operations, and decides on a materiality standard for adding issues to the audit. The materiality standard can vary from year-to-year and taxpayer-to-taxpayer, although thresholds for a taxpayer may cover all years under examination. New issues by the IRS and new claims by the taxpayer that are below the threshold cannot be raised. Claims above the threshold must be filed by a specified date. The thresholds do not apply to mathematical errors and accounting errors or omissions.

For the taxpayer, the LIFE process requires providing computations for agreed-on issues, filing claims by an agreed-on date, with supporting documentation, and only when the disputed liability is above the materiality threshold. The taxpayer must agree to response times for information document requests and must discuss issues as they arise. The IRS examiner for a LIFE must:

- Involve the taxpayer more in the planning process;
- Respond timely to taxpayer information; and
- Agree to use appropriate issue resolution programs.

Industry Issue Focus (IIF). LMSB unveiled the IIF approach in March 2007 as part of its overall issue management strategy. The IIF will be used to audit the most important issues—ones most prevalent across industry lines and those posing the greatest compliance challenges. The strategy is designed to respond to a changing business environment of global corporations and complex transactions and to maximize results from limited LMSB resources. LMSB expects the IIF Program also to improve the currency of audits by focusing on issues with the highest risk.

> **COMMENT**
>
> Practitioners expect the program to provide more centralized handling of issues and to promote greater consistency. The strategy appears to involve identifying an issue within a particular industry, although many issues are cross-cutting. Practitioners, however, are concerned that the strategy will slow down the audit process rather than improve its timeliness. Another concern is that additional coordination may encourage additional involvement by the IRS Chief Counsel's office.

IIF issues are identified through examinations, disclosure statements, review of Schedule M-3s, and other sources. Issues are then referred to the IRS's Compliance Strategy Council for approval. Industry directors must submit a description of the issue, legal opinions, the number of returns and taxpayers, revenue impact, IRS function impact, and the proposed strategy for the issue.

All tax shelter listed transactions are Tier I issues, as are two new categories of potentially abusive tax shelters. Tier I includes another dozen Tax Code provisions and categories of transactions, including:

- Justice Department settlements;
- Backdated stock options;
- The domestic production activities deduction;
- Foreign earnings repatriation;
- Foreign tax credit generators;
- International hybrid instruments;
- Nonqualified deferred compensation;
- The research and experimental credit; and
- Cost-sharing transfer pricing issues.

LMSB identified another dozen issues as Tier II issues, including:

- Casualty losses;
- The enhanced oil recovery credit;
- Deferral of gift card income;
- Healthcare accounting issues;
- Merchant discount fees; and
- The super completed contract method.

Tier I and Tier II issues would be assigned an *issue owner executive* who would be the focal point and ultimate decision maker for actions affecting that issue.

The IIF strategy provides for Tier III issues, but so far none has been identified. These issues would be specific to a particular industry. There would not be an issue owner executive, and line authority managers would decide the disposition of the issue.

Prefiling Agreements (PFAs)

In Rev. Proc. 2007-17, LMSB extended its PFA program through December 31, 2008. Under the program, taxpayers may request to enter into a PFA with LMSB regarding the determination of facts or the application of well-established legal principles to known facts that would otherwise be the subject of an audit. The taxpayer requests an audit of a transaction for the current year after the transaction has taken place but before the return has been filed. A PFA can also be requested for any prior taxable year for which the original return is not yet due (counting extensions) and can be applied to the same transaction for four years into the future.

Almost any issue is eligible for the program, except for transfer pricing and accounting issues. There is a $50,000 user fee to participate, assessed for each separate issue. If the IRS and the taxpayer agree on the issue(s), they will enter into a closing agreement.

The process is resource intensive and narrowly focused. Few taxpayers have applied for PFAs. Those that have are satisfied with the process. For example, in 2005 the IRS reported that 38 taxpayers applied to participate in the program and 27 entered into agreements. The average duration for each PFA increased to 360 days in 2004. However, most taxpayers indicated they were highly satisfied with the process and would recommend it to others.

STUDY QUESTIONS

8. For situations in which the taxpayer exhibits a cooperative attitude and there are few material identifiable issues, which type of examination is most suitable?

   a. Limited Issue Focused Examination
   b. Joint Audit Planning Process
   c. Prefiling Agreement
   d. Industry Issue Focus

> **9.** A downside to using Prefiling Agreements is that:
>
> **a.** The legal principles involved are ground-breaking issues that may consume more time to resolve than an alternative audit approach.
> **b.** There is a $50,000 user fee to participate.
> **c.** The PFA's focus is too broad to manage expeditiously.
> **d.** So many taxpayers have taken advantage of the program that it has experienced a substantial backlog of cases.

TAX SHELTERS

A discussion of audits and enforcement would not be complete without covering tax shelters. Shelters have been the number one audit priority of IRS upper management throughout the past three years, and abusive shelters are shaping up to hold examiners' attention for at least another two years. Although some of IRS tax shelter activity remains in the discovery stage, the IRS is now anticipating an active several years of litigation as it tries to apply maximum penalties to offenders that it has uncovered during the past five years. The IRS intends to deal harshly with taxpayers and promoters to send a clear message that any resurgence of tax shelter activity will not go unpunished.

Tax shelter audits cut across all four IRS divisions. Nevertheless, the LMSB Division administers the tax shelter reporting regulations as well as runs the general "command center" of IRS's "war against tax shelters." But although some of the most egregious abuses of tax shelters—measuring in the hundreds of millions and even billions of tax dollars—have involved large corporations, abusive arrangements used by small businesses or wealthy individuals have been no more tolerated.

Disclosure

The reporting obligation under the regulations applies to *listed* and other *reportable transactions* identified by the IRS, including:

- Confidential transactions;
- Transactions with contractual protection;
- Loss transactions; and
- Transactions involving a brief asset-holding period.

The IRS has identified more than 35 listed transactions as abusive tax shelters.

Disclosures of tax shelters are sent to the Office of Tax Shelter Analysis to determine whether a transaction is worth further investigation. The information collected through the reportable transaction provisions can help the IRS respond to transactions of interest. The sooner the IRS identifies the transaction, the more quickly it can take action against an abusive shelter. Information analyzed by the office helps the IRS address policy concerns as well as compliance concerns.

Material advisors to a tax shelter arrangement must disclose a tax shelter on Form 8918, Material Advisor Disclosure Statement, and maintain for seven years a list of investors in the tax shelter, to be provided to the IRS within 20 days upon request. The organizer of the tax shelter must apply for a registration number for the shelter on Form 8264. The list should identify:

- Any related documents;
- The amount invested; and
- Any other material advisors to the transaction.

Disclosure forms are sent to the IRS Service Center in Ogden, Utah, for scrutiny. The material advisor may also be the organizer.

> **COMMENT**
>
> An advisor who claims a privilege for withholding the list nevertheless must maintain the information.

Disclosure and list maintenance are required if the advisor provided assistance or advice regarding organizing, managing, promoting, selling, or implementing the transaction. The advisor must have made a statement regarding the tax consequences of the transaction and must have received income of $50,000 or more from an individual (or a minimum of $10,000 for a listed transaction) and $250,000 from an entity (just $25,000 for a listed transaction). The transaction must have been implemented.

Investor Reporting

Required disclosures and penalties. Investors in the shelter are required to disclose their participation in a registered tax shelter on Form 8271. Investors and material advisors must make a complete disclosure of the transaction. Penalties of $50,000 are a strong deterrent to taking shortcuts.

Transactions of interest. The IRS issued regulations in 2007 to implement changes made to the reporting rules by the American Jobs Creation Act of 2004, primarily affecting changes in the disclosure requirements for material advisors. The number of disclosures filed after the 2004 Jobs Act was 73 times the number prior to its enactment. The regulations added a new category of reportable transaction: *transactions of interest*. The IRS will identify these transactions in published guidance and, subsequently, once sufficient information has been submitted to the IRS, will take one of three actions:

- Eliminate the transaction from being reportable;
- Designate the transaction as a listed transaction; or
- Identify a new category of reportable transaction.

Final regulations for this category became applicable to transactions entered into after November 1, 2006. The IRS designated its first two transactions of interest in August 2007.

> **COMMENT**
>
> Treasury says that identifying a transaction of interest will not necessarily be a precursor to listing the transaction as an abusive tax shelter. This determination will depend on the information received after the designation.

Summons Enforcement

The IRS, represented by the Justice Department, continued a campaign of summons enforcement to obtain investor lists that tax shelter promoters, such as law and accounting firms, have claimed are privileged. Although rulings in some cases initially upheld the claimed privilege not to disclose names, decisions of more recent cases have required the firms to disclose their clients' names. The government has also been effective in pursuing John Doe summonses to obtain names and information from American Express, MasterCard, and Visa about potential overseas bank accounts used to hide funds.

International Taxation

The IRS has created a new deputy commissioner position for international taxes in the LMSB division. The IRS plans to devise a strategy document for international compliance and enforcement.

The IRS uses information exchanges with other countries to develop leads for its examiners. Information provided through the Joint International Tax Shelter Information Center (JITSIC), made up of Canada, Australia, the United States, the United Kingdom, and more recently, Japan, led to enforcement cases against abusive tax shelters domestically and in Canada. Information is also provided through the Organization for Economic Cooperation and Development (OECD), the seven-country group, and through treaties with other countries. Article 26 of the new U.S. Model Tax Treaty addresses information sharing. Tax information exchange agreements (TIEAs) provide a mechanism for the United States and a partner country to request information from one another about specific taxpayers.

The IRS had a withholding and reporting agent voluntary compliance initiative for agents required to withhold tax on payments to nonresident aliens under Code Sec. 1441. More than 400 agents filed 1,200 amended or delinquent Forms 1042 to attain compliance. The IRS reported that it is increasing its audits of withholding and reporting agents and is looking at payments of interest, dividends, royalties, and rents.

STUDY QUESTIONS

---

10. Although tax shelter audits encompass instances cited in all four IRS divisions, the _____ Division administers tax shelter reporting regulations and serves as the "command center" of the IRS prosecutions of abusive tax shelters.

   a. Wage and Investment Income
   b. Small Business and Self-Employed
   c. Large and Mid-Size Business
   d. Tax Exempt and Government Entities

11. All of the following are resources for revealing abusive international tax shelters *except:*

   a. Organization for Economic Cooperation and Development (OECD)
   b. Joint International Tax Shelter Information Center (JITSIC)
   c. Tax Information Exchange Agreements (TIEAs)
   d. All of the above are resources for the exchange of information about international tax shelter schemes

---

APPEALS

The appeals process is very much part of the audit continuum. It is in a sense a taxpayer's second shot at success in an audit. The taxpayer's hope is that the IRS examiner shows bias, ignorance of the applicable law, or failure to weigh all the facts and circumstances of the situation. The taxpayer can request an impartial look at the case—albeit by an IRS employee who, although not apt to give the taxpayer the benefit of the doubt, is obliged to give him or her a fair hearing.

When the IRS examiner and the taxpayer fail to agree on the results of the taxpayer's audit, the taxpayer has the right to have the case heard by the Appeals Office. Appeals is independent of any other IRS office and will take a fresh look at the taxpayer's case. Unlike examiners, the Appeals Office personnel can consider the hazards of litigation in weighing the IRS's position. Appeals spokespeople say that its mission is to resolve tax controversies without litigation in a fair and impartial manner that will enhance voluntary compliance and confidence in the IRS.

If the total tax liability for any year is $25,000 or less, the taxpayer can make a *small case request* by submitting a letter to the office that sent the taxpayer the IRS auditor's decision. For larger amounts, the taxpayer must prepare a formal written protest. The protest must list the auditor's proposed changes that the taxpayer disagrees with, the facts supporting the taxpayer, and the law on which the taxpayer is relying. Formal protests also are required, regardless of the dollar amount, for partnerships, S corporations, employee plans, and exempt organization cases.

The IRS states that a taxpayer should be contacted by Appeals staff within 90 days after filing a protest. A taxpayer who is not contacted within the 90-day period should seek help from the exam office or from an Appeals Account Resolution Specialist in Fresno Appeals who may be reached at (559) 456-5931. Once the case lands in Appeals, the IRS says that it can take 90 days to a year to resolve the case.

STUDY QUESTIONS

12. A major difference between the case examiner and the Appeals Office representative is that:

    a. The case examiner is authorized to grant an offer in compromise to close a case.

    b. The Appeals Office staffperson can consider the hazards of litigation in deciding whether to pursue the case.

    c. The Appeals Office staffperson is more interested in bringing the taxpayer into compliance, whereas the examiner is charged with resolving tax controversies without litigation.

    d. The tax examiner acts to enhance voluntary compliance and confidence in the IRS, whereas the Appeals Office representative focuses on closing a case with maximum remittance.

13. A representative of the Appeals Office is charged with contacting the taxpayer within _____ after he or she files a protest.

    a. 30 days
    b. 60 days
    c. 90 days
    d. 120 days

ALTERNATIVE DISPUTE RESOLUTION (ADR) PROGRAMS

The IRS has devised several programs in an attempt to speed up the examination and appeals process and to resolve issues at earlier stages, thus reducing the overall time that the IRS has the case. These ADR programs include:

- Fast Track Settlement;
- Fast Track Mediation;
- Early Referral;

- Mediation;
- Tax-Exempt Bond Mediation; and
- Binding Arbitration.

All are optional programs and do not eliminate a taxpayer's right to a hearing before Appeals or a conference with an examination manager. Most of these programs are popular and successful at shortening the length of time that the IRS has a taxpayer's issues under consideration. The exception is Binding Arbitration, which very few taxpayers are willing to try.

Fast Track Settlement (FTS)

Large and Mid-Size Business Division. The Fast Track Settlement program gives taxpayers managed by the Large and Mid-Size Business Division an opportunity to resolve issues before they are formally referred to Appeals. The IRS says this program has shortened the combined audit-appeals process by two years. Fast Track Settlement is available for factual and legal issues, and all cases under LMSB's jurisdiction, including listed transactions and appeals coordinated issues (ACI). An ACI is an issue of IRS-wide impact that requires coordination by Appeals to ensure uniformity and consistency nationwide among within Appeals. An Appeals officer must get the approval of the ACI coordinator before finalizing a settlement.

The IRS must determine that the issue(s) being referred can be resolved within 120 days. The Appeals Officer serves as a neutral mediator to work with the parties or to recommend the officer's own analysis of the issue. The taxpayer may withdraw from the mediation, and the IRS may terminate the process if the parties are not making meaningful progress.

The process takes place after the IRS issues a notice of proposed adjustment but before the IRS issues a 30-day letter, which would give the taxpayer the right to take the case to Appeals. FTS provides Appeals resources while the case is still with LMSB compliance. Either the taxpayer or LMSB may propose the case for Fast Track Settlement. Information on the program is set out in Rev. Proc. 2003-40.

Small Business/Self-Employed Division. The IRS has begun a pilot program to offer FTS to taxpayers under the authority of the SB/SE Division. The pilot was introduced for six months in Chicago, St. Paul, and Houston. After the pilot program, SB/SE expanded the program nationwide. The pilot program was described in Announcement 2006-61.

Fast Track Mediation (FTM)

FTM, also offered to SB/SE taxpayers, resolves most issues within 40 days. It addresses issues ranging from an examination, offers in compromise, and trust fund recovery penalties, to other collection actions. The case stays within the SB/SE Division. An Appeals or settlement officer trained in mediation works with the parties to resolve the case. The process is described in Rev. Proc. 2003-41. FTM will not take on issues that have no legal precedent or when the courts disagree.

Early Referral

For a case under audit, a taxpayer can request Early Referral from Compliance to Appeals of one or more developed, unagreed upon issues, at the same time that other issues continue to be addressed in the audit. The IRS says that the early resolution of a key issue may facilitate agreement on other issues in the case. Early Referral can also be requested for employment tax, employee plans, exempt organizations, and involuntary changes of accounting method. Regular Appeals procedures apply to the issue referred to Appeals. The process is described in Rev. Proc. 99-28.

Mediation

Mediation is an extension of the appeals process. If the parties have not come to an agreement in Appeals, the taxpayer may request mediation. Mediators come from the Appeals Office; a non-IRS comediator can be used at the taxpayer's expense. Mediation is available for both factual issues, such as valuation, and legal issues. It may also be available after an unsuccessful attempt to enter into a closing agreement. The procedures for mediation are described in Rev. Proc. 2002-44.

Tax-Exempt Bond Mediation

The TEB Mediation Dispute Resolution Program is an optional program that uses Appeals officers, trained in mediation and having a bonds background, to resolve factual disputes between bond issuers and the IRS on cases under examination. The bond issuers may bring in a non-IRS comediator at their own expense. The service is available after the IRS advises the issuer of its proposed adverse finding, and the issuer provides a written response, but before the IRS sends out a proposed adverse determination letter. There must be a limited number of unagreed upon issues, and factual issues must be fully developed. The process is designed to be completed within 60 days. TEB mediation is not available for legal issues that have no precedent.

If agreement is reached on any issue, TEB will use traditional issue or case-closing methods, including closing agreements and no-change letters. Any issue that is not resolved may be addressed through the traditional appeals process. Either party may withdraw from the mediation; the IRS mediator may suspend the process if there is no meaningful progress.

Binding Arbitration

Although most of these programs have accomplished their goals, the Binding Arbitration program has not been a success. Taxpayers may request arbitration for factual issues being considered by Appeals. The parties may jointly request binding arbitration and sign a model arbitration agreement to guide the process. The program does not address legal issues, Appeals-coordinated issues, and certain collection issues. The program is described in Announcements 2000-4 and 2002-60.

STUDY QUESTIONS

14. Alternative Dispute Resolution programs are:

   a. Unpopular because they rule out the taxpayer's right to an Appeals hearing

   b. Largely unsuccessful in bringing wayward taxpayers into compliance

   c. Largely unsuccessful except for the popular Binding Arbitration program

   d. Helpful in shortening the length of IRS consideration of a taxpayer's issues

15. Mediators used in the Mediation process under Appeals are:

   a. Members of the Appeals staff, although a taxpayer can use a non-IRS comediator at personal expense

   b. Court appointed in the most complex audit cases

   c. Available for legal issues but not factual issues

   d. None of the above

CONCLUSION

The IRS is pursuing enforcement on a number of fronts. Every taxpayer, whether large or small, business, personal, or tax-exempt, is under IRS scrutiny. The sizable tax gap will keep the IRS's attention focused on enforcement matters. The IRS seeks to apply the tax law fairly. No group of taxpayers should have a free ride; no group should be persecuted. Enforcement methods should be applied appropriately to the taxpayer's level of noncompliance. In some cases, this means programs to improve cooperation with taxpayers under audit, settle disputes, and stretch the reach of limited IRS resources. At the same time, the IRS continues to provide greater taxpayer service. This includes new programs to help taxpayers understand their obligations. The IRS will continue to implement service and enforcement programs to improve taxpayer compliance.

MODULE 3 — CHAPTER 8

Major Tax Law Developments in 2007

This chapter discusses the top tax news developments of 2007. As in past years, tax news was dominated by major legislation passed by Congress. After months of political wrangling, Congress passed The Small Business and Work Opportunity Tax Act of 2007, a significant piece of legislation that targets nearly $5 billion in tax incentives principally to small businesses. However, 2007 also saw the IRS and Treasury Department issue a wave of important guidance and the courts hand down decisions significantly affecting tax law. The 2007 rulings, guidance, and decisions from the IRS, as well as the decisions from the courts significantly affected all types of taxpayers—individuals, businesses, tax-exempt organizations, and self-employed individuals.

LEARNING OBJECTIVES

Upon completion of this chapter you will be able to:

- Describe important tax incentives created by the Small Business and Work Opportunity Tax Act of 2007;
- Identify how the significant tax law developments of 2007 affect individuals, businesses, and tax-exempt organizations; and
- Discuss the important cases decided against the IRS in 2007 and how the courts' decisions might affect the future tax planning and compliance of individuals and businesses.

INTRODUCTION

The year 2007 turned out to be an unusually active year for tax law developments. The Small Business and Work Opportunity Tax Act of 2007 is an obvious choice for any top 10 list of 2007 tax developments and is covered first in this chapter because of its importance. Much more, however, also happened in the federal tax world. Many notable, even groundbreaking, tax developments for 2007 came not out of Congress, but rather originated at the IRS and the Treasury Department or ended with later resolution in the courts. Many of 2007's notable tax developments resulted from the IRS and Treasury's interpretation of recent tax legislation. Others were the result of tremendous political pressure exerted on the IRS and Congress to stop tax cheats from avoiding their fair share of taxes. Still other notable 2007 developments have an eclectic aspect, arising out of an unexpected judicial opinion or industry issue.

With that broad view in mind—and remembering that for any particular client the development most important to him or her is the one that addresses that client's particular issues—following is the list of the Top 10 Federal Tax Developments of 2007:

1. 2007 Small Business Tax Act;
2. PPA guidance;
3. IRS enforcement and the tax gap;
4. Tax shelters: IRS tax shelters: cases;
5. New Form 990;
6. E-Filing;
7. Roth 401(k)s;
8. Code Sec. 199 deduction;
9. Advisory fees; and
10. Major IRS court losses in 2007.

TOP DEVELOPMENT #1:
THE 2007 SMALL BUSINESS TAX ACT

The most significant piece of tax legislation passed in 2007 came relatively early in the legislative year. By May 25, 2007, Congress had passed and President Bush had signed into law the Small Business and Work Opportunity Tax Act of 2007 (2007 Small Business Tax Act). The 2007 Small Business Tax Act targeted nearly $5 billion in tax incentives principally to small businesses and primarily to counterbalance the cost to such businesses of an increase in the federal minimum wage. But some larger businesses also benefited, as did businesses affected by Hurricane Katrina. In addition, the final bill included an important package of S corporation reforms.

Unfortunately, the 2007 Small Business Tax Act was not a one-sided tax giveaway. Revenue raising provisions totaling nearly $5 billion in the same bill foretell more taxes for certain taxpayers (and penalties for tax practitioners in some cases). One such provision—an expansion of the kiddie tax to apply to children who are under age 19 or who are full-time students up to age 24—will potentially affect millions of families. Another provision—tougher return preparer penalties—placed tax practitioners themselves in the cross-hairs of future IRS enforcement efforts.

Small Business Tax Incentives

The small business tax incentives are designed to help businesses absorb the cost of complying with the increase in the federal minimum wage passed under the Fair Minimum Wage Act of 2007. The new law gradually raises the minimum wage to $7.25 during a period of two years. Highlights of the small business tax incentives include:

- An extended and enhanced small business Code Sec. 179 expensing;
- A FICA tip credit calculation that ignores the new hike in the minimum wage; and
- An extended and enhanced work opportunity tax credit.

Small Business Expensing

Almost every new tax law passed during the last several years has tweaked small business expensing under Code Sec. 179, and the 2007 Small Business Tax Act was no exception. The dollar and investment limitations for expensing were increased retroactively to January 1, 2007, and were extended through 2010.

Because of the extension of enhanced Section 179 expensing, taxpayers now have more certainty. The significantly more generous tax break is not only extended through 2010, it is also indexed for inflation. If Congress had not acted, the dollar limitation would have plummeted to $25,000 and the investment limitation to $200,000 after 2009. But because the deduction is completely phased out under the new levels for qualifying purchases exceeding $625,000, the deduction continues to be confined generally to the relatively small business.

Dollar limitation. Under the new law, the base $100,000 limit ($112,000 as indexed for inflation for 2007) is increased to $125,000 for tax years beginning in 2007 through 2010.

Investment limitation. The maximum deduction is phased out by the amount by which all qualifying property placed in service during the tax year exceeds the investment limitation. The investment limitation for property placed in service in tax years beginning in 2007 was formerly $450,000, as indexed for inflation. The new law retroactively raises the investment limitation to $500,000 for tax years beginning in 2007 through 2010. The $500,000 amount is indexed for inflation in tax years beginning after 2007 and before 2011.

STUDY QUESTIONS

1. The federal minimum wage is being raised during a period of _____ to _____ per hour.
   a. One year; $6.25
   b. One year; $6.75
   c. Two years; $7.25
   d. Three years; $7.55

> **2.** Which of the following is *not* a change to small business expensing made by the 2007 Small Business Tax Act?
>   **a.** The tax break is indexed for inflation.
>   **b.** The dollar and investment limitations were extended through 2010.
>   **c.** The deduction is phased out entirely for qualifying business purchases exceeding $625,000.
>   **d.** All of the above are changes made by the Act.

FICA Tip Credit

Under the 2007 Small Business Tax Act, the FICA tip credit (also known as the Sec. 45B credit) will continue to be based on the old minimum wage of $5.15 per hour, rather than the new minimum wage, which will reach $7.25 at the end of the next two years. As a result, even though the minimum wage has increased, the amount of the tip credit applicable to the food and beverage industry will not be reduced. Alternative minimum tax (AMT) relief is also included for these employers. The provisions apply with respect to tips received for services performed after December 31, 2006.

Work Opportunity Tax Credit

The 2007 Small Business Tax Act extends the work opportunity tax credit (WOTC) through August 31, 2011. It had been set to expire for employees hired after December 31, 2007. The new law also broadens the scope of the credit. The expanded WOTC is effective starting May 26, 2007.

The WOTC provisions are in large part companions to the portion of the larger bill that raises the minimum wage. They help employers hire entry-level workers at the new minimum wage. The credit encourages employers to hire individuals from various economically challenged populations and receive a tax credit based on part of their first two years' wages.

The 2007 Small Business Tax Act also expands one of the groups targeted for the credit: the veterans' community. The new law adds to the group veterans with service-connected disabilities who have been unemployed for six months or more during a one-year period ending on the hire date (the six months do not have to be consecutive) and are hired within one year after having been discharged from the military or released from active duty. Additionally, the new law raises the qualified wage threshold for the expanded veterans' groups (from $6,000 to $12,000). The high-risk youth and vocational rehabilitation referral targeted groups have also been expanded.

Family Business Tax Simplification

Under the 2007 Small Business Tax Act, spouses who jointly operate an unincorporated business and who file a joint return can elect not to be treated as a partnership for federal tax purposes. This treatment is available for tax years beginning after December 31, 2006. The purpose of this provision is to help ensure that when a married couple jointly owns and participates in a small business the spouses both can get credit for paying Social Security and Medicare taxes.

Each spouse may now take into account his or her share of income, gain, loss, and other items as a sole proprietor. They do not have to file a partnership return (Form 1065) and report two Schedule K-1s. Instead, spouses will each report their share of income on Form 1040, Schedule C.

The husband and wife can be the only members of the joint venture. If there are other individuals in the enterprise, the provision does not apply. Additionally, both spouses must materially participate in the business.

S Corporations

The 2007 Small Business Tax Act includes a package of S corp reforms. The changes impact the treatment of passive investment income, partial sale of qualified subchapter S subsidiaries (QSubs), interest deduction by electing small business trusts (ESBT), reduction of earnings and profits (E&P), and banks operating as S corps.

The new S corp provisions are designed to make it easier for small businesses to retain S corp status. In two cases—ESBT interest and E&P reduction—they also encourage use of the S corp business entity by effectively reducing the taxes owed by shareholders.

Passive investment income. The passive investment income test has long been a trap for S corps that convert from C corp status. The 2007 Small Business Tax Act eliminates some of that worry and does an about-face by no longer treating capital gain from the sale or exchange of stock or securities as an item of passive investment income.

Partial sale of QSubs. A qualified subchapter S corporation is a wholly owned subsidiary that an S corp elects to treat as a *QSub*. Under the 2007 Small Business Tax Act, a sale of QSub stock that terminates the QSub election and creates a deemed new corporation is now treated as a sale of an undivided interest in the assets of the QSub. This treatment eliminates the danger of an avalanche of gain being recognized by a sale of only a partial, but substantial (that is, more than 20 percent), interest in the subsidiary.

ESBT interest. The 2007 Small Business Tax Act allows an electing small business trust (ESBT) to deduct interest paid on money borrowed to acquire S corp stock. Although Treasury regulations allocated the interest to the S corporation portion of the ESBT, they did not allow a deduction.

Leveraging S corp ownership in an ESBT becomes economically more feasible under the new law because the leveraged interest is now deductible against income otherwise taxed at the 35 percent rate.

E&P reduction. The new law allows a corporation that was an S corp before 1983, but was not an S corp for its first tax year that began after December 31, 1996, to eliminate its pre-1983 earnings and profits (E&P) from the corporation's accumulated E&P balance. This benefit had previously been available only to a corporation that was an S corp for its first taxable year after 1996. The result is that S corps to which this new provision applies may be able to reduce the amount of distributions treated as taxable dividends.

Banks as S corps. The 2007 Small Business Tax Act eliminates the treatment of restricted bank director stock as outstanding stock that threatened S corp status under the single-class-of-stock rule. It also alters the treatment of accounting adjustments caused by a bank changing its method of accounting.

STUDY QUESTIONS

3. The intent of the work opportunity tax credit changes made by the 2007 Small Business Tax Act is to:
   a. Phase in the increases to the minimum wage during 2008 and 2009 for new hires with increases in tax credit offsets
   b. Encourage hiring individuals from economically challenged populations with employer tax credits based on their first two years of pay
   c. Create rebates to employers hiring workers from economically challenged populations during 2007 and 2008
   d. Supplement employee's base wages through tax refunds if they are hired at the existing $5.15 per hour minimum wage.

4. The purpose of the family business tax simplification feature of the 2007 Small Business Tax Act is to:
   a. Encourage formation of family limited partnerships by spouses
   b. Enable each spouse working in an unincorporated business to get credit for Medicare and Social Security payments
   c. Allow couples to include other family members to participate in their unincorporated business without filing and partnership returns Schedule K-1s
   d. All of the above are effects of the Act

Katrina Recovery Tax Incentives

The 2007 Small Business Tax Act extends and enhances some of the tax incentives in the Gulf Opportunity Zone Act of 2005 and Katrina Emergency Tax Relief Act of 2005. These include the extension of special expensing for qualified property, an enhanced low-income housing credit, and flexible tax-exempt bond financing rules.

Revenue Raisers

Not all provisions in the 2007 Small Business Tax Act are pro-taxpayer. In fact, half of them are not. Some of the revenue raisers will hit a lot of taxpayers in their wallets. The measures are expected to raise almost $5 billion throughout 10 years, making the new law fully offset.

Major "Kiddie Tax" Changes

Older "kiddies" subject to the tax. The 2007 Small Business Tax Act has extended the reach of the "kiddie tax" by raising the age limit to include:

- All children younger than age 19 (previously under age 18); and
- Students younger than age 24.

Both changes are effective for tax years beginning after May 25, 2007—i.e., January 1, 2008 for most calendar-year individuals.

The actual computation of the kiddie tax remains the same. The net unearned income of the child (for 2007, generally unearned income of more than $1,700 ($1,800 for 2008)) is taxed at the parents' marginal tax rates, if their rates are higher than the child's tax rates.

Good news/bad news. The effective date for the new kiddie tax provision offers both good news and bad news. For calendar year taxpayers, the higher age limit starts in 2008. The last hike in the kiddie tax, from age 14 through age 17, in TIPRA '06 was made retroactive to the beginning of 2006. This time, the change is not retroactive and was not effective immediately, making tax planning for the remainder of 2007 critical. Parents have the option to sell appreciated assets quickly in 2007, while the old rule is still in effect.

The new age limit for the kiddie tax generally tracks the age test for a *qualifying child* under the uniform definition of *child* first put into place by the Working Families Tax Relief Act of 2004.

If the earned income of a student older than age 17 exceeds half of the student's support, the kiddie tax no longer applies. Scholarships are not counted in the support test for this purpose.

Interest and Penalty Suspension

The 2007 Small Business Tax Act doubles the period before which accrual of interest and certain penalties are suspended, from 18 months to 36 months, after the filing of a tax return if the IRS has not sent the taxpayer a notice specifically stating the liability and the basis for the liability. The 36-month period is effective for IRS notices issued after November 25, 2007. As has been the case since 1998, the suspension is available only for individuals and applies only to income taxes.

Other Revenue Raisers

Other significant "revenue raisers" that constitute the remainder of the $5 billion that the IRS plans to collect from the 2007 Small Business Tax Act include those covered here.

New penalty for erroneous refund claims. This penalty plugs a loophole used by some taxpayers who overwithhold and claim credits that technically might be sheltered from accuracy-related penalties. A person who files a claim for a refund or credit for income tax for an excess amount will be subject to a penalty equal to 20 percent of the excess amount claimed. The penalty does not apply to earned income credit claims (which have their own set of rules) or the claims for refund or credit already subject to accuracy-related or fraud penalties.

Employment tax levies. The 2007 Small Business Tax Act excludes certain employment tax levies from collection due process (CDP) hearings. Congress had suspected that some employers use the prelevy CDP hearing to delay or prevent collection. Under the new law, the IRS now may deny a prelevy CDP hearing for employment taxes anytime when a previous CDP hearing request has been made for unpaid employment taxes arising in the two-year period before the beginning of the tax period for which the more recent employment tax levy is served.

Bounced check fees. The new law raises the IRS bad check fee to $25 for filers with insufficient checking account funds to cover payments. This amount applies to checks and money orders of $1,250 or less. The minimum fees had been $15 on amounts of $750 or less. The penalty is 2 percent for amounts exceeding $1,250.

Permanent user fees. The 2007 Small Business Tax Act makes permanent the IRS's authority to charge user fees related to requests for letter rulings, determination letters, opinion letters, or other similar rulings or determinations. The IRS's authority to charge user fees was originally granted by the Revenue Act of 1987 and has been extended since.

Corporate estimated tax. The 2007 Small Business Tax Act increases the corporate estimated tax payments for corporations having assets of at least $1 billion that will be due in July, August, and September 2012 from 106.25 to 114.25 percent of the payment otherwise due, with the next payment being reduced accordingly. This budgeting "wizardry" was designed to increase revenues and keep the tax cuts offset by accelerating tax payments.

New Reporting Standards for Preparers and Practitioners

One of the more controversial developments of 2007 affecting many tax professionals involved new tax return preparer standards and increased penalties that were introduced as part of the 2007 Small Business Tax Act. Predictions are that the imposition of the new standards and increased penalties will trigger a flood of disclosures for routine tax return positions by cautious practitioners who must remain obedient to these rules while protecting their clients' interests.

The 2007 Small Business Tax Act made several important changes to the reporting standards of tax return preparers. The 2007 Small Business Tax Act raised the return preparer reporting standard under Code Sec. 6994 for undisclosed, nontax-avoidance items from the "realistic possibility of success" to the "more-likely-than-not" standard. *More likely than not* is generally understood to mean that the position has a greater than 50 percent likelihood of being sustained on the position's merits, whereas the old realistic possibility of success standard was understood to mean a one-in-three likelihood of success. For disclosed positions, the 2007 Small Business Tax Act also raised the bar, by replacing the nonfrivolous standard with the requirement that there be a reasonable basis for the tax treatment of the position.

The 2007 Small Business Tax Act also expanded the scope of the penalty provisions of Code Sec. 6694, which had applied only to income tax return preparers, to cover all return preparers. Now, the return preparer penalties apply to all types of returns, including income tax, information, and employment tax returns, among others. Congress also significantly raised the penalties under Code Sec. 6694(a) for an "unrealistic position" from $250 to the greater of $1,000, or 50 percent of the income derived or to be derived by the preparer. The penalty for willful or reckless conduct in Code Sec. 6694(b) also increased, from $1,000 to the greater of $5,000, or 50 percent of the income derived or to be derived by the preparer.

The new return preparer standards also raised concerns during 2007 in other ways. Most notably, the American Institute of Certified Public Accountants (AICPA), National Association of Enrolled Agents (NAEA), and other tax professionals urged Congress to equalize the return reporting standards for preparers with the lower standards currently applicable to self-preparers. With no quick resolution in sight, the battle may continue well into 2008.

TOP DEVELOPMENT #2: PPA GUIDANCE

The IRS was busy—perhaps even overwhelmed—issuing a flood of guidance in 2007 under the Pension Protection Act of 2006 (PPA). Issues that required guidance, because they were left by Congress for the Treasury and the IRS to fill in, included those addressing retirement savings held in IRAs, 401(k)s, defined benefit plans, and Code Sec. 409A nonqualified deferred compensation plans, among other areas. This "first round of guidance" issued under the PPA in 2007 (yes, more needs to be done) also covered the following:

Distributions from IRAs to charitable organizations;

- Rollovers for nonspouse beneficiaries under Code Sec. 402(c)(11);
- Interest rates for defined benefit limits;
- Hardship distributions from certain employee benefit plans, including 401(k) plans and governmental employee 403(b) tax-sheltered annuities;
- Vesting of nonelective contributions; and
- Distributions for public safety officers.

Perhaps the most anticipated set of guidance released in 2007 involved regulations issued on nonqualified deferred compensation under Code Sec. 409A. The guidance (T.D. 9231) released under Code Sec. 409A clarified and finally liberalized rules (the best it could do so, that is, considering a fairly strict Internal Revenue Code) for deferral elections, timing of payouts, valuation, and plan documents, among other areas. Although nonqualified deferred compensation that is included under the new rules was defined broadly by Congress in Code Sec. 409A, its reach did not hit home and surprise many businesses and employees until this 2007 set of guidance was issued. The looming effective date for these new rules—January 1, 2008—also came as a shock to many taxpayers despite the fact that it represented a one-year postponement by the IRS of the original rules. In September the IRS gave these taxpayers a one-year reprieve, to January 1, 2009, to bring all plan documents up to date. However, no extension of the deadline for operational compliance has been made. For those who blunder into being operationally noncompliant, however, the IRS is offering a voluntary compliance program under which defects can be remedied, if compliance is then made retroactive to January 1, 2008.

PPA guidance issued in 2007 also explained changes to the limits on deductible pension contributions (T.D. 9319). The IRS also issued long-awaited phased retirement regulations (T.D. 9325), which permit in-service distributions (*partial retirements*) and include safe harbors and variable effective dates depending on the type of plan. The IRS also unveiled comprehensive final rules (T.D. 9319) on Code Sec. 415 limits on contributions and benefits under qualified retirement plans. The regulations apply to benefits provided by qualified defined plans and to contributions and additions to qualified defined contribution plans.

Finally, the IRS and Treasury Department released regulations (NPRM REG-113891-07) to follow through on PPA-designated rules to curb the payment of benefits by underfunded defined benefit pension plans unless the troubled plans increase funding to meet required levels. These regulations also introduced a comprehensive set of guidance (the second in an anticipated series) and transitional rules regarding the use by underfunded defined benefit plans of two types of credit balances established under Code Sec. 430(f):

- Prefunding balances; and
- Funding standard carryover balances, which consist of employer contributions that exceed the required minimum contribution for a plan year.

The regulations provide that the sponsor of an underfunded defined benefit plan may use these balances to offset its minimum contribution requirements in later years.

STUDY QUESTIONS

> **5.** The 2007 Small Business Tax Act extended and enhanced tax incentives enacted in the Gulf Opportunity Zone Act of 2005 but terminated those in the Katrina Emergency Tax Relief Act of 2005. **_True or False?_**
>
> **6.** All of the following are revenue raisers in the 2007 Small Business Tax Act intended to compensate for all of the tax reductions in the Act **except:**
>
> **a.** Increased estimated tax payments of individuals, which must equal 95 percent of the actual year's tax liability
>
> **b.** Doubled length of time before accrual of interest and penalties are suspended for income tax liabilities
>
> **c.** Increased bounced check fees from $15 to $25 for bad checks submitted to the IRS
>
> **d.** All of the above are part of the Act's revenue-raising provisions

TOP DEVELOPMENT #3:
IRS ENFORCEMENT AND THE TAX GAP

In 2007, the IRS increased its commitment to reducing the *tax gap*—the difference between what taxpayers owe and what they actually pay—by enhancing compliance initiatives and revamping enforcement activities and audit processes. The tax gap is estimated at $345 billion.

In part, the IRS is focusing on enforcement out of organizational self-preservation. Many congressional leaders have expressed outrage at the size of the shortfall due to lack of enforcement. During the past year, they have directly threatened IRS leadership with solutions ranging from a draconian management shakeup to entirely eliminating the income tax in favor of a more direct, value-added tax or other system.

Existing and Future NRP Studies of the Tax Gap

Initial tax gap findings originated from the IRS's three-year National Research Program (NRP) study, the compliance study of individual taxpayers that the IRS uses to select returns for audit on an annual basis. As part of its continuing effort to understand the tax gap and compliance issues, in October 2007, the IRS began a new NRP study, which will examine meticulously about 13,000 individual income tax returns from the 2006 tax year. As this special audit program begins, however, the IRS also has plans to increase the number and the rate of its regular audits for both individuals and businesses.

Industry Issue Focus Business Audit Strategy

The IRS Large and Mid-Sized Business Division (LMSB) also announced a new audit strategy, known as the Industry Issue Focus (IIF), intended to concentrate on high-risk tax issues. Under the IIF approach, compliance issues are identified through field examinations, Schedule M-3 reviews, and other sources. The issues are then prioritized, or tiered, based on their prevalence across industry lines and the level of compliance risk they represent:

- Tier I issues are of high strategic importance to the LMSB and significantly affect one or more industries; and
- Tier II issues are areas of potentially high noncompliance and/or significant compliance risk to the LMSB or an industry.

Revision of Offer-in-Compromise Program

In March 2007 the IRS released a revised offer-in-compromise (OIC) application package, Form 656, with some key changes for taxpayers (IR-2007-50, FS-2007-16). Form 656 was principally revised to reflect procedural changes to the OIC program by the Tax Increase Prevention and Reconciliation Act of 2005 (TIPRA). The form is designed as both an OIC application and a guide for taxpayers to determine their eligibility for an OIC. To the consternation of many taxpayer advocates, however, the IRS has been sticking to a policy of granting offers-in-compromise only when there is clear doubt about collectability or doubt as to the IRS's legal position in a dispute. The IRS will not use the OIC program to "make deals" in order to reduce its caseload or reduce the tax gap. The IRS continues to maintain that Congress would need to change the law for the Service to do so. Although some bills have been introduced to liberalize the OIC program, none has yet been put to a vote.

Issuance of Temporary Regs for Installment Agreements

The IRS also created new temporary rules governing installment agreements, from their submission to acceptance or rejection, including appeals of rejections. The new proposed rules reflect longstanding IRS administrative practices and incorporate important legislative changes made by the IRS Restructuring and Reform Act 1998, American Jobs Creation Act of 2004, Taxpayer Bill of Rights II, and TIPRA. Those new rules, although "temporary" in the sense they are subject to change, do signal a willingness on the part of the IRS to help taxpayers work out a reasonable payment plan. But, again, the IRS continues to refuse to reduce the amount owed as part of the installment agreement process.

STUDY QUESTION

---

7. Tier I of the Industry Issue Focus program concentrates on:
  a. Areas of potentially high noncompliance with LMSB rules
  b. Areas of significant compliance risk to an industry
  c. Issues of high strategic importance to the LMSB that affect one or more industries
  d. None of the above is the focus of the IIF program

TOP DEVELOPMENT #4: TAX SHELTERS

IRS Actions

The IRS stepped up its campaign against abusive tax shelter transactions in 2007. After remaining stagnant for more than two years, the IRS's roster of *listed transactions* welcomed "loss importation transactions" in 2007. A *loss importation transaction* is essentially a transaction in which a U.S. taxpayer uses offsetting positions with respect to foreign currency or other property for the purpose of importing a loss, but not the corresponding gain, in determining U.S. taxable income.

With this addition, there are now 32 listed transactions. The IRS also designated two types of transactions as its first *transactions of interest (TOI)* since the category was created, thereby subjecting these transactions to the strict disclosure requirements and penalty provisions of Code Secs. 6111 and 6112. The first TOI, designated by Notice 2007-72, involves the manipulation of charitable deduction valuations of real property subject to a long-term lease. The second TOI, designated in Notice 2007-73, involves transactions that manipulate grantor trusts to reduce tax liabilities.

The IRS also established the exclusive procedures for requesting rescission of tax shelter disclosure penalties on tax advisors who fail to file informational returns and taxpayers who fail to disclose reportable transactions. In Rev. Proc. 2007-21, the IRS fixed strict ground rules for its staff to follow when considering requests for abatement or rescission of penalties. A rescission or abatement will be allowed only on reportable transactions that are not listed transactions.

The IRS's campaign against abusive tax shelters, in addition to setting up tough rules, continued to bring large amounts of revenue into government coffers. In fact, 2007 was a record year for tax shelter-generated tax revenues. It included what the IRS reported as its biggest tax shelter settlement agreement: with Merck & Company for its use of minority equity interest financing transactions. The settlement resulted in the defendant paying approximately $2.3 billion in federal tax, net interest, and penalties.

Also in the IRS's gunsights in 2007 was the participation of tax-exempt entities in the facilitation of abusive tax shelter arrangements. Regulations (IR-2007-73, NPRM REG-156779-06) limiting use of foreign tax credits outside the jurisdiction of the U.S. rules were also issued (IR-2007-143, Notice 2007-72 & 73) focusing on circumscribing the use of tax-exempt organizations within the United States, such as public charities, in accepting income that was otherwise taxable in an arrangement that then offloaded deductions or credits onto taxable participants.

In the Courts

The IRS experienced a series of major courtroom victories—and defeats— in 2007 in its battle against abusive tax shelters. IRS's aggressive pursuit of tax shelters that began in 2002 finally resulted in several high-profile cases coming to trial after pretrial maneuverings came to a halt and settlement offers were rejected. IRS's successes came early in 2007, but taxpayers had to wait until late summer for their stunning victory.

IRS victories. The IRS's successes in 2007 against tax shelter investors and promoters rested largely on the use of two theories:
- The economic substance doctrine; and
- The substance-over-form doctrine.

In *Klamath Strategic Investment Fund, LLC* (DC Tex., 2007-1 USTC ¶50,223, 472 FSupp2d 885) the IRS asserted the economic substance doctrine to defeat a Son of BOSS (an option sales strategy) style of tax scheme. The federal district court determined that, although the transaction at issue was supported by a technical reading of the relevant provisions of the Tax Code individually, taken as a whole it was a variation of the Son of BOSS tax scheme that lacked economic substance. As a result, the court denied the company $50 million in purported losses.

Nevertheless, the court rejected the government's demand for penalties, finding that the investors had obtained opinions of counsel and relied on substantial authority before making their investments. This part of the *Klamath* decision may play importantly for investors in future litigation because the court looked at the actions and circumstances of the particular investors instead of automatically imposing penalties on an abusive tax shelter investment. Moreover, in 2007, the Supreme Court declined to review two major tax shelter cases won by the IRS using the economic substance doctrine: *Dow Chemical Co.* (CA-6, 2006-1 USTC ¶50,126, 435 F3d 594, *cert. denied,* 127 S. Ct. 1251), and *Coltec Industries, Inc.* (CA-FC, 2006-2 USTC ¶50,389, 454 F3d 1340, *cert. denied,* 127 S. Ct. 1261).

In *BB&T Corporation,* DC N.C., 2007-1 USTC ¶50,130, the IRS also won big using the substance-over-form doctrine in a tax shelter case involving a lease-in, lease-out (LILO) transaction. The district court in the case disregarded the income and denied the deductions claimed by the taxpayer. The court focused on the substance of the transaction, rather than its form.

IRS defeat. In auditing a corporation for a sale-in, lease-out (SILO) tax-shelter transaction, the IRS requested to see the company tax lawyer's tax accrual workpapers for that year. *Textron Inc.* (DC R.I., 2007-2 USTC ¶50,605). The company refused and in a summons enforcement action by the IRS. The district court agreed with the company.

The work product privilege applies to materials prepared by an attorney in anticipation of litigation. It allows a lawyer to develop legal theories and strategy free from unnecessary intrusion by his or her adversaries. The privilege can be overcome by a substantial need, but opinion work product is accorded "nearly absolute" protection, the court found.

The court rejected the IRS's argument that the workpapers were not prepared for litigation but in the ordinary course of business and to satisfy various SEC and tax-return preparation requirements. Although most tax practitioners hailed the decision as major, correct, and for the right reasons, the IRS chief counsel was not among them. He continued to maintain that the documents were not work product and that the IRS would be vindicated on appeal.

Clearly, the final chapter has not yet been written on the ultimate viability and reach of the economic substance and substance-over-form doctrines that gave the IRS its 2007 victories. Nor has the final chapter been written on the viability of the work product doctrine as it relates to information on tax-shelter activities. Although decisions in 2007 provided the start of much-needed judicial resolution of these competing interests, the decisions by no means provide a conclusion.

STUDY QUESTIONS

8. In Rev. Proc. 2007-21, the IRS imposed strict ground rules for its staff that allow a rescission or abatement of tax shelter penalties only:

   a. On certain listed transactions
   b. On reportable transactions that are not listed transactions
   c. On self-reported listed transactions
   d. A rescission or abatement of penalties is not allowed for reportable transactions, including listed transactions

9. Which of the following cases brought the IRS a defeat in its campaign against abusive tax shelters?

   a. *Coltec Industries*
   b. *Klamath Strategic Investment Fund*
   c. *BB&T Corp.*
   d. *Textron, Inc.*

TOP DEVELOPMENT #5: NEW FORM 990

Tax-exempt organizations have grown exponentially during the past five years, both in number and in size. These groups have also seen an exponential growth in abuses, both in actions not staying true to their exempt purpose and in abusing their tax-exempt status to absorb taxable income from taxable entities or individuals. To stop these increasing abuses, the IRS looked in 2007 to "transparency." The IRS began insisting on raising the bar on the level at which the exempt organization should be required to reveal information on operations and cash flow to the IRS on an annual basis. The vehicle it is using to do so is a revised, next-generation version of the Form 990, Annual Return for Tax Exempt Organizations. The much-anticipated first draft of Form 990 was released in early summer 2007. The new draft form represents the first major revision of Form 990 since 1979.

The draft form consists of a one-page summary, nine-page core form for all organizations to complete, and 15 schedules for organizations that conduct particular activities. The previous Form 990 had only two schedules. However, most organizations will likely not experience a reduced filing burden. The new core form seeks information about governance, management, and financial reporting, including executive and board compensation. Several of the 15 schedules are new or have been revised. New schedules request information specific to foreign activities, hospitals, tax-exempt bonds, and noncash contributions. A form on compensation was substantially revised to gather information about additional forms of compensation, such as deferred compensation, bonuses, and incentive compensation. The IRS plans to begin use of the final version of Form 990 for 2008, to be filed in 2009.

TOP DEVELOPMENT #6: E-FILING

The IRS continued to promote e-filing in 2007, both because of its congressionally mandated goal of having 80 percent of all individual returns filed electronically by 2010 and because it is simply less expensive for the IRS to receive and process e-filed documents. In 2007, the IRS reported that a record 76 million electronically filed individual tax returns were filed in 2006, well above its target goals.

For the first time in 2007, mandatory electronic filing (e-filing) was required of midsize corporations (those with assets between $10 million and $50 million), as well as all corporations with assets more than $10 million that annually file 250 or more returns, such as Forms W-2 and 1099. Partnerships with more than 100 partners have been required to file the tax returns in electronic format since tax year 2000, and corporations with assets of more than $50 million that file 250 or more returns annually have been required to e-file since 2005.

Moreover, for the first time in 2007, individual taxpayers, whether using the regular Form 1040, Form 1040-EZ, or other iteration of short form, or Form 1040s accompanied by trade or business Schedule C, were able to file their income tax returns online. E-filing by individuals is not mandatory, but the IRS is making the process so enticing that the IRS hopes that it will never be an absolute requirement. For the 2006 tax year, the IRS reported receiving more than 68 million individual e-filed returns, representing a majority of returns for the first time during any filing season.

The IRS also made two significant additions to its Online Payment Agreement (OPA) tool in 2007:

- Individuals who have not received a balance due notice can nevertheless access OPA to establish preassessed agreements on Form 1040 liabilities; and
- Practitioners with valid authorizations can request agreements for multiple clients.

TOP DEVELOPMENT #7: ROTH 401(k)s

The Roth 401(k), born in the Economic Growth and Tax Relief Reconciliation Act of 2001 but with a delayed effective date of January 1, 2006, finally came into its own in 2007. The legislation left it up to the employer/sponsor of a 401(k) plan to decide whether to amend the plan to allow for Roth contributions. However, 2007 saw employers jumping onto the Roth bandwagon as IRS guidance made compliance more streamlined and the Roth feature itself was made permanent by the Pension Protection Act of 2006.

Final regulations on Roth 401(k) plans in 2007 addressed the taxation of distributions from a designated Roth account under Code Sec. 402A, maintained in connection with a 401(k) plan or a 403(b) tax-sheltered annuity, as well as how amounts in a designated Roth account can be rolled over, after a termination of employment, into a Roth individual retirement arrangement (IRA) maintained under Code Sec. 408A (T.D. 9324). New regulations also addressed reporting and recordkeeping requirements, as well as a safe-harbor rule that enabled employers to make midyear changes to implement a qualified Roth contribution program or insert a hardship withdrawal provision (Announcements 2007-55 and 2007-59).

STUDY QUESTIONS

10. Which of the following is **not** information reportable on the revised Form 990?

  a. Compensation of executives and members of the board of directors

  b. Governance information

  c. Additional forms of compensation

  d. All of the above are reportable

11. Which of the following developments was **not** a reason for increased employer participation in Roth 401(k) plans in 2007?

  a. Elimination of the hardship withdrawal provision formerly required for qualified plans

  b. Release of IRS guidance streamlining compliance terms

  c. Pension Protection Act provision making the Roth feature permanent

  d. All of the above were factors listed as contributing to the growing popularity of Roth 401(k) plans

TOP DEVELOPMENT #8: CODE SEC. 199 DEDUCTION

The Section 199 qualified domestic production activities deduction finally was noticed in 2007, transforming from a sleeping giant of a deduction, largely ignored for the first two years of its existence, to a useful tax reduction tool. One reason for its slow start was simply that it was new; the other was that it began as saving a relatively small amount and began to be "phased in" to significant numbers only starting in 2007. The deduction, which was added to the Tax Code by the American Jobs Creation Act of 2004, began as equal to 3 percent of the lesser of the taxpayer's taxable income or qualified production activities income. The deduction grew to 6 percent in 2007 and will rise to 9 percent after 2009.

Although the term *domestic production activities,* to describe actions that qualify for the deduction, is defined broadly, the high-tech sector was disappointed with the IRS's decision in 2007 to issue final regulations (T.D. 9317) that deny the Code Sec. 199 deduction for most online or "hosted" computer software. On the other hand, 2007 brought good news for the film industry.

Proposed reliance regulations (NPRM REG-103482-07) issued under Code Sec. 199 deduction provide major changes beneficial to the film industry in qualifying for the deduction, such as more flexible tests for film-related compensation, taxpayer participation in production, and related safe harbors.

For partners and shareholders of passthrough entities engaged in qualifying domestic production activities, 2007 saw the IRS issue Rev. Proc. 2007-24, which allows items applicable to the Code Sec. 199 deduction to be calculated at the entity level and then allocated to each partner or shareholder. The procedure describes eligibility, cost allocation methods, and more. A second important revenue procedure issued in 2007 under Code Sec. 199 (Rev. Proc. 2007-35) outlines requirements for statistical sampling for purposes of the deduction as well as the appropriateness of statistical sampling. Both are key to supporting Code Sec. 199 deductions.

TOP DEVELOPMENT #9: ADVISORY FEES

The IRS issued proposed regulations (NPRM REG-128224-06) to clarify and create a uniform, bright-line rule for determining which estate and trust expenses for portfolio advisory fees are subject to the 2-percent floor for itemized deductions under Code Sec. 67(a). The IRS's move came as a surprise in light of the Supreme Court's grant of certiorari in *W.L. Rudkin Testamentary Trust* (CA-2, 2006-2 USTC ¶50,569, 467 F3d 149), in which the Court of Appeals for the Second Circuit concluded that the fees were subject to the 2-percent floor. That holding created a split among the circuits.

The general rule under Code Sec. 67(e) provides that the adjusted gross income (AGI) of an estate or trust is computed in the same manner as for an individual, except that deductions for costs paid in connection with the administration of the estate or trust, and which would not have been incurred if the property were not held in the trust or estate, are allowed in full in determining AGI. The underlying issue is whether portfolio advisory fees come under that category of fees; that is, whether they are paid more for investment advice or rather to safeguard the trustee or executor from fiduciary liability for an inappropriate investment.

The regulations propose a *uniqueness test* for determining what expenses are subject to the 2-percent floor. The distinction would depend on whether the costs are unique to an estate or a trust; if the costs are unique, they are deductible. The regulations define *unique costs* as costs that could not be incurred by an individual in connection with property not held in a trust or an estate.

Also moving to the forefront in 2007 was the issue of whether advisory fees for individuals are deductible only as a miscellaneous itemized deduction or whether the fees can be added to the basis of shares purchased, held, or sold resulting from such advice. Reversing what had been assumed to be the IRS's previous position, the IRS chief counsel, in CCA 200721015, ruled that an annual fee paid by an investor on his or her brokerage account in lieu of commissions paid on each trade should not be considered a "carrying charge" for the account. As a result, and contrary to what has been the practice of many investors, the IRS chief counsel is taking the position that taxpayers having these *wrap accounts* may not elect to capitalize the fees under Reg. §1.266-1(b) and add the amount to the basis of their investments pro rata. Instead, the fee can only be treated as a Schedule A miscellaneous itemized deduction, which is subject to an overall 2-percent AGI floor. Although a miscellaneous itemized deduction may offset ordinary income, getting past the 2-percent AGI floor is usually difficult for those wealthy enough to find themselves in flat-fee arrangements.

STUDY QUESTIONS

12. Which industry was disappointed in 2007 by being denied the Code Sec. 199 qualified domestic production activities deduction?

   a. High-tech industries

   b. Film industry

   c. Food production

   d. Motor vehicle

13. Items eligible for the Code Sec. 199 deduction for partnerships engaging in qualifying domestic production activities are calculated at the entity level and then allocated to partners on the basis of their distributive share of income and expenses of the partnership. ***True or False?***

TOP DEVELOPMENT #10: MAJOR IRS COURT LOSSES IN 2007

The IRS wins the major portion of cases that it litigates. When it does lose, more frequently than not it is over the interpretation of facts rather than a dispute over what constitutes correct law. When the IRS does lose over an interpretation of tax law, therefore, it is usually notable. 2007 has seen the IRS's litigation track record on the whole remain about the same as in past years. But as in past years, the taxpayers have won several cases that are notable in that they will affect how other taxpayers approach certain compliance or planning challenges in the future. Those cases and their significance are summarized here.

Deductibility of Start-up Expenses: *J.A. Toth*

In a decidedly pro-taxpayer opinion, the Tax Court held in *J.A. Toth* (128 TC 1, No. 1, Dec. 56,801 (2007)) that initial operating expenses incurred by a taxpayer in connection with expenses paid for the production of income from a horse boarding and training facility were deductible business expenses under Code Sec. 212, not start-up expenditures that must be capitalized under Code Sec. 195. Code Sec. 212 provides, in part, that individuals may deduct all ordinary and necessary expenses paid or incurred for the production of income.

Start-up costs are those incurred in investigating or creating an active trade or business before the day on which the active trade or business begins. Under Code Sec. 195, a taxpayer who actually enters the investigated or self-created business can deduct up to $5,000 of start-up costs for expenses paid or incurred after October 22, 2004. The $5,000 deduction is reduced dollar-for-dollar to the extent start-up expenses exceed $50,000. Excess start-up costs are amortized over a 180-month period (15 years).

The IRS argued the taxpayer's expenditures were nondeductible start-up expenses under Code Sec. 195(a) and had to be capitalized because they were incurred in anticipation of the Code Sec. 212 activity becoming a trade or business.

The court rejected the IRS's argument. According to the court, the taxpayer's expenses were incurred from activities engaged in for profit and were fully deductible under Code Sec. 212. She had been operating her horse boarding and training activities for profit and continued to engage in the same activities through the date of trial. Once the taxpayer began her Code Sec. 212 activity, the court ruled that the deduction of ordinary and necessary expenses paid or incurred in connection with the activity is not precluded by Code Sec. 195, regardless of whether the activity is subsequently transformed into a trade or business.

Tax Accrual Workpapers Protected by Work Product Privilege: *Textron Inc.*

The IRS suffered a major defeat in August 2007 in **Textron Inc.** (DC R.I., 2007-2 USTC ¶50,605), when a District Court denied the IRS access to a corporation's tax accrual workpapers. The court held that the corporation's tax accrual workpapers were protected by the work product privilege, which protects materials prepared or gathered by an attorney in anticipation of possible litigation or preparation for trial. The documents were also protected by the tax practitioner–client privilege under Code Sec. 7525. The court determined that the documents sought contained attorney and tax practitioner advice and opinion regarding the possibility of, and chances of prevailing in, any future litigation with the IRS. Moreover, the workpapers had been prepared to ensure that the taxpayer had an adequate reserve for any potential disputes or litigation, thus bringing the documents within the work product privilege. The court did observe that the IRS had a legitimate, good-faith purpose for requesting the workpapers: to determine the taxpayer's tax liability. Nevertheless, the documents were protected.

The court also ruled that the company's disclosure of the documents to an independent auditor was not inconsistent with keeping the workpapers confidential and did not waive the work product privilege because it did not substantially increase the likelihood that the workpapers would be disclosed to a potential adversary, in this case the IRS. The IRS has vowed to appeal the case to the First Circuit Court of Appeals, as well as to maintain its policy of requesting tax accrual workpapers.

Basis Overstatement Does Not Trigger Extended Limitations Period: *Bakersfield Energy Partners*

Rebuffing the IRS, in *Bakersfield Energy Partners, LP* (128 TC No. 17, Dec. 56,966 (2007)), the Tax Court held that an overstatement of basis is not an omission of gross income triggering an extended statute of limitations. The Tax Court held that the extended limitations period under Code Sec. 6501(e)(1)(A) is limited to situations in which specific receipts or accruals of income are excluded from the computation of gross income. Although the IRS must generally assess tax within three years after a return is filed, the period of limitations on assessment is extended to six years if a substantial amount of gross income is omitted from an income tax return.

A *substantial omission* consists of omitting from gross income an amount exceeding 25 percent of the gross income shown on the tax return.

Under *Colony, Inc.* (SCt, 58-2 USTC ¶9593, 357 US 28, 78 SCt 1033), the extended limitations period applies when specific income receipts have been "left out" of the gross income computation, not when an understatement results from overstatement of reported basis. The IRS's argument that the *Colony, Inc.* holding should be limited to the sale of goods or services by a trade or business was rejected. The court ruled that when an understatement of gross income results from an overstatement of basis but gross receipts have been fully reported, the extended limitations period is not triggered. Thus, as long as gross receipts are fully accounted for and included, any basis understatement will not enable the IRS to apply an extended statute of limitations on assessment of income.

Estate Entitled to Refund of Remittance as Deposit Payment, Not Overpayment of Tax: *Huskins*

The Court of Federal Claims ruled in *J. Huskins* (FedCl, 2007-1 USTC ¶60,538, 75 FedCl 659), that the IRS was required to refund a remittance paid by an estate because the remittance was a deposit, not an overpayment of tax, and therefore was not bound to the three-year statute of limitations on claims for refunds.

Unless a taxpayer is under examination or has received a statutory notice of deficiency, remittances not specifically designated by the taxpayer as deposits are automatically treated as payments and applied against any outstanding liabilities. In this case, the taxpayer (an estate) agreed to deposit proceeds from the sale of property into an escrow account that was later transferred to the IRS to cover any estate tax liability that might be claimed. When the estate later filed a return claiming no estate tax liability, the IRS failed to honor the estate's request for a refund of the remittance it already paid. The IRS argued that the estate was required to make its claim for "overpayments" of tax within three years of making a tax liability payment and that the estate had missed the deadline by a year and one-half.

The court agreed with the taxpayer that, because the IRS never imparted any tax liability to the estate, the remittance was a deposit, not a payment of tax. Accordingly, under Rev. Proc. 84-58, a taxpayer may elect to have the tax deposit returned to them at "any time before the issuance of a revenue agent's or examiner's report." The Revenue Procedure also provides that any undesignated remittance made before any liability is proposed is treated as a deposit.

Innocent Spouse Relief cases:
Wilson, Cumings, Smith, Farmer, and Van Arsdalen

Taxpayers prevailed in a number of innocent spouse relief cases resolved in 2007 in favor of the taxpayer:

- *J.M Wilson* (93 TCM 1242, Dec. 56,941(M), TC Memo 2007-127);
- *M.E. Cumings* (T.C. Summ. Op. 2007-77);
- *L.J. Smith* (T.C. Summ. Op. 2007-57);
- *L.D. Farmer* (93 TCM 1052, Dec. 56,881(M), TC Memo 2007-74); and
- *D. Van Arsdalen* (93 TCM 953, Dec. 56,852(M), TC Memo 2007-48).

The Tax Court in many of these cases determined that the IRS abused its discretion in denying the taxpayer equitable relief from joint and several liability. In these cases, the Tax Court, in exercising its jurisdiction over innocent spouse petitions, determined that many of the factors set forth in Rev. Proc. 2000-15 (still applicable in many of the cases, although superseded by Rev. Proc. 2003-61) favored granting the taxpayer innocent spouse relief under Code Sec. 6015(f), or were neutral. Rev. Proc. 2003-61 (and Rev. Proc. 2000-15, although superseded) sets forth the criteria under which relief will ordinarily be granted and includes a nonexhaustive list of factors to determine whether it would be inequitable to hold the requesting spouse jointly and severally liable for a deficiency or an unpaid liability.

Although the decisions in each case rested heavily on the facts, factors the courts found important involved:

- The economic hardship of the ex-spouse;
- Failure to significantly benefit from the former spouse's underpayment of tax; and
- The ex-spouse's lack of knowledge that there was an understatement or underpayment of tax liability.

Whether the IRS will back off on the number of innocent spouse claims that it denies as the result of these consistent rebukes by the Tax Court, however, remains to be seen.

Medical Residents May Qualify for FICA Tax Exemption: *Mount Sinai Medical Center of Florida, Inc.*

In a case of first impression, the Eleventh Circuit ruled against the IRS in *Mount Sinai Medical Center of Florida, Inc.* (CA-11, 2007-1 USTC ¶50,525, 486 F3d 1248), and held that medical residents may qualify for the IRS's student exemption from Federal Insurance Contributions Act (FICA) tax. The court ruled that services performed by medical students are not categorically ineligible for the student exemption from FICA tax.

The Eleventh Circuit held the language of Code Sec. 3121(b)(10) itself is clear and unambiguous; therefore, the district court improperly considered the statute's legislative history. Congress's repeal of the entirely separate intern exemption is irrelevant to whether residents qualify for the student exemption. The intern exemption applied to a type of service, but "[b]y its plain terms, the student exemption does not limit the types of services that qualify for exemption," the court said.

The Eleventh Circuit further ruled that a case-by-case analysis is required to determine a medical resident's student exemption eligibility. Specifically, Code Sec. 3121(b)(10) requires a determination both about whether the hospital qualifies as a "school, college, or university" and whether medical residents qualify as "students."

Despite this taxpayer victory, teaching hospitals and similar institutions should proceed cautiously when determining whether to file for a refund under Code Sec. 3121(b)(10) in light of the Eleventh Circuit's decision. In 2004 the IRS issued final regs applicable for services performed on or after April 1, 2005, and incorporating a *primary function standard* for determining whether an organization qualifies as a school, college, or university for purposes of Code Sec. 3121(b). An organization whose primary function is to carry on educational activities qualifies as a school, college, or university for purposes of the student FICA exemption. The case at hand involved years before the final regs took effect, a circumstance that may have enough administrative authority behind it to counterbalance the Eleventh Circuit's decision. Moreover, with a split among the circuits as to medical residents' eligibility for the FICA exception, the issue is ripe for review by the Supreme Court.

Attorney's Fees Claimed as Estate Expenses Not Proven to Be Improper: *Kessler*

In *J. Kessler* (DC Cal., 2007-2 USTC ¶60,544), the government was not entitled to summary judgment because it failed to establish that the attorneys' fees of all of the parties to a will contest claimed as estate expenses under Code Sec. 2053 were inappropriate. A decedent created two wills, naming different executors, who were also beneficiaries under both wills, and altering the distribution of her estate.

The estate's personal representative filed an amended federal estate tax return claiming the attorneys' fees as an estate administration expense and sought a refund of $529,103. Code Sec. 2053 permits "administration expenses" of an estate that "are allowable by the laws of the jurisdiction...under which the estate is being administered." California probate law provides only for the payment by the estate of attorneys' fees incurred by an executor or personal representative. Thus, the attorneys' fees of the will-contestant beneficiaries were not deductible under Code Sec. 2053.

The court found that the government failed to show that attorneys' fees for all parties to the contest could not be properly deducted as estate expenses under Code Sec. 2053. Although there was no basis under state law to charge some of the parties' fees to the estate, the IRS failed to show that none of the fees could be properly claimed as estate expenses, the court found. In addition, the reasonableness of the executor's attorneys' fees was a factual issue and not subject to determination on summary judgment.

E-mails of Chief Counsel Office Subject to Disclosure; Not Protected by Two-Hour Rule: *Tax Analysts*

A unanimous D.C. Circuit Court of Appeals held in *Tax Analysts* (CA-DC, 2007-2 USTC ¶50,553), that the IRS is required to disclose e-mails containing legal advice, which it had withheld under its *two-hour rule* that effectively shields advice rendered in less than two hours from disclosure, sent by lawyers in the IRS Office of the Chief Counsel (OCC) to IRS field personnel. The court ruled that the documents constituted "chief counsel advice," which the IRS is required to publicly disclose under Code Sec. 6110. The IRS could not rely on its two-hour rule to avoid disclosure.

The D.C. Circuit ruled that the e-mails fell within the broad definition of *chief counsel advice* and therefore, under the plain language of the statute, the IRS was required to disclose the documents. The court ruled that the IRS's two-hour rule was contrary to the statutory directive that a written determination, including, without exception, chief counsel advice, must be open to public inspection. The documents sought fell within the statutory description because they were written interpretations of revenue provisions prepared by lawyers in the OCC and sent to field personnel. The advice did not have to be formally issued as an official position to fall under the statutory definition of chief counsel advice, which encompasses not only a formal position or policy concerning a revenue position but also any legal interpretation of a revenue position. Also, the statutory phrase that the advice be prepared by any national office "component" of the OCC included advice prepared by an individual OCC lawyer, whether he or she be considered a "component" of the OCC or simply a member of an institutional component who prepares the opinion on its behalf.

Whether the latest court case will persuade the chief counsel to return to telephone-only advice is uncertain. In most cases, however, the Freedom of Information Act (FOIA) disclosure process is sufficiently lengthy and the redaction process sufficiently thorough that the current court victory will provide practitioners with no clear window to current information on pending matters.

STUDY QUESTIONS

14. In *J.A. Toth*, the Tax Court ruled that expenses incurred from a horse boarding and training facility were:

  a. Start-up expenses that must be capitalized under Code Sec. 195

  b. Initial operating expenses deductible as business expenses under Code Sec. 212

  c. Expenses to be allocated, with a portion treated as start-up costs and the rest as operating expenses

  d. None of the above was the ruling

15. All of the following were factors the courts considered important in deciding innocent spouse relief cases in favor of the taxpayer during 2007 *except:*

  a. Failure to acquire significant benefit from the former spouse's underpayment

  b. Economic hardship of the ex-spouse claiming relief

  c. Amount of property or other divorce settlements granted subsequently to the spouse claiming relief

  d. Lack of knowledge of the underpayment or understatement

CONCLUSION

The year 2007 was a big year for tax law developments that affected tax-payers across the board; no one and no entity was left unaffected by the numerous changes. Tax law is an amalgam of complex and complicated—if not convoluted—rules that continue to change. The IRS and Treasury, Congress, and the courts all played a hand in shaping the tax laws of 2007, adding new rules while tweaking existing ones. With a presidential election around the corner, issues such as the unresolved AMT and a number of controversial proposed tax plans, will undoubtedly mean that 2008 will also be an active year for tax law.

CPE NOTE: When you have completed your study and review of chapters 7 and 8, which comprise this Module, you may wish to take the Quizzer for the Module.

For your convenience, you can also take this Quizzer online at **www. cchtestingcenter.com**.

TOP FEDERAL TAX ISSUES FOR 2008 CPE COURSE
Answers to Study Questions

MODULE 1: HOT BUSINESS TOPICS—CHAPTER 1

1. d. Correct. The SEC enforces the provisions of FIN 48, which was developed by FASB. The IRS has expressed an interest in FIN 48 disclosures but does not enforce FIN 48. The PCAOB does not have an enforcement role with FIN 48.
a. Incorrect. The IRS has expressed an interest in FIN 48 disclosures but does not enforce FIN 48.
b. Incorrect. FASB developed FIN 48 but does not enforce it.
c. Incorrect. The PCAOB does not have an enforcement role with FIN 48.

2. a. Correct. FIN 48 applies to accounting for uncertainty in income taxes. It does not apply to estate, gift, value-added, or other taxes.
b. Incorrect. FIN 48 does not apply to estate, and gift taxes.
c. Incorrect. FIN 48 does not apply to value-added taxes.
d. Incorrect. FIN 48 does not apply to all of the above taxes.

3. b. Correct. Practitioners claimed that the probable recognition threshold was not consistently understood and applied.
a. Incorrect. Either threshold could examine the same areas, such as workpapers, SEC filings, and minutes of audit committee meetings.
c. Incorrect. The overstatement was not an issue for applying the more-likely-than-not threshold rather than the probable threshold.
d. Incorrect. FASB considered but rejected using best estimate as the threshold for measuring the tax benefit under FIN 48.

4. c. Correct. All available evidence is used to evaluate the organization's position but is essentially a matter of judgment.
a. Incorrect. Prior financial statements are not the basis of the determination.
b. Incorrect. FASB had selected best estimate as the threshold for measuring the tax benefit under FIN 48, but commentators felt this approach would yield counterintuitive results.
d. Incorrect. One of the choices reflects the appropriate unit of account.

5. a. Correct. FASB stipulates that derecognition should occur in the first subsequent financial reporting period in which that threshold is no longer met.

b. *Incorrect.* The derecognition should occur as of the time the position is "effectively settled," not upon initiation of an examination.

c. *Incorrect.* FASB does not call for a restatement.

d. *Incorrect.* A revised projected earnings statement is not the requirement of FASB when a previously reported tax position no longer meets the threshold.

6. c. *Correct.* FASB decided to change the threshold from "highly unlikely" to "remote" based on commentator views about the language for effective settlements.

a. *Incorrect.* FASB staff presented the option to the Board to leave the wording as it stood for enterprises that had to determine whether their position was effectively settled, but the Board rejected that option.

b. *Incorrect.* Guidelines for enterprises, not the taxing authority, were issued in the FSP.

d. *Incorrect.* One of the choices reflects the final action of FASB following issuance of FSP FIN 48-a.

7. a. *Correct.* FASB Statement 109 does not contain specific guidance for addressing uncertainty in account for income tax assets and liabilities, and the need to clarify FASB Statement 109 triggered the development of FIN 48.

b. *Incorrect.* Rules for covered opinions in Circular 230 use similar more-likely-than-not language in developing opinions about the likelihood that the taxpayer's opinion will prevail.

c. *Incorrect.* Code Sec. 6664(d) applies more-likely-than-not language to support reasonable cause for reportable transaction understatements.

d. *Incorrect.* One of the choices is not guidance having language similar to that of FIN 48.

8. True. *Correct.* For example, unrecognized tax benefits could decrease because of audit settlements or the closing of the statute of limitations on certain tax years.

False. *Incorrect.* Although FIN 48 uses the more-likely-than not recognition threshold, disclosures may reveal tax positions that enterprises expect will change.

9. a. *Correct.* FIN 48 is effective for fiscal years beginning after December 15, 2006.

b. *Incorrect.* December 31, 2006 is not the effective date

c. *Incorrect.* January 1, 2007 is not the effective date.

d. *Incorrect.* December 15, 2007 is not the effective date.

10. a. *Correct.* The "Field Examiners Guide" does not indicate that the tax position as measured under international accounting standards would be a FIN 48 disclosure.

b. *Incorrect.* The IRS "Field Examiners Guide" indicates that a description of tax years that remain subject to examination by major tax jurisdictions would be a FIN 48 disclosure.

c. *Incorrect* The IRS "Field Examiners Guide" indicates that penalties and interest would be a FIN 48 disclosure.

d. *Incorrect.* One of the choices is not a FIN 48 disclosure discussed in the "Field Examiners Guide."

11. False. *Correct.* Similar or identical tax positions in periods that have not been examined are not settled when such a position is resolved for a different tax period.

True. *Incorrect.* Although when an examination closes there is effective settlement of all uncertain tax positions for the examined year, the effective settlement of a tax position for that year does not result in effective settlement of such positions in unexamined periods.

12. True. *Correct.* According to IRS Chief Counsel Donald Korb and other senior IRS officials, FIN 48 workpapers are tax accrual workpapers and are subject to the IRS' policy of restraint.

False. *Incorrect.* The IRS is treating FIN 48 workpapers as tax accrual workpapers, which are subject to the IRS' policy of restraint.

13. d. *Correct.* All three choices depict differences between effective tax rate reconciliation workpapers and audit or accrual workpapers.

a. *Incorrect.* Being prepared by the taxpayer, effective tax rate reconciliation workpapers are not equivalent with audit workpapers.

b. *Incorrect.* Unlike audit workpapers, effective tax rate reconciliation workpapers do not reflect the processes performed by auditors.

c. *Incorrect.* Auditors do not prepare effective tax rate reconciliation workpapers to determine the proper amount of reserve for contingent tax liabilities.

14. c. *Correct.* The initiative aimed to expedite the examination and resolution of filed or to be filed returns.

a. *Incorrect.* Issues or transactions designated for litigation were outside the scope of the initiative.

b. *Incorrect.* Issues and transactions were excluded from consideration under the initiative if a fraud penalty had been issued or if the IRS notified the taxpayer of an impending fraud penalty.

d. Incorrect. Tax-related issues under criminal investigation were considered outside of the initiative's scope.

15. a. Correct. Nondomestic companies could access U.S. capital markets under this proposal.
b. Incorrect. Such unification regarding disclosures was not the SEC's proposed change.
c. Incorrect. Such standardization is not the intent of the SEC proposal.
d. Incorrect. One of the choices reflects the change to U.S. accounting applications that would result from adoption of the SEC proposal.

MODULE 1—CHAPTER 2

1. c. Correct. Per Notice 2007-78, all written plans must fully comply with the final regulations on January 1, 2009.
a. Incorrect. This date was the deadline for amending a pre-2005 plan for good faith compliance according to Notice 2005-1.
b. Incorrect. January 1, 2008, is the proposed effective date of the final regulations for written plans under TD 9321.
d. Incorrect. One of the dates is the full compliance date for the final regulations under Code Sec. 409A for all plan documents.

2. c. Correct. This period is beyond the inclusion period for either of the VCPs requested by the ABA Section of Taxation.
a. Incorrect. The ABA requested a short-term program to cover this transition period.
b. Incorrect. These dates comprise the compliance period that follows the full compliance date of January 1, 2009.
d. Incorrect. One of the choices was not a period for which the ABA requested a voluntary corrections program.

3. a. Correct. Contributions under a salary reduction agreement not includible in the employee's gross income include cafeteria plan contributions, qualified transportation fringe benefits, a 401(k) plan, or a 403(b) annuity.
b. Incorrect. Professional service fees are not open to elections about whether the payments are compensation.
c. Incorrect. To the extent the amounts are includible in gross income or excludable as foreign earned income.
d. Incorrect. Only one of the choices is available for the election not to be included as compensation.

4. d. Correct. Written plans must specify the deferred amount due to the service provider, the payment schedule, or payment-triggering events.

a. Incorrect. Written plans must specify the amount to which the service provider has a right to be paid.

b. Incorrect. The payment schedule is required unless the plan is set up for certain events to trigger payment.

c. Incorrect. The terms of any formula to be used to determine deferred amounts payable must be specified in written plans.

5. True. Correct. The employee owns the policy under a loan regime, so the arrangement is not deferred compensation unless the employee's payments are waived, cancelled, or forgiven.

False. Incorrect. Unlike arrangements under the economic benefit regime in which the employer owns the policy, loan-regime arrangements are not deferred compensation unless the employee is excused from loan payments.

6. b. Correct. Setting aside assets in a trust outside the United States is a taxable property transfer under Code Sec. 83, even if the funds are available to satisfy creditors' claims.

a. Incorrect. The employment contract's terms do not drive the tax liability for the trust assets.

c. Incorrect. Trust termination does not drive the period in which the tax liability occurs.

d. Incorrect. One of the choices describes the circumstance in which the assets are taxed.

7. b. Correct. If a collective bargaining agreement stipulate the terms of separation pay, it is not considered to be deferred compensation.

a. Incorrect. These are not the criteria for excluding the separation pay from being considered deferred compensation.

c. Incorrect. One exclusion is for separation pay not in excess of twice, not three times, the service provider's annualized compensation.

d. Incorrect. New employment does not qualify the former employee to exclude the separation pay from being considered deferred compensation. The employee must terminate employment with all employers.

8. a. Correct. Services provided to any recipient cannot exceed 70 percent of the total compensation received by the contractor in order for Code Sec. 409A not to apply.

b. Incorrect. Statutory employees are eligible under certain circumstances to qualify for deferred compensation subject to Code Sec. 409A.

c. Incorrect. If services to any one recipient are more than 70 percent of the total compensation, Code Sec. 409A applies to the independent contractor.

d. Incorrect. The Code Sec. 409A exclusion applies to only one of the choices.

9. a. *Correct.* Code Sec. 409A applies to reimbursement arrangements that are taxable to the service provider.
b. *Incorrect.* The Code Sec. 409A provisions do not apply to these reimbursement arrangements.
c. *Incorrect.* Health savings accounts (HSAs) are not considered deferred compensation under Code Sec. 409A.
d. *Incorrect.* Code Sec. 409A does not apply to Archer medical savings accounts or any medical reimbursement arrangement not includible in the employee's income.

10. c. *Correct.* The exclusion from the Code Sec. 409A rules applies only if the option is not changed so that it is treated as the grant of a new option.
a. *Incorrect.* Under some circumstances, the statutory option is not excluded.
b. *Incorrect.* The employee may terminate employment up to three months before exercising the option.
d. *Incorrect.* Stock options and employee stock purchase plan options are not always considered to be deferred compensation.

11. d. *Correct.* The initial election must be made before the taxable year in which the services are rendered for which the compensation is deferred.
a. *Incorrect.* The only one-time retroactive election permitted is for the employee during the first year after plan benefits accrue under a nonelective excess benefits plan.
b. *Incorrect.* A plan may enable the initial election to be changed anytime up to the last date established for making the election.
c. *Incorrect.* This is not the permissible time for making the deferral election.

12. b. *Correct.* Unless the arrangement has a performance-based vesting requirement, the compensation is not considered performance-based.
a. *Incorrect.* Under certain circumstances, the compensation is considered performance-based compensation.
c. *Incorrect.* This set of employees is not the only group to which performance-based compensation may be offered.
d. *Incorrect.* Instead of requiring the election before the beginning of the tax year of the deferral, an initial election to defer performance-based compensation may be made no later than six months before the end of the performance period.

13. a. Correct. Payments for creditors in bankruptcy proceedings are not eligible for acceleration.
b. Incorrect. Scheduled payments may be accelerated in order to pay employment taxes or income tax withholding imposed on the FICA amount.
c. Incorrect. Upon disability of the service provider, accelerated payments are permitted.
d. Incorrect. Acceleration of scheduled payments is allowed when amounts are included in income because of compliance failures.

14. b. Correct. Payers reporting amounts deferred by nonemployees use Form 1099-MISC, whereas for employees, Form W-2 is used.
a. Incorrect. Form W-3 is a transmittal form used to submit copy A of Form W-2.
c. Incorrect. Form W-2 is used to report nonqualified plan deferrals for employees or to include income recognized when a plan fails to meet Code Sec. 409A requirements.
d. Incorrect. One of the choices is the correct form for reporting amounts deferred by nonemployees.

15. a. Correct. Even if they relied on earlier guidance for calendar year 2005, employers and payers must file original or corrected information returns (due February 28, 2007) and payee statements for 2005 (due January 31, 2007).
b. Incorrect. The corrected information may not be submitted with the 2006 returns.
c. Incorrect. Employers are not required to report amounts in this way for calendar years 2005 and 2006.
d. Incorrect. One of the above choices is the process to use under the transitional reporting rules for 2005.

MODULE 1—CHAPTER 3

1. d. Correct. A succession plan for transferring a business to the next generation commonly includes how ownership will be transferred, how assets will be transferred, and how the knowledge and skills of the current generation will be transferred.
a. Incorrect. Passing along business knowledge and special skills acquired by the owner of the current generation to the owner of the next generation is an element of a typical succession plan. This element may even be transferred to a different individual than other elements are conveyed.
b. Incorrect. Whether and how the ownership will be transferred in its entirety or spread among multiple recipients in the next generation is a typical element of a succession plan.

c. *Incorrect.* The means by which assets will be transferred is an essential element of a typical succession plan.

2. d. *Correct.* All three choices are issues whose proper timing helps to ensure the successful transition of control for the small business.
a. *Incorrect.* Emotional as well as financial factors affect when and how the current-generation owner decides to transfer control of the business.
b. *Incorrect.* Because transitional periods are stressful for all concerned, good timing of the transition is an important issue for transferring control of a small business.
c. *Incorrect.* Business owners affected by a disaster must choose whether to elect to recognize losses on a prior year's return, when to file returns and submit payments, and how to have late payment penalties abated.

3. b. *Correct.* Under the proposed regulations, the IRS considers that an unsecured or secured annuity can be valued at the time it is received in exchange for property. The transferor of property and the transferee are in the same position as if the transferor sold the property for cash then used to purchase an annuity.
a. *Incorrect.* The fair market value of the annuity is not determined when payments begin.
c. *Incorrect.* The contract is not valued at the death of the transferor.
d. *Incorrect.* One of the choices is the time of valuation for an annuity contract according to the IRS proposed regulations.

4. c. *Correct.* No gift tax is due as long as transferred property does not exceed the prevent value of the payments, and estate tax is not due when the transferor dies because the value of the business is not included in his or her gross estate for tax purposes.
a. *Incorrect.* No estate tax is due upon the senior family member's death because the value of the business is not included in the gross estate for tax purposes.
b. *Incorrect.* Income tax on the appreciation of the transferred property is deferred by the transferor.
d. *Incorrect.* One of the choices is the tax treatment of transfers in traditional private annuity arrangements.

5. c. *Correct.* To qualify for the exclusion, a gift must be for a present interest.
a. *Incorrect.* This is not the reason that the transfer is disqualified from the gift tax exclusion.
b. *Incorrect.* Although the grantor may claim these deductions and credits, the transfer is not qualified for the exclusion for another reason.

d. *Incorrect.* Transfers of assets to GRATs do not qualify for the annual gift tax exclusion for donors.

6. d. *Correct.* All three choices cause the transfers to be considered completed gifts.

a. *Incorrect.* Removal of the assets from the parent's estate causes the transfer to be considered a completed gift.

b. *Incorrect.* If an immediate economic benefit occurs as a result of the transfer, the transaction is considered to be a completed gift.

c. *Incorrect.* If the gifted interest's taxable value is a fraction of the full asset value, the transfer is considered a completed gift.

7. a. *Correct.* Professional appraisers may use traditional market-based valuation methods including industry averages and comparable sales.

b. *Incorrect.* The capitalized earnings method is a historical earnings valuation method that includes the value of intangible assets that requires using a required rate of return on the business in the future.

c. *Incorrect.* Net book value is an asset-based, not market-based, valuation method.

d. *Incorrect.* The discounted cash flow method is not market-based; rather it employs expected growth and intangible asset values in its calculations.

8. a. *Correct.* Net tangible assets are valued and the value of goodwill extracted by capitalizing earnings in excess of a reasonable return on the net tangible assets.

b. *Incorrect.* Discounted cash flow is a separate valuation method with the advantage of capturing expected growth and intangible assets values, but it is subjective and may have inaccurate assumptions in its projections.

c. *Incorrect.* The capitalized earnings method does include valuation of intangible assets but is a historical earnings valuation method not necessarily focused on goodwill.

d. *Incorrect.* Net book value is an asset-based method that primarily reflects market value of commodities.

9. c. *Correct.* Businesses reporting taxes greater than $50,000 during the lookback period are required to deposit employment taxes more frequently.

a. *Incorrect.* The cutoff for more frequent filing is a higher minimum.

b. *Incorrect.* This is not the minimum threshold for requiring more frequent deposits.

d. *Incorrect.* The cutoff is a lower amount for triggering more frequent deposits.

10. b. *Correct.* Half of self-employment tax may be claimed as an adjustment to income on Form 1040.
a. *Incorrect.* This fraction is lower than that allowed to sole proprietors as a deduction on Form 1040.
c. *Incorrect.* This is not the fraction of self-employment tax allowed as a deduction for sole proprietors.
d. *Incorrect.* This fraction is higher than the allowed deduction of self-employment tax for sole proprietors.

MODULE 2: WEALTH-BUILDING STRATEGIES—CHAPTER 4

1. d. *Correct.* Although TIPRA benefited taxpayers by enabling nonrefundable personal credits to offset the AMT, it neither increased nor lowered the general AMT tax rate.
a. *Incorrect.* The Tax Reform Act of 1986 increased the AMT tax rate from 20 to 21 percent and phased out the exemption amount for individuals having AMTI of more than $150,000 for joint-filing taxpayers or $112,500 for single-filing taxpayers.
b. *Incorrect.* OBRA 1990 increased the individual AMT tax rate from 21 percent to 24 percent.
c. *Incorrect.* OBRA 1993 increased the rate to 26 percent and 28 percent.

2. b. *Correct.* Unmarried individuals (single filers) are subject to the phaseout if their AMTI exceeds $112,500.
a. *Incorrect.* The phaseout begins at $75,000 for married couples filing separately, not single filers.
c. *Incorrect.* The $150,000 figure is only applied to surviving spouses and joint-filing couples.
d. *Incorrect.* One of the choices is the phaseout threshold for single-filing taxpayers.

3. d. *Correct.* The adoption credit, child credit, and saver's credit are allowed to the full extent of both the regular tax and AMT liability.
a. *Incorrect.* The saver's credit is allowed to the full extent of the individual's regular tax and AMT liability.
b. *Incorrect.* The child credit is available to offset both the regular tax and AMT liability.
c. *Incorrect.* The adoption credit continues to be applicable for offsetting both the regular tax liability and AMT liability.

4. c. *Correct.* Interest on any mortgage resulting from refinancing a taxpayer's main or second home is deductible only to the extent that the refinanced mortgage amount does not exceed the amount of the debt prior to refinancing.

a. Incorrect. Whether a mortgage is an ARM or fixed loan does not affect its deductibility for the AMT.

b. Incorrect. The same deductibility rule applies to both a principal/primary residence and second/vacation home of the taxpayer.

d. Incorrect. A limited deduction for mortgage interest is permitted under the AMT.

5. b. Correct. Either the lesser of the amount of the deduction attributable to NOLs or 90 percent of the AMTI determined excluding the deduction applies.

a. Incorrect. The deduction is a lower percentage than 100 percent.

c. Incorrect. The maximum deduction is not based on 75 percent of AMTI excluding the deduction.

d. Incorrect. A higher percentage than 50 percent is used to establish the maximum deduction.

6. a. Correct. Subtracting the alternative tax NOL deduction is the last step in computing AMTI.

b. Incorrect. An earlier step involves adding the accelerated depreciation or amortization of property, which is a preference item.

c. Incorrect. Adding tax refunds is one of the first steps in calculating the AMTI, as such deductions allowed under the regular tax are disallowed under the AMT and are added back.

d. Incorrect. One of the choices describes the final step in figuring AMTI.

7. d. Correct. All three choices reflect reasons married taxpayers are more likely to be subject to the AMT in 2007.

a. Incorrect. Married taxpayers tend to have higher household incomes than single taxpayers do and fewer of their deductions for regular tax apply to the AMT.

b. Incorrect. Married taxpayers with children may claim more miscellaneous itemized deductions for children's expenses and also claim personal exemptions for the children under regular tax but not the AMT.

c. Incorrect. The identical tax rates increase the chance that married taxpayers will be subject to the AMT.

8. c. Correct. High state and local taxes reduce regular tax liability, thus increasing the likelihood that the taxpayer will owe AMT.

a. Incorrect. The state or local tax rates have no direct influence on the tax rates established for the AMT.

b. Incorrect. No correlation between high state and local taxes and the amount of taxpayers' discretionary income is proven for the AMT.

d. Incorrect. Higher state and local taxes do make individuals more likely to owe AMT.

9. a. Correct. This timing enables taxpayers to claim high enough income so AMT is not triggered and to claim the deductions in regular tax years that are not available under AMT.
b. Incorrect. Charitable contributions are an allowed deduction reducing AMTI.
c. Incorrect. Preference items are taxable under AMT and thus should not be timed for an AMT year. Postponing income into a regular tax year may trigger the AMT.
d. Incorrect. State and local tax payments are itemized deductions for regular tax purposes that are not deductible in an AMT year.

10. a. Correct. With the 4 percent tax, the top effective tax rates on ordinary income and capital gains would remain below 39.6 percent and 20 percent.
b. Incorrect. The Tax Policy Center's plan does not involve raising tax rates for all but the 10 percent bracket filers.
c. Incorrect. This recommendation is from the American Enterprise Institute to reform but not repeal the AMT by capping deductions, cutting exemptions, and lowering AMT tax rates.
d. Incorrect. The Tax Policy Center did not recommend a flat tax to replace the AMT.

MODULE 2—CHAPTER 5

1. c. Correct. No withholding is deducted from distributions to FLP partners because distributive shares are not considered earnings. A partner may also be an employee of the partnership, however, in which case wages would be subject to withholding.
a. Incorrect. Although FLP partners may be required to file estimated tax payments, that is not the reason withholding is not applied to their partnership distributions.
b. Incorrect. Although assets are held by the partnership and the FLP is a flowthrough entity, partners are required to render tax for their distributive portion of partnership income.
d. Incorrect. Although the FLP is a flowthrough entity not subject to tax at the partnership level, partners are required to pay tax on their distributive portions of partnership income at the individual level.

2. b. Correct. Transfer of wealth while simultaneously retaining control of the assets in the partnership is a major attraction of the FLP structure.

a. Incorrect. The FLP is structured to award only nonvoting interests to the children or other beneficiaries of the FLP.

c. Incorrect. A written agreement specifying the terms of the FLP is not a requirement, although it is highly recommended.

d. Incorrect. Percentages are usually not balanced equally. The general partner (older family member) typically receives no more than a 2 percent general partnership interest but a large limited partnership interest, which he or she gradually transfers to the younger partners as he or she deems fit.

3. b. Correct. A senior family member can transfer fractional interests by gift, bequest, or intrafamily sales of FLP interests without breaking up business and investment assets.

a. Incorrect. The management structure of family businesses is not directly associated with the financial umbrella of the FLP.

c. Incorrect. Younger family members typically do not have interests that provide voting rights in administering the businesses.

d. Incorrect. One of the choices reflects the benefit of operational unit afforded to FLP assets.

4. a. Correct. The FLP's partnership agreement can stipulate that partners transfer their interests back to the partnership in case of divorce.

b. Incorrect. Limited partners have no voting rights in the partnership.

c. Incorrect. As a flowthrough entity, an FLP does not have an entity-level tax liability. Partners are taxed on their distributive shares of FLP net profits.

d. Incorrect. Without written partnership agreement provisions for a buy-back it might prove problematic to apply. In addition, most younger-generation partners do not typically have voting rights in the partnership.

5. a. Correct. EGTRRA left the gift tax in place, and the gift and estate taxes have not been considered unified since 2004.

b. Incorrect. EGTRRA did not lower the lifetime gift exclusion.

c. Incorrect. The exclusion amounts were not altered identically for the gift and estate taxes.

d. Incorrect. EGTRRA specified that the gift tax should remain in force.

6. a. Correct. Public entities are not usually comparable to FLPs in valuations because publicly traded securities do not have the two discounts applied in valuing FLP assets.

b. Incorrect. The IRS scrutinizes FLPs that claim substantial discounts when their assets include marketable securities.

c. Incorrect. Combined lack of control and lack of marketability discounts typically range from 20 to 40 percent, not as high as 50 percent.

d. Incorrect. Only one of the choices is not an action that spurs IRS scrutiny.

7. d. Correct. Under EGTRRA the estate tax is repealed entirely for the sole year 2010.

a. Incorrect. A later year is scheduled under EGTRRA to shelter a higher dollar amount from estate tax.

b. Incorrect. The lifetime credit does not shelter the greatest amount from estate tax liability in 2008.

c. Incorrect. Although the dollar limit of $3.5 million applies to estates for decedents during 2009, under EGTRRA the tax is repealed altogether for just one year, so the entire estate would have no estate tax liability.

8. c. Correct. Because the partnership's profits and losses are reported on individuals' income tax returns rather than entity-level returns, older-generation partners may pass income to or enable deductions by younger partners without the tax liability that would occur with a corporate structure.

a. Incorrect. Quarterly estimated taxes must still be paid if the partners' income level requires them.

b. Incorrect. Although passthrough entities create no income tax liability at the entity level, the investment company exception applies to disallow nonrecognition of gain if the partnership essentially functions as an investment company.

d. Incorrect. Only one of the choices is a tax advantage of FLPs.

9. b. Correct. The lack of control and loss of marketability of the assets within the FLP are advantages of this entity due to the resulting valuation discounts that result from these impairments to the assets.

a. Incorrect. The IRS issued Technical Advice Memorandum 9436005 analyzing gift transfers of FLP interests that resulted in swing votes, creating governance as well as gift tax issues for the FLP.

c. Incorrect. Kiddie tax rules do apply to the partnership income of partners younger than age 24.

d. Incorrect. The cost of legal fees to establish an FLP may run tens of thousands of dollars.

10. b. Correct. Code Sec. 721(b) describes the investment company exception to the general nonrecognition rule for contributions of property to an FLP.

a. Incorrect. Income shifting is not the focus of Code Sec. 721(b).

c. *Incorrect.* Code Sec. 704(e) details the rules for disregarded young family members' interests in the FLP unless they have a legitimate capital interest.

d. *Incorrect.* One of the choices describes the intent of Code Sec. 721(b).

11. b. *Correct.* The IRS held that Code Sec. 2704(b) should not apply because the restriction on the limited partner's right to withdraw is not a restriction on the ability to liquidate the entity.

a. *Incorrect.* "Applicable restrictions" under Code Sec. 2704(b) require limitations that are *more* restrictive than limitations under state law. An applicable restriction under Code Sec. 2704 requires three elements: the restriction must limit the partners' ability to liquidate the partnership; must allow any lapses in the ability to liquidate to be removable by the transferor or the transferor's family; and must be more restrictive than state and federal law. If any of these requirements is not met, the restriction is not an applicable restriction and will not case the restriction to be disregarded for valuation purposes under Code Sec. 2704(b).

c. *Incorrect.* The reasoning was not one of taxpayer ignorance involving terms of the partnership agreement.

d. *Incorrect.* One of the choices was the reason behind the rulings' rejection of the IRS position.

12. b. *Correct.* The IRS applied such an analysis in **Church** and **Strangi,** but the courts rebuked the IRS position.

a. *Incorrect.* The gift on creation argument holds that forming an FLP is itself a gifting transaction.

c. *Incorrect.* The "applicable restrictions" provision of Code Sec. 2704(b) involves limitations on the ability to liquidate the FLP entity.

d. *Incorrect.* The step transaction doctrine analyzes whether forming an FLP close in time to a decedent's death and the transfer of partnership interests or testamentary transfers should be viewed as one testamentary transaction.

13. a. *Correct.* Although rent accrued in the FLP's books, it was not paid for more than two years after Mr. Strangi's death.

b. *Incorrect.* This was one of the justifications of the Fifth Circuit in determining that Mr. Strangi continued to control the FLP's assets by an implied agreement.

c. *Incorrect.* The lack of substantial business purpose was a sign that the FLP was created essentially to minimize tax.

d. *Incorrect.* Paying for personal posthumous expenses from the FLP signaled that the partnership was not a separate entity.

14. a. *Correct.* Because the transferred tree farm property was intended to be a long-term venture, the family's LLC did not qualify for the annual gift tax exclusion.

b. *Incorrect.* A donor may make excludible gifts to any donee, regardless of their relationship. The Hackls' LLC was subjected to the gift tax for a different reason.

c. *Incorrect.* Under the operating agreement, the LLC members had no such rights.

d. *Incorrect.* The operating agreement allowed none of the members to receive distributions except on dissolution of the company.

15. c. *Correct.* Individuals forming FLPs should avoid such special allocations of income for specific assets.

a. *Incorrect.* Funding the partnership first indicates that the entity is not solely created to avoid tax.

b. *Incorrect.* Matching the amount of partnership interests to the partners' contributions indicates that the FLP makes arm's length transactions.

d. *Incorrect.* Proving a nontax motive for establishing an FLP is key for upholding its legitimacy.

MODULE 2—CHAPTER 6

1. a. *Correct.* Under the passive activity rules, active participation applies to rental real estate activities.

b. *Incorrect.* Nonpassive substantial participation is not the name of the type of participation applicable to rental real estate activities.

c. *Incorrect.* Passive substantial participation is not the name of the type of participation applicable to rental real estate activities.

d. *Incorrect.* One of the choices is the term applicable to rental real estate activities under the passive activity rules.

2. d. *Correct.* All three choices are circumstances constituting exceptions to the general treatment of rental activity income.

a. *Incorrect.* An exception to the passive activity rules is allowed for an active participant in the activity whose gross income is less than $100,000, owns at least 10 percent of the property, and is not a limited partner.

b. *Incorrect.* These circumstances constitute an exception to the passive activity income rules.

c. *Incorrect.* The real estate professional having material participation in the rental is excepted from the passive activity loss rules.

3. b. *Correct.* The passive activity credit is only applied against a tax liability allocable to the taxpayer's passive activities.

a. Incorrect. The credits, unlike deductions, may not be group together to net against all future passive activities.

c. Incorrect. Any disallowed credit is treated as a credit from the activity to which it is allocated for the taxpayer's immediately succeeding tax year.

d. Incorrect. One of the choices is applicable to passive activity credits in excess of liabilities.

4. d. Correct. Income/gain from investing working capital, from intangible property created by the taxpayer, and cancellation of debt not allocated to passive activities are all exceptions to the passive activity loss rules.

a. Incorrect. The income or gain from investments of working capital is an exception from the definition of passive activity income.

b. Incorrect. Such intangible property is excepted from the passive activity loss rules.

c. Incorrect. Cancellation of debt income is excepted if it is not allocated to passive activities under interest expense allocation rules.

5. d. Correct. None of the three choices is the special rule for treating gain for property converted to inventory as passive income.

a. Incorrect. The special rule requires property to be treated as originally held unless held for sale to customers at least 80 percent of the time.

b. Incorrect. Gain from property originally held as inventory is not required to be treated as passive income.

c. Incorrect. Gain from such property must be treated as rental activity, a passive activity.

6. b. Correct. The taxpayer claiming material participation must participate at least as much as any other participating individual, whether workers or owners of interests in the activity.

a. Incorrect. The material participation for 5 out of 10 years is required in another test, the five-out-of-ten-years' participation test.

c. Incorrect. The three-year personal activity test is different from the equal participation test.

d. Incorrect. All of the material participation tests take into account participation by the taxpayer's spouse.

7. b. Correct. Significant participation activities must total at least 500 hours for the income and losses to be considered nonpassive.

a. Incorrect. The 100-hours amount is the minimum number required for the activity to be considered a business. Significantly more hours are required for the gains and losses from the activity to be considered nonpassive.

c. Incorrect. The measurement of significant participation activities is not tied to business or calendar quarters.

d. Incorrect. Fewer hours of participation are required for income and losses to be considered nonpassive.

8. d. Correct. All three choices are requirements for treatment of a limited partner's income or loss from a partnership to be considered nonpassive.
a. Incorrect. Taxpayers must substantiate their participation in partnership activities.
b. Incorrect. The partner must actually participate in the activity in a role considered to be material.
c. Incorrect. The partner must satisfy the requirements of either the 500 minimum hours, five-out-of-ten years, or three-year personal service activity tests.

9. d. Correct. No one choice is disallowed in establishing material participation.
a. Incorrect. Time reports and logs are reasonable methods of substantiating material participation.
b. Incorrect. The *any reasonable means* requirement mandates identification of services performed over a period of time.
c. Incorrect. Such tools are sufficient to establish the period of time and approximate number of hours spent performing such services.

10. b. Correct. The active participation rule excludes the amount allowable to a surviving spouse.
a. Incorrect. Beneficiaries' actions are not considered in applying the allowance.
c. Incorrect. Trusts, even grantor retained annuity trusts, may not take advantage of the active participation allowance.
d. Incorrect. Only one of the choices reflects a condition for claiming the active participation allowance.

11. d. Correct. The threshold employee activity in closely held C corporations enables the closely held C corporation to qualify for material participation.
a. Incorrect. The minimum amount of outstanding stock held is just 50 percent.
b. Incorrect. This is not a minimum requirement for material participation in closely held C corporations.
c. Incorrect. The active participation requirement does not in itself meet the material participation requirement, even by the majority shareholder.

12. d. Correct. This advantage is an improvement over the one-half of all trades and 750 hours of service rules applicable to individual real estate professionals.
a. Incorrect. This is not the correct level of material participation for closely held c corporations involved in real estate.
b. Incorrect. Net receipts are not used to substantiate material participation for closely held C corporations.
c. Incorrect. These criteria apply to real estate individuals, not closely held C corporations in real estate activities.

13. a. Correct. No other notification is permitted, and the taxpayer cannot make the election on an amended return or during a tax audit.
b. Incorrect. Taxpayers cannot use an amended income tax return to notify the IRS of the election.
c. Incorrect. Neither means is an acceptable method of notifying the IRS of the grouping election.
d. Incorrect. One of the choices is the correct method of notifying the IRS about the grouping election.

14. a. Correct. Calculating AMTI using lowered deductions may even turn a passive activity loss into a net gain.
b. Incorrect. Allowable deductions under AMT are usually much lower than under the regular tax system.
c. Incorrect. The carryforward period is not directly changed under the AMT.
d. Incorrect. One of the choices reflects the major effect of the AMT on the AMTI calculation for passive activity losses and tax liability.

15. b. Correct. Interest paid for secondary or vacation homes is not deductible or considered a passive activity loss for the AMT.
a. Incorrect. The percentage of deduction is not higher under the AMT.
c. Incorrect. Home improvement indebtedness is included in qualified housing interest for the taxpayer's primary residence.
d. Incorrect. One of the choices reflects how qualified housing interest affects interest deductions under the AMT.

MODULE 3: NEW TAX LAW/IRS—CHAPTER 7

1. d. Correct. Congress slashed the IRS enforcement budget and mandated the agency to be devoted to taxpayer service.
a. Incorrect. IRS personnel were given a different focus than enforcement following the hearings.

b. Incorrect. Following RRA 98 the IRS enforcement budget was slashed.

c. Incorrect. Both the number of IRS liens and property seizures dropped in response to the outcry by Congress.

2. a. Correct. The IRS has maintained its level of taxpayer service as the agency's enforcement budget has slowly increased recently.

b. Incorrect. Taxpayer service has been maintained, but the funding for enforcement has not remained level.

c. Incorrect. The IRS budget has not shifted funding away from enforcement to supplement taxpayer service.

d. Incorrect. There has not been a dramatic increase in funding for either focus of IRS programs.

3. b. Correct. Audits of individuals having incomes of $1 million or more increased by 33 percent, to 17,000 audits, or 6 percent of taxpayers in that income bracket. However, the most audits were conducted for taxpayers with incomes less than $25,000 were most common, with 1.035 million taxpayer returns audited that year.

a. Incorrect. Statistics were not listed for taxpayers in this highest income bracket.

c. Incorrect. Taxpayer audits for individuals having incomes of $100,000 or more increased 18 percent in 2006, but this was neither the greatest percentage increase in the number of audits nor the highest number of returns audited.

d. Incorrect. Although the IRS conducted the most audits for any income level for returns of these lower-income taxpayers (1.035 million returns audited), this bracket did not have the greatest increase in **percentage** of returns examined.

4. a. Correct. Although face-to-face audits were used for 40,000 returns, the audits were not line-by-line but rather from third-party information and other sources beside taxpayers.

b. Incorrect. Face-to-face audits were conducted for 40,000 of the 46,000 returns.

c. Incorrect. Information from the 2001 study was incorporated into new discriminant formulas aiding in selecting returns to be audited.

d. Incorrect. One of the choices is not a method employed in the study.

5. b. Correct. Audit rates for individuals filing Schedule C increased from 3.65 percent to 3.90 percent for gross receipts of $100,000 and more in FY 2006.

a. Incorrect. Statistics were not present for small business and self-employed taxpayers reporting more than $1 million in gross receipts for FY 2006.
c. Incorrect. Audit levels remained at 2.1 percent from 2005 to 2006 for this bracket of gross receipts.
d. Incorrect. Although audit rates rose from 3.68 percent to 3.8 percent for taxpayers having gross receipts of less than $25,000 from FY 2005 to 2006, this was not the greatest rate increase based on receipts.

6. c. Correct. Audit coverage levels for 2006 were slightly above FY 2005 but well below those of FY 1997.
a. Incorrect. The 2.22 percent rate did not apply to FY 2006, nor did the 0.80 rate apply to FY 1997.
b. Incorrect. Audit coverage levels for 2006 were well below FY 1997.
d. Incorrect. The audit rate for C corporations was not the highest in FY 2005.

7. a. Correct. The Employee Plans Compliance Unit was established in 2005 to provide "soft" contacts with plans having problems or questionable items. The EPCU had performed more than 4,700 compliance checks by mid-2007.
b. Incorrect. The EO unit will initiate a project for employment taxes using data from this system, administered by the Social Security Administration.
c. Incorrect. EO plans to conduct a compliance project of community foundations, which have grown significantly in number, size, and complexity.
d. Incorrect. For 2008 the EO unit is developing a project to review how unrelated business income is calculated and how income and expenses are allocated within large university systems.

8. a. Correct. LIFE examinations should help the IRS focus on fewer issues than would arise during a traditional audit, and taxpayers must provide computations for agreed-on issues and submit supporting documentation.
b. Incorrect. Although the Joint Audit Planning Process also relies on co-operation between the IRS and taxpayer, this program features step-by-step planning for all issues throughout the audit process
c. Incorrect. The intent of PFAs is to determine before the taxpayer files a return how legal principles will be applied to transactions that would be subject to audit.
d. Incorrect. The IIF focuses on the issues most prevalent across industry lines and those that pose the greatest compliance challenges. This approach differs from one taken to focus on few issues for which the taxpayer provides extensive paperwork.

9. b. *Correct.* This user fee is assessed for each separate issue under consideration for a PFA.
a. *Incorrect.* The PFA focuses on applying well-established legal principles to known facts that would otherwise be subject to audit.
c. *Incorrect.* The PFA process is resource intensive and narrowly focused.
d. *Incorrect.* Although program participants have been highly satisfied with the process, few taxpayers have applied for PFAs.

10. c. *Correct.* LMSB channels audits for tax shelter schemes regardless of which division normally oversees an organization.
a. *Incorrect.* The Wage and Investment Income Division is not the authority for the IRS tax shelter initiative.
b. *Incorrect.* SB/SE is not the focal point for investigations of abusive tax shelters.
d. *Incorrect.* The TE/GE Division is the "hot spot" for tax audits investigating misdeeds of tax-exempt organizations and government entities and their bond and employee plan programs.

11. d. *Correct.* The OECD, JITSIC, and TIEAs all are mechanisms for exchanging information about tax and tax avoidance.
a. *Incorrect.* The OECD exchanges information among treaty member countries.
b. *Incorrect.* JITSIC led to pressing enforcement cases against abusive tax shelters in the United States and Canada. JITSIC members encompass Canada, Australia, the United States, the United Kingdom, and Japan.
c. *Incorrect.* TIEAs provide a mechanism for exchange of information between the United States and another country about specific taxpayers.

12. b. *Correct.* The Appeals Office representative weighs the IRS's position to determine whether it is financially prudent to litigate a case.
a. *Incorrect.* A case examiner cannot address an offer in compromise. A collection officer can accept an offer in compromise, but if the offer is rejected, the taxpayer can solicit acceptance of the offer from an Appeals Office representative.
c. *Incorrect.* Just the opposite is the case: The Appeals Office staffperson's stated mission is to resolve tax controversies without litigation, whereas the tax examiner's top priority is pressing for the greatest payment of the liability.
d. *Incorrect.* Just the opposite is true: The Appeals Office representative aims to promote voluntary compliance, whereas the examiner wishes to extract payment of the tax liability.

13. c. Correct. The IRS mandates that the Appeals Office representative contact a taxpayer within 90 days after he or she files a protest.
a. Incorrect. The grace period for an IRS response is longer than 30 days.
b. Incorrect. The response period for the IRS is not two months.
d. Incorrect. The turnaround time for responding to the protest is shorter, although the IRS states that it can take between 90 days and a year to resolve a case under protest.

14. d. Correct. Most programs—with the notable exception of Binding Arbitration—have been successful in trimming the examination period.
a. Incorrect. These programs do not eliminate the taxpayer's right to an Appeals hearing.
b. Incorrect. Most of the programs have succeeded at shortening the time that the IRS considers a taxpayer's issues.
c. Incorrect. Binding Arbitration is one of the only programs not popular with taxpayers, and it has not succeeded at shortening the time that the IRS considers a taxpayer's issues.

15. a. Correct. Although the Appeals Office supplies a mediator, a taxpayer may opt to use a non-IRS comediator at personal expense.
b. Incorrect. The court does not appoint mediators; these representatives are not slated only for highly complex cases.
c. Incorrect. Mediation is available for both factual and legal issues.
d. Incorrect. One of the choices reflects the actual status of mediators in the Appeals Office process.

MODULE 3—CHAPTER 8

1. c. Correct. The minimum wage will increase to $7.25 per hour during a two-year phase-in period.
a. Incorrect. The terms of the change to the minimum wage are different.
b. Incorrect. The minimum wage is being changed differently under the new law.
d. Incorrect. These do not represent the period or the hourly rate of the change to the minimum wage.

2. d. Correct. The 2007 Small Business Tax Act indexed both the dollar base limitation (to $125,000) and the investment limitation (upward from $500,000 beginning after 2007 and before 2011), extended the duration of the break, and phased out the deduction for qualifying purchases of more than $625,000.

a. *Incorrect.* Under the 2007 Small Business Tax Act, the expensing is indexed for inflation, both in the base dollar limitation and the investment limitation.

b. *Incorrect.* Had the Act not made these extensions, after 2009 the dollar limitation would have decreased to $25,000 and the investment limitation to $200,000.

c. *Incorrect.* The deduction is generally confined to small businesses because of the phaseout of qualifying purchases exceeding $625,000.

3. b. *Correct.* The tax credit to employers is based on part of the employees' first two years' wages.

a. *Incorrect.* The tax credits are not increased to phase in the new minimum wage.

c. *Incorrect.* The Act does not create employer rebates.

d. *Incorrect.* The Act does not issue tax refunds to employees.

4. b. *Correct.* Spouses in an unincorporated business can elect not to be treated as a partnership for federal tax purposes and each spouse can receive credit for Medicare and Social Security taxes paid.

a. *Incorrect.* These features do not encourage spouses to form FLPs.

c. *Incorrect.* If other individuals become involved in the spouses' joint venture, the election by spouses does not apply.

d. *Incorrect.* Only one choice describes the effect of the simplification features for family businesses under the Act.

5. False. *Correct.* The 2007 Small Business Tax Act extended and enhanced some tax incentives in both of the previous acts.

True. *Incorrect.* The 2007 Small Business Tax Act enhanced incentives enacted in both of the previous relief acts.

6. a. *Correct.* The Act did not change the terms related to estimated tax payments of individuals. The Act increased the estimated payments due by corporations having assets of at least $1 billion, to 114.25 percent of the payment otherwise due.

b. *Incorrect.* The period before which suspension begins doubled from 18 months to 36 months.

c. *Incorrect.* For amounts less than $1,250, the fee increased by $10. Amounts greater than $1,250 are charged 2 percent of the payment amount for bounced checks.

d. *Incorrect.* One of the choices is not a revenue-raising feature of the Act.

7. c. Correct. This top tier concentrates on high-risk issues of high strategic importance to the LMSB that significantly affect one or more industries.
a. Incorrect. These areas are the purview of Tier II.
b. Incorrect. Areas presenting a significant compliance risk are Tier II issues.
d. Incorrect. One of the choices describes the focus of the IIF program.

8. b. Correct. The IRS will allow a rescission or abatement only on reportable transactions that are not listed transactions.
a. Incorrect. Rev. Proc. 2007-21 does not stipulate that rescissions or abatements are allowable in these cases.
c. Incorrect. Self-reporting is not the criterion for allowing a rescission or abatement of penalties for tax shelters.
d. Incorrect. IRS rules allow for rescission or abatement of penalties for only certain transactions.

9. d. Correct. The district court agreed that Textron did not have to allow the IRS access to its tax accrual workpapers in a SILO tax-shelter transaction because the documents were protected by the work product privilege.
a. Incorrect. The U.S. Supreme Court declined to review this case, which was decided in favor of the IRS.
b. Incorrect. The IRS succeeded in its assertion of the economic substance doctrine against Klamath's Son of BOSS tax scheme.
c. Incorrect. In this case the IRS prevailed against BB&T's LILO tax-shelter transaction.

10. d. Correct. All three choices are types of information reportable on the revised Form 990 and its schedules.
a. Incorrect. Executive and board member compensation is to be listed on the new core form.
b. Incorrect. The organization must report governance information on the new core form.
c. Incorrect. The form on compensation was revised to include types of additional compensation.

11. a. Correct. New regulations enabled employers to implement hardship withdrawal provisions midyear to their Roth 401(k) plans.
b. Incorrect. IRS guidance in 2007 made compliance more streamlined.
c. Incorrect. Provisions in the PPA made the Roth feature permanent.
d. Incorrect. One of the choices was not a contributing factor to the growth in popularity of Roth 401(k)s.

12. a. ***Correct.*** The IRS's final regulations deny the deduction to most online or "hosted" computer software.

b. ***Incorrect.*** Major changes to the Code Sec. 199 deduction are beneficial to film companies' compensation, taxpayer participation in production, and safe harbors.

c. ***Incorrect.*** Food production companies were not a major focus of the final regulations for Code Sec. 199 deductions.

d. ***Incorrect.*** The motor vehicle industry was not directly affected by Code Sec. 199 regulations, although companies using statistical sampling may benefit from requirements helping to support Code Sec. 199 deductions.

13. True. ***Correct.*** The deduction is passed through to partners and shareholders of passthrough entities.

False. ***Incorrect.*** Rev. Proc. 2007-24 allows items eligible for the deduction to be calculated at the partnership level and allocated to each partner.

14. b. ***Correct.*** The Tax Court determined the initial operating costs to be deductible business expenses under Code Sec. 212.

a. ***Incorrect.*** The Tax Court did not consider the expenses to be Code Sec. 195 start-up costs requiring capitalization.

c. ***Incorrect.*** The Tax Court did not require the expenses to be allocated.

d. ***Incorrect.*** One of the choices reflects the Tax Court's decision.

15. c. ***Correct.*** Size of any subsequent divorce settlements was not a factor in deciding for innocent spouse relief.

a. ***Incorrect.*** The lack of substantive benefit from the ex-spouse's understatement or underpayment was a factor in the Tax Court's decisions.

b. ***Incorrect.*** The Tax Court considered the economic hardship of spouses claiming relief.

d. ***Incorrect.*** Lack of the ex-spouse's knowledge of the underpayment or understatement was a factor in the innocent spouse decisions.

TOP FEDERAL TAX ISSUES FOR 2008 CPE COURSE

Index

TOP FEDERAL TAX ISSUES FOR 2008 CPE COURSE

CPE Quizzer Instructions

The CPE Quizzer is divided into three Modules. There is a processing fee for each Quizzer Module submitted for grading. Successful completion of Module 1 is recommended for **7 CPE Credits.*** Successful completion of Module 2 is recommended for **6 CPE Credits.*** Successful completion of Module 3 is recommended for **6 CPE Credits.*** You can complete and submit one Module at a time or all Modules at once for a total of **19 CPE Credits.***

To obtain CPE credit, return your completed Answer Sheet for each Quizzer Module to **CCH Continuing Education Department, 4025 W. Peterson Ave., Chicago, IL 60646,** or fax it to (773) 866-3084. Each Quizzer Answer Sheet will be graded and a CPE Certificate of Completion awarded for achieving a grade of 70 percent or greater. The Quizzer Answer Sheets are located after the Quizzer questions for this Course.

Express Grading: Processing time for your Answer Sheet is generally 8-12 business days. If you are trying to meet a reporting deadline, our Express Grading Service is available for an additional $19 per Module. To use this service, please check the "Express Grading" box on your Answer Sheet and provide your CCH account or credit card number **and your fax number.** CCH will fax your results and a Certificate of Completion (upon achieving a passing grade) to you by 5:00 p.m. the business day following our receipt of your Answer Sheet. **If you mail your Answer Sheet for Express Grading, please write "ATTN: CPE OVERNIGHT" on the envelope.** NOTE: CCH will not Federal Express Quizzer results under any circumstances.

NEW ONLINE GRADING gives you immediate 24/7 grading with instant results and no Express Grading Fee.

The **CCH Testing Center** website gives you and others in your firm easy, free access to CCH print Courses and allows you to complete your CPE Quizzers online for immediate results. Plus, the **My Courses** feature provides convenient storage for your CPE Course Certificates and completed Quizzers.

Go to **www.cchtestingcenter.com** to complete your Quizzer online.

---

* Recommended CPE credit is based on a 50-minute hour. Participants earning credits for states that require self-study to be based on a 100-minute hour will receive ½ the CPE credits for successful completion of this course. Because CPE requirements vary from state to state and among different licensing agencies, please contact your CPE governing body for information on your CPE requirements and the applicability of a particular course for your requirements.

Date of Completion: The date of completion on your Certificate will be the date that you put on your Answer Sheet. However, you must submit your Answer Sheet to CCH for grading within two weeks of completing it.

Expiration Date: December 31, 2008

Evaluation: To help us provide you with the best possible products, please take a moment to fill out the Course Evaluation located at the back of this Course and return it with your Quizzer Answer Sheets.

CCH is registered with the National Association of State Boards of Accountancy (NASBA) as a sponsor of continuing professional education on the National Registry of CPE Sponsors. State boards of accountancy have final authority on the acceptance of individual courses for CPE credit. Complaints regarding registered sponsors may be addressed to the National Registry of CPE Sponsors, 150 Fourth Avenue North, Suite 700, Nashville, TN 37219-2417. Web site: www.nasba.org.

CCH is registered with the National Association of State Boards of Accountancy (NASBA) as a Quality Assurance Service (QAS) sponsor of continuing professional education. State boards of accountancy have final authority on the acceptance of individual courses for CPE credit. Complaints regarding registered sponsors may be addressed to NASBA, 150 Fourth Avenue North, Suite 700, Nashville, TN 37219-2417. Web site: www.nasba.org.

CCH has been approved by the California Tax Education Council to offer courses that provide federal and state credit towards the annual "continuing education" requirement imposed by the State of California. A listing of additional requirements to register as a tax preparer may be obtained by contacting CTEC at P.O. Box 2890, Sacramento, CA, 95812-2890, toll-free by phone at (877) 850-2832, or on the Internet at www.ctec.org.

Processing Fee:	**Recommended CPE:**	
$84.00 for Module 1	7 hours for Module 1	
$72.00 for Module 2	6 hours for Module 2	
$72.00 for Module 3	6 hours for Module 3	
$228.00 for all Modules	19 hours for all Modules	
CTEC Course Number:	**CTEC Federal Hours:**	**CTEC California Hours:**
1075-CE-7473 for Module 1	3 hours for Module 1	N/A for Module 1
1075-CE-7483 for Module 2	3 hours for Module 2	N/A for Module 2
1075-CE-7493 for Module 3	3 hours for Module 3	N/A for Module 3
	9 hours for all Modules	N/A for all Modules

One **complimentary copy** of this Course is provided with certain copies of CCH Federal Taxation publications. Additional copies of this Course may be ordered for $29.00 each by calling 1-800-248-3248 (ask for product 0-0987-200).

TOP FEDERAL TAX ISSUES FOR 2008 CPE COURSE

Quizzer Questions: Module 1

Answer the True/False questions by marking a "T" or "F" on the Quizzer Answer Sheet. Answer Multiple Choice questions by indicating the appropriate letter on the Answer Sheet.

---

1. FIN 48 applies to all tax positions taken on all of the following income tax returns *except*:

    a. International taxing authorities
    b. Local taxing authorities
    c. State taxing authorities
    d. FIN 48 applies to all of the above

2. Which of the following is *not* a FASB recommended area to review to identify tax positions?

    a. SEC filings
    b. Projected earnings statements
    c. Settlements
    d. All of the above are recommended for review

3. FIN 48 is a _____ step process involving _____.

    a. One; recognition
    b. Two; recognition and measurement
    c. Three; recognition, measurement, and payment
    d. None of the above describes the process

4. For purposes of FIN 48, before a tax position may be considered settled, the enterprise must consider it:

    a. Highly unlikely that the taxing authority will subsequently examine or reexamine any aspect of the tax position included in the completed examination
    b. Remote that the taxing authority will subsequently examine or reexamine any aspect of the tax position included in the completed examination
    c. Probable that the taxing authority will subsequently examine or reexamine any aspect of the tax position included in the completed examination
    d. Definite that the taxing authority will subsequently examine or reexamine any aspect of the tax position included in the completed examination

5. The recognition step of a FIN 48 analysis requires that an enterprise determines whether it is _____ that a tax position will be sustained upon examination.

    a. Probable
    b. Remote
    c. Highly unlikely
    d. More-likely-than-not

6. Although FIN 48 is intended to provide additional transparency of financial conditions to investors, many practitioners are concerned that:

    a. The disclosures will ward off potential investors.
    b. The disclosures of interest and penalties paid for tax positions will trigger repercussions from corporate audit committees and large shareholders.
    c. The change from "highly unlikely" to "remote" for effective settlements is too vague.
    d. The disclosures will be a roadmap for the IRS.

7. FIN 48 is effective for fiscal years beginning:

    a. Before December 15, 2006
    b. After December 15, 2006
    c. After January 1, 2008
    d. After December 15, 2008

8. Currently, the IRS is treating FIN 48 workpapers as:

   a. Miscellaneous workpapers
   b. Tax accrual workpapers
   c. Filings
   d. None of the above

9. The IRS's policy of restraint in requesting tax accrual workpapers is:

   a. Mandated by Congress
   b. Required by statute
   c. Self-imposed
   d. Required by the courts

10. What was the purpose of the special IRS FIN 48 initiative?

   a. To manage the transition to the FIN 48 disclosure requirements
   b. To expedite resolution of uncertain tax positions in tax returns
   c. To assist taxpayers with compliance in their financial accounting years ending before December 31, 2007
   d. To assist both parties to litigation related to uncertain tax positions

11. The 2006 IASB–FASB roadmap for convergence includes all of the following active agenda items **except:**

   a. Subsequent events
   b. Performance reporting
   c. Revenue recognition
   d. Liability and equity distinctions

12. In June 2007 the SEC proposed use of what accounting standards for non-U.S. companies participating in U.S. capital markets?

   a. Use of the IFRS instead of U.S. GAAP
   b. Use of both the IFRS and U.S. GAAP
   c. Use of either the IFRS or U.S. GAAP
   d. Use of the accounting convergence standards developed by the IASB and FASB

13. If a non-U.S. based enterprise issues financial statements reconciled to U.S. GAAP, FIN 48 requirements apply to them. **True or False?**

14. In response to objections about FIN 48's implementation date, FASB delayed implementation until December 15, 2007. **True or False?**

15. The IRS, in its "FIN 48 Field Examiners Guide," predicts that disclosures required are specific enough to give the IRS a perfect view of taxpayers' uncertain tax positions. *True or False?*

16. Which of the following is *not* a penalty for violating regulations in Code Sec. 409A?

   a. 20 percent penalty
   b. Inclusion of deferred amount in income
   c. Interest accrual on deferred amount
   d. All of the above are penalties for violating Code Sec. 409A

17. All of the following compose guidance issues addressed in notices, announcements, and revenue rulings for Code Sec. 409A *except:*

   a. Treatment of losses that follow inclusion of deferred amounts in income before they are paid
   b. Reporting and withholding
   c. Application to split-dollar life insurance
   d. Interaction of Code Secs. 409A and 457

18. Plan amendments that increase an employee's deferral amount are not considered established:

   a. Unless all key or highly-compensated employees are made subject to the same amended amounts
   b. Until the amendment is included in the written plan's documents
   c. Until the first payout of the increased amount
   d. Until the end of the second quarter following the tax year in which the legally binding right arises

19. If the employer owns an employee's split-dollar life insurance policy, the arrangement is taxed:

   a. By splitting the tax liability equally between employer and employee
   b. As a loan to the employee
   c. Under the economic benefits regime
   d. The arrangement is untaxed if the employer retains ownership of the policy

20. Short-term deferrals are amounts paid to employees within _____ after the end of the year in which the employee earned the compensation.

   a. 2 months
   b. 2½ months
   c. 3 months
   d. 6 months

21. The maximum length of time a window program applies to separation pay under specified circumstances is:

   a. To the end of the same tax year as when offered to the service provider
   b. 6 months
   c. Three tax quarters
   d. 12 months

22. Code Sec. 409A does not apply to any of the following types of assets or benefits covered by other regulations **except:**

   a. Section 457(b) plans
   b. Service recipient stock
   c. Grant of a stock option under an employee stock purchase plan
   d. Code Sec. 409A does not apply to any of the above

23. Performance-based compensation is contingent on satisfying pre-established performance criteria relating to a performance period of at least _____.

   a. Two out of five past quarters
   b. 12 consecutive months
   c. Three out of five performance review periods
   d. None of the above is the period

24. A specified employee (key employee, officer, or 5 or 1 percent owner) of a publicly traded corporation cannot receive a separation from service payment until _____ or the date of death.

   a. Three months after the date of separation
   b. Six months after the date of separation
   c. The first day of the following fiscal year of the employer
   d. A specified employee is ineligible for separation from service payments

25. A beneficiary of a deceased service provider in a nonqualified deferred compensation plan:

  a. Is eligible to elect time or form changes only based on his or her different life expectancy
  b. May implement account changes through a limited window of three months following the death of the plan participant
  c. Is not subject to the rules for accelerated payments
  d. May not make changes if the account was established as a joint-and-survivor annuity

26. An election to delay payment of or change the payment form of a life annuity must be made:

  a. At the time the annuity account is established
  b. At least 12 months before the scheduled commencement of the life annuity
  c. Within six months of the initial annuity payment
  d. Life annuity payments become irrevocable upon establishment of the account and may not be delayed or changed

27. Generally, taxpayers may treat issuance of a partnership's profits or capital interest in payment of performance of services:

  a. As not resulting in a deferral of compensation
  b. As deferred compensation subject to the Code Sec. 409A regulations
  c. As subject to Code Sec. 409A upon liquidation of the partnership
  d. As subject to Code Sec. 409A when payments are issued to a partner acting in his or her capacity as a partner

28. If all of the taxpayers involved in a foreign arrangement use the accrual method of accounting, Code Sec. 409A does **not** apply. **True or False?**

29. An election to defer rather than to receive compensation immediately includes elections regarding the time of the payment, form of the payment, or both. **True or False?**

30. An employee may make an initial election to defer separation pay at the time of involuntary, but not voluntary, separation from service. **True or False?**

31. All of the following are frequent government initiatives to help business owners affected by presidentially declared disasters **except:**

    a. Abatement of penalties for late filing or late payment of income or employment taxes

    b. Temporary decreases in federal income tax and FICA withholding rates

    c. Claiming disaster losses in the tax year before the year of loss

    d. All of the above are government aids to businesses experiencing such disasters

32. Proposed regulations governing private annuities generally became effective for exchanges of property for an annuity contract after _____ and for annuity contracts received in such exchanges after that same date, with exceptions for specific transactions.

    a. January 1, 2006

    b. October 18, 2006

    c. January 1, 2007

    d. January 1, 2008

33. Valuations of noncommercial annuities based on one life are valued by the IRS using an interest rate assumption equal to _____ of the federal midterm rate for the month of interest valuation.

    a. 90 percent

    b. 100 percent

    c. 110 percent

    d. 120 percent

34. The seller's gross profit divided by the selling price of the asset is known in the installment accounting method as the:

    a. Gross profit percentage

    b. Depreciation recapture amount

    c. Installment basis amount

    d. Taxable gain percentage

35. The most common means of funding a buy-sell agreement is by:

    a. Stock redemption agreements

    b. Self-canceling installment notes

    c. Life insurance

    d. Irrevocable trusts

36. At the end of the GRAT's term, the remainder passes to the beneficiaries:

    a. Free of transfer tax
    b. Subject to a value added tax
    c. Subject to a federal excise tax
    d. Subject to federal employment taxes

37. The general rule that partners can transfer assets tax-free to a family limited partnership does **not** apply if:

    a. The limited partners (generally, children) have a legitimate capital interest in the partnership
    b. Discounts are applied to the transfer
    c. The FLP is an investment partnership
    d. All of the above trigger taxation of transfers to the FLP

38. The annual limit on employee earnings for Social Security tax is known as the:

    a. Employment tax limit
    b. Withholding maximum
    c. Taxable wage base
    d. OASDI trigger

39. Under current law, business sellers who use the accrual accounting method cannot defer recognition of income until payments are received from the buyers. **True or False?**

40. There is no taxable wage base for Medicare tax purposes. **True or False?**

Quizzer Questions: Module 2

> Answer the True/False questions by marking a "T" or "F" on the Quizzer Answer Sheet. Answer Multiple Choice questions by indicating the appropriate letter on the Answer Sheet.

41. For the 2007 tax year, the exemption amount for AMT for joint filers if not "patched" by Congress is scheduled to be:

   a. $42,000
   b. $45,000
   c. $53,000
   d. $60,000

42. The AMT exemption amount is phased out for married taxpayers filing jointly with more than $150,000 of AMTI on what percentage basis?

   a. Dollar for dollar
   b. 50 percent (reducing the AMT exemption by $1 for every $2 of AMTI above $150,000)
   c. 25 percent
   d. 10 percent

43. For what reason is the number of taxpayers subject to the AMT expected to increase substantially for the 2007 tax year?

   a. The maximum income level subject to social security tax is higher for 2007.
   b. AMT exemption levels are scheduled to be lower than in recent years while phaseout levels will not be adjusted for inflation.
   c. Indexing the AMT exemption levels resulted in more taxpayers becoming subject to the tax.
   d. Many of the tax credits formerly used to offset AMT liability have sunsetted in 2007.

44. Medical expenses are an itemized deduction for AMT purposes only to the extent they exceed _____ of the taxpayer's AGI.

  a. 7.5 percent
  b. 10 percent
  c. 12.5 percent
  d. Medical expenses are never deductible for AMT purposes

45. All of the following are types of taxpayer situations that make individuals more likely to be subject to the AMT *except:*

  a. Marriage, because the exemption rate for joint filers is not double that of single filers
  b. Extensive medical expenses, because the threshold for deducting them is higher for the AMT than for regular tax
  c. Smaller family size, which lowers the standard exemption total for regular tax
  d. All of the above make taxpayers more likely to be subject to the AMT

46. All of the following are disadvantages of exercising incentive stock options for individuals subject to AMT liability *except:*

  a. Income from exercising options is immediately taxable under AMT but not until stock is sold under regular income tax rules.
  b. If the stock price falls, the taxpayer may still have a substantial AMT liability without any profit from selling the stock.
  c. Even if the stock eventually earns a profit upon sale, the AMT paid earlier is not credited against the gain for regular income tax.
  d. All of the above are disadvantages of exercising the options.

47. If a taxpayer's investment earns very large long-term capital gains, it might affect his or her AMT liability because:

  a. Capital gains over a certain amount are taxed at the same rate as other AMT income under the AMT.
  b. Capital gains are considered a tax preference item.
  c. Capital gains, like other income, can subject the taxpayer to a higher marginal AMT rate and a phased-out exemption amount.
  d. None of the above may be the result of recognizing large capital gains in an AMT year.

48. Changes to the AMT under the Small Business and Work Opportunity Tax Act of 2007:

    a. Reduced the tentative minimum tax to zero for determining tax liability limitation for certain business tax credits

    b. Eliminated the AMT adjustment for the MACRS depreciation allowance

    c. Indexed the basic AMT exemption to the national inflation index

    d. Reduced marginal tax rates for all filing statuses of the AMT

49. The same AMT rules apply to estates and trusts as apply to individuals. **True or False?**

50. For 2007 the AMT exemption level for married taxpayers filing jointly is exactly double the exemption allowed for married taxpayers filing separately. **True or False?**

51. The general partner of an FLP must own at least _____ interest in the partnership.

    a. 1 percent

    b. 25 percent

    c. 51 percent

    d. 75 percent

52. Which of the following is **not** a valid nontax reason for establishing an FLP?

    a. Shielding assets from creditor claims

    b. Lowering the costs of administering investments of family assets

    c. Retaining interests in the event of divorce of one or more partners

    d. All of the above are valid nontax reasons for establishing an FLP

53. All of the following are reasons to include transfer restrictions in the limited partnership agreement **except:**

    a. To create discounts for lack of marketability and lack of control for the value of partnership interests

    b. To specify whether and how substitute partners may be admitted

    c. To outline transfer rights of partners

    d. To allow members of the younger generation the right to access their portions of the partnership assets before the senior member's death

54. Which should come first?

    a. Transfers of limited partnership interests to members of the younger generation family members

    b. Transfers of assets to an FLP

    c. Specifications of earmarked partnership assets to family members in the senior member's will

    d. Election of senior partners for the FLP who will determine allocation of distributions based on the senior member's designations

55. If the patriarch and matriarch of the Astor family decide to gift their two children the maximum amount as gifts in 2007, what is the total amount of their excludible gift without recourse to using their lifetime gift tax exclusion?

    a. $12,000

    b. $24,000

    c. $36,000

    d. $48,000

56. Which of the following reflects the future of the estate tax under EGTRRA?

    a. The credit against estate tax will be $3.5 million in 2009.

    b. There will be no estate tax applied to estates of decedents dying in 2010.

    c. The estate tax credit will be only $1 million in 2011.

    d. All three choices describe the true status.

57. An FLP may constitute an investment company if a total of _____ or more of the value of the FLP's assets result from partners' contributions of assets such as securities or real estate investment trusts.

    a. 50 percent

    b. 60 percent

    c. 70 percent

    d. 80 percent

58. All of the following may constitute costs for establishing and managing an FLP *except:*

    a. Appraisal fees for valuing interests in setting up the FLP

    b. Kiddie tax rules applied to income of younger family members

    c. The inability to allocate a disproportionate share of partnership losses to partners

    d. All of the above are possible or probable costs of the FLP

59. The reasoning that the IRS has applied to claim an FLP has no business purpose beside transfer of wealth to family members is the:

    a. Step transaction doctrine

    b. Adequate and full consideration test

    c. Substance over form doctrine

    d. Applicable restriction doctrine

60. The reasoning used by the IRS in court to justify that partnership transfers occurring close in time to a decedent's death should be treated as part of the decedent's testamentary transfers is the:

    a. Step transaction doctrine

    b. Adequate and full consideration test

    c. Substance over form doctrine

    d. Applicable restriction doctrine

61. To escape having property included in a decedent's gross estate under the retained interest provision of Code Sec. 2036(a), the transfer must both:

    a. Be completed at least two years before the death and be a sale to a current limited partner

    b. Be a bona fide sale to the donee and transferred for adequate and full consideration

    c. Be paid for within 60 days of the transfer and be treated by all partners as made to a separate entity

    d. Require active participation in FLP management by the donees and retain the donor's general partnership interest in the FLP following the transfer

62. In the **Kimbell** case, the court ruled the $2.5 million transfer to the FLP met the criteria for exclusion from the decedent's estate because:

    a. The decedent remained the general partner and actively participated in the management of the partnership until her death.
    b. She retained just a 1 percent interest in her FLP and maintained management control until her death.
    c. It met the adequate and full consideration and bona fide sale tests.
    d. None of the above constituted criteria used to exclude the FLP assets from the estate.

63. Why is it generally **not** advantageous to transfer assets to an FLP after gifts of the limited partnership interests are made?

    a. The IRS and the courts treat such subsequent gifts as gifts of future interests subject to gift and estate tax.
    b. Percentages of the partnership interests may have changed since the original funding of the FLP, complicating allocation of later contributions.
    c. The same valuation method cannot be applied properly to initial and later gifts.
    d. The later transfers may constitute indirect gifts of underlying FLP assets subject to gift tax.

64. FLPs, unlike S corporations, may distribute special allocations of profits, losses, and deductions for their operating businesses. **True or False?**

65. Loans from an FLP to partners do not affect the independence of the partnership under Code Sec. 2036(a). **True or False?**

66. Individuals, trusts and estates, personal service corporations, and closely held C corporations may deduct their passive activity losses **only:**

    a. For two out of four accounting periods
    b. From net income for the current year without offsetting income of previous or future years
    c. From passive activity income
    d. For rental activity income of real estate professionals

67. Passive activity deductions in excess of passive activity gross income (i.e., passive activity losses) in a particular year:

   a. Are unavailable to carry back or forward as offsets
   b. Are carried forward indefinitely to be deducted from subsequent years' passive gross income
   c. Are carried forward for a maximum of three tax years
   d. May offset passive activity income in the same or subsequent years

68. Taxpayers are not required to allocate gain for disposing of interest in a multiple-use passive activity or property used in such an activity if their interest in the property is no more than the lesser of:

   a. $20,000 or 25 percent of the FMV
   b. $10,000 or 10 percent of the FMV
   c. $20,000 or 15 percent of the FMV
   d. $100,000 or 10 percent of the FMV

69. All of the following are taxpayers subject to the passive loss limitation **except:**

   a. Closely held C corporations
   b. Personal service corporations
   c. S corporations
   d. Trusts

70. Which of the following is **not** a factor examined in the seven tests for material participation in an activity?

   a. Material participation by the taxpayer in prior tax years
   b. Number of hours of participation by the taxpayer during the tax year
   c. Facts and circumstances of the taxpayer's relationship with the business
   d. All of the above are factors

71. In the personal service activity test, an individual is considered to have materially participated in any year if he or she materially participated in the activity for any consecutive or nonconsecutive _____ preceding the tax year.

   a. 6 months
   b. 12 months
   c. 2 tax years
   d. 3 tax years

72. Which of the following is **not** one of the six exceptions to the *per se* passive activity treatment of rental activities?

   a. Incidental exception
   b. Providing-property exception
   c. Nonbusiness hours exception
   d. All of the above are exceptions

73. The active participation allowance that Congress created to offer relief to taxpayers with modified AGIs of less than $100,000 who receive rental income has a maximum of:

   a. $10,000 annually
   b. $15,000 annually
   c. $20,000 annually
   d. $25,000 annually

74. To qualify as a real estate professional for the rules of *per se* passive activities, one must has performed more than _____ of services during the tax year in that real property trade or business.

   a. 100 hours
   b. 250 hours
   c. 500 hours
   d. 750 hours

75. Which of the following describes the active participation standard?

   a. It is more strenuous than the material participation standard.
   b. It does not include the making of management decisions.
   c. It does not require regular, continuous, and substantial involvement in operations.
   d. None of the above describes the active participation standard.

76. Which type of trust is excluded from the passive activity rules under Reg. § 1.469-1T(b)(2)?

    a. Testamentary trusts
    b. Grantor trusts
    c. Revocable trusts
    d. Irrevocable trusts

77. Why do taxpayers elect to group related activities into a single one in order to avoid the passive activity loss rules?

    a. Fewer passive activity losses may be offset when passive activity gains are aggregated through grouping.
    b. Grouping activities enables taxpayers to prove material participation of the group as a whole rather than for each individual activity.
    c. Grouping related activities is the method used for consolidated reporting of affiliated groups having passive income and losses.
    d. None of the above is the primary reason for grouping.

78. Any net passive activity income may be offset by deductions or credits available to reduce ordinary income. *True or False?*

79. Passive activity income is determined by examining how active the taxpayer receiving the income was in its generation but not at the income source itself. *True or False?*

80. Work such as monitoring the finances or operations of the activity by an investor counts toward the qualifying material participation requirement. *True or False?*

Quizzer Questions: Module 3

> Answer the True/False questions by marking a "T" or "F" on the Quizzer Answer Sheet. Answer Multiple Choice questions by indicating the appropriate letter on the Answer Sheet.

81. The IRS cut back enforcement programs in the 1990s following criticism by members of Congress related to which act?

  a. Tax Reform Act of 1986
  b. Taxpayer Relief Act of 1997
  c. IRS Reform and Restructuring Act of 1998
  d. Tax Relief Extension Act of 1999

82. Former Commissioner Everson's formula for increasing taxpayer compliance with federal income tax was _____ + Enforcement = Compliance.

  a. Penalties
  b. Service
  c. Amnesty
  d. Examinations

83. Data on return filing compliance and tax payment compliance will be updated beginning with 2006 returns by which staff group within the IRS?

  a. Taxpayer Compliance Measurement Program
  b. National Research Program
  c. Compliance Assurance Process of the Large and Mid-Size Business Division
  d. Limited Issue Focused Examinations Program of the Large and Mid-Size Business Division

84. Which IRS organization has become a "hot spot" for enforcement actions because of recently uncovered abuses?

  a. TE/GE Division
  b. EO unit
  c. LMSB Division
  d. SB/SE Division

85. The Pension Protection Act of 2006 imposed new reporting requirements for noncash donations exceeding:

    a. $25
    b. $100
    c. $500
    d. $10,000

86. Which of the following is **not** a new emphasis of the EO unit?

    a. Compliance Assurance Process
    b. Gaming activities
    c. Community foundations
    d. College and university UBIT project

87. Which of these is **not** an Exempt Organization unit follow-up activity for charities that previously violated the prohibition on political activities?

    a. Continued monitoring of state election databases
    b. Contacting organizations that may have violated the rules in 2004 and 2005
    c. Monitoring political contributions by charities to candidates and political organizations
    d. All of the above are follow-up activities planned by the EO unit

88. On the newly revised Form 990, the IRS queries tax-exempt _____ about their community benefit, billing and collection practices, and management companies and joint ventures.

    a. Municipal service consultants
    b. Fundraising consultants
    c. Social service agencies
    d. Hospitals

89. Because interest earned on state, municipal, hospital, and community development investments has been mischanneled, Exempt Organizations and the _____ are investigating potentially abusive transactions

    a. Office of Professional Responsibility
    b. Industry Issue Focus
    c. Compliance Assurance Process
    d. Tax-Exempt Bonds office

90. Which of the following is *not* a reportable transaction for tax shelters scrutinized by the IRS?

    a. Confidential transactions
    b. Masked gain transactions
    c. Transactions involving a brief holding period
    d. Transactions with contractual protection

91. Taxpayers may make a small case request for appeal by sending a request letter to the office issuing the auditor's decision if the total tax for the year is no more than:

    a. $10,000
    b. $15,000
    c. $20,000
    d. $25,000

92. The pilot program adapting an alternative dispute resolution technique from the Large and Mid-Size Business Division to the Small Business/Self-Employed Division is:

    a. Fast Track Settlement
    b. Fast Track Mediation
    c. Tax Exempt Bond Mediation
    d. Offer in Compromise

93. If a taxpayer decides to use the TEB Mediation Dispute Resolution Program:

    a. He or she may propose an unlimited number of unagreed issues for the mediator's ruling.
    b. The process must be completed within one year.
    c. The taxpayer must elect to use the program before the IRS issues a proposed adverse determination letter.
    d. The IRS mediator is prohibited from using traditional case-closing methods.

94. Because of emphasis on closing audits of large companies, the IRS has substantially ignored any pressure to close audits of small businesses because records tend to be retained better in smaller concerns. *True or False?*

95. Former IRS Commissioner Everson has stated that the most effective way to close the tax gap is through increased rates of more thorough audits. **True or False?**

96. The tax incentives for small businesses in the 2007 Small Business Tax Act were intended to:

   a. Encourage research and experimental activities in small businesses
   b. Replace tax credits for small businesses that were eliminated by the Act
   c. Counterbalance the costs of the increase in the federal minimum wage
   d. All of the above were intentions of the Act

97. The effects of the small business expensing changes mandated by the 2007 Small Business Tax Act were to:

   a. Lower the maximum of Section 179 expensing in early years but index the tax break for inflation
   b. Index the dollar limitation to $125,000 for tax years 2007–2010 but offset the break amount by lowering the investment limitation during the same period to $450,000
   c. Raise the investment limitation to $650,000 by 2010 but lower the base dollar limitation to $100,000 during that same period
   d. None of the above describes the effects of the changes

98. All of the following are reforms made to S corporations by the 2007 Small business Tax Act **except:**

   a. Sale of a partial interest in a QSub is now treated as a sale of an undivided interest in the QSub's assets
   b. Reduction of accumulated earnings and profits by its pre-1983 accumulated E&P
   c. No longer treating capital gain from the sale or exchange of securities as passive investment income
   d. All of the above are reforms to S corporations made by the Act

99. Under the 2007 Small Business Tax Act, the kiddie tax for 2008 calendar-year taxpayers applies to full-time students until they are age:

   a. 18
   b. 22
   c. 24
   d. 26

100. The more-likely-than-not standard for tax return preparers means that the tax position should have more than a _____ likelihood of being sustained on its merits.

    a. 50 percent
    b. 51 percent
    c. 66 percent
    d. 75 percent

101. Stricter reporting standards for tax preparers and practitioners enacted in the 2007 Small Business Tax Act raised the Code Sec. 6694(a) penalties from $250 to _____ for an "unrealistic position."

    a. The greater of $500 or 50 percent of the income derived by the preparer
    b. The greater of $750 or 51 percent of the income derived by the preparer
    c. The greater of $1,000 or 50 percent of the income derived by the preparer
    d. The greater of $1,500 or 75 percent of the income derived by the preparer

102. All of the following are balances that an employer may use to credit balances for employer contributions to defined benefit plans **except:**

    a. Prefunding balances
    b. Use of benefits unclaimed by retired or terminated employees
    c. Funding standard carryover balances
    d. All of the above may be used as offsets

103. Which of the following was **not** an IRS action in 2007 to address the tax gap?

    a. Temporary rules governing installment agreements
    b. Industry Issue Focus (IIF) program
    c. Offer in compromise (OIC) program
    d. All of the above were actions to narrow the gap

104. The newest type of listed transactions for abusive tax shelters is:

    a. Transactions of interest
    b. Loss importation transactions
    c. Son of BOSS shelters
    d. None of the above

105. In which 2007 case did the court side with the company in refusing the IRS access to the lawyer's tax accrual workpapers?

    a. *Textron Inc.*
    b. *Klamath Strategic Investment Fund*
    c. *Dow Chemical Company*
    d. *Coltec Industries*

106. For the first time in 2007, mandatory e-filing was required of:

    a. Sole proprietors in their first year of Schedule C filing
    b. Family limited partnerships
    c. Midsize corporations and corporations filing 250 or more returns annually
    d. Estates and trusts

107. For 2007 the qualified domestic production activities deduction is _____ of the lesser of the taxpayer's taxable income or qualified productive activities income.

    a. 3 percent
    b. 5 percent
    c. 6 percent
    d. 9 percent

108. As a result of the 2007 Small Business Tax Act, treating restricted bank director stock as outstanding stock terminates an organization's status as an S corp. *True or False?*

109. The IRS chief counsel ruled during 2007 that taxpayers having wrap accounts must treat advisory fees as Schedule A miscellaneous itemized deductions. *True or False?*

110. In the *Tax Analysts* case, the D.C. Circuit Court of Appeals upheld the IRS's nondisclosure of e-mails containing legal advice under its two-hour rule. *True or False?*

TOP FEDERAL TAX ISSUES FOR 2008 CPE COURSE   (0747-3)

Module 1: Answer Sheet

NAME _____

COMPANY NAME _____

STREET _____

CITY, STATE, & ZIP CODE _____

BUSINESS PHONE NUMBER _____

E-MAIL ADDRESS _____

DATE OF COMPLETION _____

CFP REGISTRANT ID (for Certified Financial Planners) _____

CRTP ID (for CTEC Credit only) _____(CTEC Course # 1075-CE-7473)

On the next page, please answer the Multiple Choice questions by indicating the appropri-ate letter next to the corresponding number. Please answer the True/False questions by marking "T" or "F" next to the corresponding number.

A $84.00 processing fee wil be charged for each user submitting Module 1 for grading.

Please remove both pages of the Answer Sheet from this book and return them with your completed Evaluation Form to CCH at the address below. You may also fax your Answer Sheet to CCH at 773-866-3084.

You may also go to **www.cchtestingcenter.com** to complete your Quizzer online.

METHOD OF PAYMENT:

| ☐ Check Enclosed ☐ Visa ☐ Master Card ☐ AmEx |
| ☐ Discover ☐ CCH Account* _____ |
| Card No. _____ Exp. Date _____ |
| Signature _____ |
| * Must provide CCH account number for this payment option |

EXPRESS GRADING: Please fax my Course results to me by 5:00 p.m. the business day following your receipt of this Answer Sheet. By checking this box I authorize CCH to charge $19.00 for this service.

☐ Express Grading $19.00   Fax No. _____

CCH
a Wolters Kluwer business

Mail or fax to:
CCH Continuing Education Department
4025 W. Peterson Ave.
Chicago, IL 60646-6085
1-800-248-3248
Fax: 773-866-3084

PAGE 1 OF 2

TOP FEDERAL TAX ISSUES FOR 2008 CPE COURSE   (0747-3)

Module 1: Answer Sheet

Please answer the Multiple Choice questions by indicating the appropriate letter next to the corresponding number. Please answer the True/False questions by marking "T" or "F" next to the corresponding number.

1. ___	11. ___	21. ___	31. ___
2. ___	12. ___	22. ___	32. ___
3. ___	13. ___	23. ___	33. ___
4. ___	14. ___	24. ___	34. ___
5. ___	15. ___	25. ___	35. ___
6. ___	16. ___	26. ___	36. ___
7. ___	17. ___	27. ___	37. ___
8. ___	18. ___	28. ___	38. ___
9. ___	19. ___	29. ___	39. ___
10. ___	20. ___	30. ___	40. ___

Please complete the Evaluation Form (located after the Module 3 Answer Sheet) and return it with this Quizzer Answer Sheet to CCH at the address on the previous page. Thank you.

TOP FEDERAL TAX ISSUES FOR 2008 CPE COURSE   (0748-3)

Module 2: Answer Sheet

NAME _____

COMPANY NAME _____

STREET _____

CITY, STATE, & ZIP CODE _____

BUSINESS PHONE NUMBER _____

E-MAIL ADDRESS _____

DATE OF COMPLETION _____

CFP REGISTRANT ID (for Certified Financial Planners) _____

CRTP ID (for CTEC Credit only) _____ (CTEC Course # 1075-CE-7483)

On the next page, please answer the Multiple Choice questions by indicating the appropriate letter next to the corresponding number. Please answer the True/False questions by marking "T" or "F" next to the corresponding number.

A $72.00 processing fee wil be charged for each user submitting Module 2 for grading.

Please remove both pages of the Answer Sheet from this book and return them with your completed Evaluation Form to CCH at the address below. You may also fax your Answer Sheet to CCH at 773-866-3084.

You may also go to **www.cchtestingcenter.com** to complete your Quizzer online.

METHOD OF PAYMENT:

☐ Check Enclosed   ☐ Visa   ☐ Master Card   ☐ AmEx

☐ Discover   ☐ CCH Account* _____

Card No. _____ Exp. Date _____

Signature _____

* Must provide CCH account number for this payment option

EXPRESS GRADING: Please fax my Course results to me by 5:00 p.m. the business day following your receipt of this Answer Sheet. By checking this box I authorize CCH to charge $19.00 for this service.

☐ Express Grading $19.00   Fax No. _____

.CCH
a Wolters Kluwer business

Mail or fax to:
CCH Continuing Education Department
4025 W. Peterson Ave.
Chicago, IL 60646-6085
1-800-248-3248
Fax: 773-866-3084

TOP FEDERAL TAX ISSUES FOR 2008 CPE COURSE   (0748-3)

Module 2: Answer Sheet

Please answer the Multiple Choice questions by indicating the appropriate letter next to the corresponding number. Please answer the True/False questions by marking "T" or "F" next to the corresponding number.

41. ___	51. ___	61. ___	71. ___
42. ___	52. ___	62. ___	72. ___
43. ___	53. ___	63. ___	73. ___
44. ___	54. ___	64. ___	74. ___
45. ___	55. ___	65. ___	75. ___
46. ___	56. ___	66. ___	76. ___
47. ___	57. ___	67. ___	77. ___
48. ___	58. ___	68. ___	78. ___
49. ___	59. ___	69. ___	79. ___
50. ___	60. ___	70. ___	80. ___

Please complete the Evaluation Form (located after the Module 3 Answer Sheet) and return it with this Quizzer Answer Sheet to CCH at the address on the previous page. Thank you.

TOP FEDERAL TAX ISSUES FOR 2008 CPE COURSE   (0749-3)

Module 3: Answer Sheet

NAME _____

COMPANY NAME _____

STREET _____

CITY, STATE, & ZIP CODE _____

BUSINESS PHONE NUMBER _____

E-MAIL ADDRESS _____

DATE OF COMPLETION _____

CFP REGISTRANT ID (for Certified Financial Planners) _____

CRTP ID (for CTEC Credit only) _____ (CTEC Course # 1075-CE-7493)

On the next page, please answer the Multiple Choice questions by indicating the appropriate letter next to the corresponding number. Please answer the True/False questions by marking "T" or "F" next to the corresponding number.

A $72.00 processing fee wil be charged for each user submitting Module 3 for grading.

Please remove both pages of the Answer Sheet from this book and return them with your completed Evaluation Form to CCH at the address below. You may also fax your Answer Sheet to CCH at 773-866-3084.

You may also go to **www.cchtestingcenter.com** to complete your Quizzer online.

METHOD OF PAYMENT:

☐ Check Enclosed   ☐ Visa   ☐ Master Card   ☐ AmEx

☐ Discover   ☐ CCH Account* _____

Card No. _____ Exp. Date _____

Signature _____

* Must provide CCH account number for this payment option

EXPRESS GRADING: Please fax my Course results to me by 5:00 p.m. the business day following your receipt of this Answer Sheet. By checking this box I authorize CCH to charge $19.00 for this service.

☐ Express Grading $19.00   Fax No. _____

CCH
® a Wolters Kluwer business

Mail or fax to:
CCH Continuing Education Department
4025 W. Peterson Ave.
Chicago, IL 60646-6085
1-800-248-3248
Fax: 773-866-3084

TOP FEDERAL TAX ISSUES FOR 2008 CPE COURSE   (0749-3)

Module 3: Answer Sheet

Please answer the Multiple Choice questions by indicating the appropriate letter next to the corresponding number. Please answer the True/False questions by marking "T" or "F" next to the corresponding number.

81. ___	89. ___	97. ___	104. ___
82. ___	90. ___	98. ___	105. ___
83. ___	91. ___	99. ___	106. ___
84. ___	92. ___	100. ___	107. ___
85. ___	93. ___	101. ___	108. ___
86. ___	94. ___	102. ___	109. ___
87. ___	95. ___	103. ___	110. ___
88. ___	96. ___		

Please complete the Evaluation Form (located after the Module 3 Answer Sheet) and return it with this Quizzer Answer Sheet to CCH at the address on the previous page. Thank you.

TOP FEDERAL TAX ISSUES FOR 2008 CPE COURSE   (0987-2)

Evaluation Form

Please take a few moments to fill out and mail or fax this evaluation to CCH so that we can better provide you with the type of self-study programs you want and need. Thank you.

About This Program

1. Please circle the number that best reflects the extent of your agreement with the following statements:

	Strongly Agree				Strongly Disagree
a. The Course objectives were met.	5	4	3	2	1
b. This Course was comprehensive and organized.	5	4	3	2	1
c. The content was current and technically accurate.	5	4	3	2	1
d. This Course was timely and relevant.	5	4	3	2	1
e. The prerequisite requirements were appropriate.	5	4	3	2	1
f. This Course was a valuable learning experience.	5	4	3	2	1
g. The Course completion time was appropriate.	5	4	3	2	1

2. This Course was most valuable to me because of:

    _____ Continuing Education credit   _____ Convenience of format
    _____ Relevance to my practice/   _____ Timeliness of subject matter
          employment   _____ Reputation of author
    _____ Price
    _____ Other (please specify) _____

3. How long did it take to complete this Course? (Please include the total time spent reading or studying reference materials and completing CPE Quizzer).

    Module 1 _____   Module 2 _____   Module 3 _____

4. What do you consider to be the strong points of this Course?

5. What improvements can we make to this Course?

TOP FEDERAL TAX ISSUES FOR 2008 CPE COURSE   (0987-2)

Evaluation Form *cont'd*

General Interests

1. Preferred method of self-study instruction:
    _____ Text   _____ Audio   _____ Computer-based/Multimedia   _____Video

2. What specific topics would you like CCH to develop as self-study CPE programs? _____

    _____

    _____

    _____

3. Please list other topics of interest to you _____

    _____

    _____

About You

1. Your profession:

    _____ CPA   _____ Enrolled Agent
    _____ Attorney   _____ Tax Preparer
    _____ Financial Planner   _____ Other (please specify)
                                 _____

2. Your employment:

    _____ Self-employed   _____ Public Accounting Firm
    _____ Service Industry   _____ Non-Service Industry
    _____ Banking/Finance   _____ Government
    _____ Education   _____ Other _____

3. Size of firm/corporation:

    _____ 1   _____ 2-5   _____ 6-10   _____ 11-20   _____ 21-50   _____ 51+

4. Your Name _____
    _Firm/Company Name_____
    Address _____
    City, State, Zip Code _____
    E-mail Address _____

THANK YOU FOR TAKING THE TIME TO COMPLETE THIS SURVEY!

NOTES

NOTES

NOTES

NOTES

NOTES

NOTES

NOTES

NOTES

NOTES

NOTES

NOTES

NOTES

NOTES

NOTES

NOTES

NOTES